Salvadorans in Costa Rica

displaced lives

Salvadorans

in

Costa

Rica

Bridget A. Hayden

The University of Arizona Press
Tucson

The University of Arizona Press
© 2003 The Arizona Board of Regents
First printing
All rights reserved

∞ This book is printed on acid-free, archival-quality paper.
Manufactured in the United States of America

08   07   06   05   04   03   6   5   4   3   2   1

Library of Congress Cataloging-in-Publication Data

Hayden, Bridget A., 1963–
   Salvadorans in Costa Rica : displaced lives / Bridget A. Hayden.
      p. cm.
Includes bibliographical references and index.
ISBN 0-8165-2294-4 (cloth : alk. paper)
1. Political refugees—El Salvador.   2. Political refugees—Costa Rica.
3. Salvadorans—Costa Rica—Social conditions.   4. Salvadorans—
Costa Rica—Economic conditions.   5. El Salvador—Emigration
and immigration—Social aspects.   6. Costa Rica—Emigration and
immigration—Social aspects.   I. Title.
   HV640.5.S24 H39 2003
   325'.21'097284097286—dc21

                        2002012326

British Library Cataloguing-in-Publication Data
A catalogue record for this book is available from the British Library.

Publication of this book is made possible in part by the proceeds of a
permanent endowment created with the assistance of a Challenge Grant
from the National Endowment for the Humanities, a federal agency.

Contents

Acknowledgments

Lo mejor de mí son los demás.
(The best of me is other people.)
—Facundo Cabral

Without the help, friendship, and encouragement of many people this project would never have been completed, much less published, and I cannot possibly do justice to them all. My first debt of gratitude is to all the Central Americans who have taught me so much about their lives, countries, and region. I am particularly grateful for the Salvadorans I knew in Costa Rica, who made this book possible. I regret that I cannot name them here, but I hope they know how much I appreciate all they did for me. Most of those who appear in the following pages directly, under pseudonyms, or indirectly have also been good friends. I hope they find no cause to regret it.

This book had its first life as my dissertation, which increases my indebtedness a great deal not only to those who most helped me get to and complete that stage, but also to those who encouraged me afterward in the process of making the dissertation into a book. I particularly want to thank Bruce Mannheim, Crisca Bierwert, Dick Ford, Gracia Clark, Nan Rothschild, Roger Rouse, Skip Rappaport, and Val Daniel. They represent different stages in this project but have been equally important to me as people and scholars. I also thank the two anonymous reviewers of the manuscript for the University of Arizona Press for their careful reading and insightful comments, even when I did not always follow their advice.

I sincerely thank other colleagues and friends who read portions of this manuscript at some point and helped me figure it all out as well as those who continue to keep me sane. Coralyn Davis, Lessie Frazier, Beth Notar, Deb Jackson, John Stiles, Tom Williamson, and Kate Zirbel were there in the initial stages of writing and so many other occasions. Laura Ahearn, Michele Gamburd, Debbie Gold, Melissa Johnson, Charles Klein, Deborah Lustig, Char Makley, Bilinda Straight and Gina Ulysse have been sources of support for more years and ways than I can count. Ellen Moodie, Charo Montoya, and Janise Hurtig have been generous friends and colleagues working on similar issues topically and regionally. Brian Larkin, Leslie Sharp, Paul Silverstein, Sandhya Shukla and Zoe Strother formed a particularly congenial writing group when I began turning the dissertation into a book manuscript.

A Fulbright-Hays dissertation fellowship made the research for this book possible. Further financial assistance came from a grant from the Horace Rackham School of Graduate Studies at the University of Michigan and the Latin American and Caribbean Studies program at the University of Michigan.

Finally, as always I thank my extended and immediate family for more than I will even try to put into words.

Introduction:
Displaced
Lives

Salvadorans in Costa Rica

It was a day like almost any other at OARS, an office in Costa Rica that gave aid to Salvadoran refugees, when *doña* Alicia arrived hoping to sell some Salvadoran *colones*. The office was nearly empty, except for the ghostly remembrances of the activities that used to take place there. The office used to be a busy, well-known place. Now there were shelves and drawers of papers no longer consulted. There was an aging sign on the wall near the front door requesting donations of leftover medicines for others. The first room on the first floor still showed signs of when it had been a cooperative providing both employment and low-cost groceries to the poorest Salvadoran refugees. In back the *salón* had layers of faded and fading decorations from past celebrations hanging under the now leaking corrugated metal roof. On the first floor, parallel to the staircase, was a long, paneled painting done by a European volunteer many years before. On occasion I saw it used by parents to show children Salvadoran history. The painting showed *campesinos* in the fields, workers, soldiers with their guns. At least once I did the same with children who were playing with me while their parents or grandparents did other things. There were rural literacy campaigns, the *guerrilla, Monseñor*. Salvadorans unaffiliated with the office were surprised it still existed when they spoke with me. Really?! Why? Who goes there? Is the *padre* still there? The office still had a medical clinic twice a week, literacy and sewing classes in the salón on weekends, some emergency aid given to help the poorest Salvadorans with living expenses, and loans. So some people still frequented the office, although it would soon close and was quiet compared to the 1980s. Doña Alicia came periodically to clean and also to wait for her bus or rest between jobs, but on that day in May of 1994 she came to sell Salvadoran bills.

They were two bills of fifty Salvadoran colones each. Together they were worth fifteen hundred Costa Rican colones, or approximately ten U.S. dollars. Alicia had been keeping this money safe for fourteen years against the day she would return home. Finally, she was ready to sell them. She confided to me, as we sat together on the old brown couch in the reception area on the second floor, that she needed the money now and, she continued, the truth was that she would not ever be going back. There was nowhere to buy or sell Salvadoran money on the street. Not even in the banks or money changing offices had I seen Central American currencies exchanged. When people traveled, they traveled with U.S. dollars. Alicia came to the office because she was hoping one of the people there would buy them; *don* Renaldo went to El Salvador sometimes, she mentioned to me hopefully. She knew he needed to visit the office that day and she hoped to see him. I would have bought them myself, but I did not have that much cash, and the bank was already closed for the day. I was planning to go to El Salvador eventually and could have saved the bills until then. In a way, I am relieved that don Renaldo did buy them; it was not much money, but it was more than I felt I could afford on souvenirs or personal whims, and I would have felt bad spending those colones. I think I would have kept them forever in Alicia's place because those two purple bills were more than mere money by then. In another way, I am sorry I didn't save them from being recycled back into crass consumerism and pure survival.

She would have found that odd, I think; even I find it a bit weird. However, despite her matter-of-fact demeanor, this was surely a significant moment. Why had she kept them in the first place? And why sell them then? Surely she had passed equally, and probably more, difficult times before in Costa Rica. What did they mean? One does not need colones to go back to El Salvador, much less bills a decade old. The most obviously sensible thing to do is to exchange money when you go, as the accountant pointed out after she had left the office. Alicia did not do that. She kept that money believing, or at least sensing, it would take her home. When she finally admitted she was not going, the money went instead to help her survive in her new, de facto home; she used the money to pay the electric bill. In a sense, it was the second time she left El Salvador and the day she definitively settled in Costa Rica.

Alicia was one of many Salvadorans to leave her home country during the warfare of the 1980s. Salvadorans have a long history of migration out of El Salvador, the most densely populated of the Central American countries, in search of better economic prospects (Hamilton and Chinchilla 1991). In the 1980s migration rose dramatically as violence and economic insecurity both increased to levels that made life at home extremely difficult and even impossible for large segments of the population. As much as one-fourth of the population was outside of El Salvador at that time and many others were displaced within the country. The largest number of Salvadorans went to the United States, but significant numbers also went to countries within the region. Some went even farther, to South America, Europe, Canada, or Australia. This migration, despite the importance it has for Salvadoran society, has been relatively little studied and until recently most research has mainly dealt with demographic variables. Enough has been published, however, to show that the conditions of reception in each country varied dramatically and that this led to different types of Salvadoran communities and different relationships with El Salvador during and after the war. Many Salvadorans who spent the years in Costa Rica repatriated individually, as families, or in small groups when it became possible, but many also integrated permanently into that society. Salvadorans in the United States are forming transnational migrant circuits and institutions that are changing Salvadoran society (Bailey and Hane 1995; DeCesare 1998; Landolt 1997; Lungo 1997; Mahler 1995a, 1995b; Montes 1987). Those who were isolated in camps in Honduras repatriated as entire communities under the aegis of the United Nations (Fagen and Eldridge 1991; Macdonald and Gatehouse 1995). This book is solely about those Salvadorans who remained in Costa Rica after the war ended, but the contrast with Salvadorans who went to other countries will be discussed in the concluding chapter.

There were four main groups of Salvadorans in Costa Rica. First, some wealthy Salvadorans occasionally showed up in the society pages of the newspaper. On the several occasions that people I knew made mention of this group of elite expatriate Salvadorans, they were clear that the wealthy would not welcome social contact with them. This group is absent in my study and cannot be considered refugees. There were no direct social connections between its members and other Salvadorans in the country. A small, but appreciable, number of Salvadorans went to Costa Rica in the mid to late 1970s, some to work and others either to escape political persecution or because the Salvadoran government exiled them. They included students and teachers who had political problems; artisans who in some cases taught later Salvadorans, especially men, trades, particularly shoe-making; and other laborers. Many of these took an active part in assist-ing, either individually or through organizations, the later refugees who formed the largest group of Salvadorans in Costa Rica. The refugee move-ment began in 1980, when two hundred Salvadorans took over the Costa Rican embassy in El Salvador and were flown to refuge in Costa Rica by the UNHCR (United Nations High Commission for Refugees). Most refu-gees arrived in the early years of that decade, but Salvadorans have con-tinued to arrive for work, although they are now far outnumbered by Nicaraguans. With the exception of the elite, these identifiable demo-graphic cohorts of Salvadorans did not form completely separate social groups although there were tensions, as in any community, based on po-litical and/or class differences. Nearly all the Salvadorans included in my study arrived in the 1980s and almost all as a direct result of the violence.

The term "refugee" is problematic because it is at once a legal and a moral category, and these usages do not always coincide. For example, a major issue in work on Salvadorans in the United States in the 1980s was whether they were truly refugees despite the fact that few had that legal status. When I use the word "refugee" in this book I mean this group of non-elite Salvadorans and not solely those who were officially docu-mented with a refugee identity card. The exception to this is when I am explicitly discussing the legal category, especially in chapter 2.

Estimates vary, but as many as twenty thousand Salvadorans went to Costa Rica during the war, most in the early years of the decade, with the largest numbers arriving between 1980 and 1982. At that time most entered the country on tourist visas obtained at the border, visas that had to be renewed every thirty days. Between one-third and two-thirds of Salvadorans in the country subsequently requested and obtained refu-gee status.[1] Others remained undocumented or otherwise documented, at least initially, in a context of strong prejudice against refugees, who were mainly Salvadorans during the 1980 to 1983 period (Ramírez Boza 1987:76).

During the early years of the decade, Costa Rican authorities, searching for subversive materials or actions and for people working illegally, some-times harassed Salvadorans. Migration officials went to the homes of refugees to make sure they were not working and checked identification papers at the main post office in San José. Negative representations in the mass media and by government officials also made the situation for Salvadorans uncomfortable (Basok 1993b:32–33; Campos V. et al. 1985:94–95; Muñoz Jiménez 1985; Rodríguez, Francisco 1993:116–17). Until 1984, when the law was changed so they could work as wage-laborers under the same conditions as other foreigners, refugees were not permitted to work legally except in UNHCR-funded small businesses (Basok 1993b:35). It was not until 1985, however, that a mechanism for issuing them work permits was instituted (Wiley 1991:96).[2] In practice, even then legal work was difficult to attain for refugees (Basok 1993b: 32–33, Campos V. 1985:94–95, Muñoz Jiménez 1985).

In 1983 Costa Rica began enforcing stricter control over tourist visas for Salvadorans. This is the explanation analysts commonly gave for a dramatic drop in Salvadoran immigration after 1982 (Asociación Nacional de ONG's de Costa Rica 1991:9; Basok 1990, 1993b:30).[3] A combination of factors indubitably contributed to the decline, but I doubt Costa Rican policies alone could have significantly reduced migration. The country remained unable to control its Nicaraguan border and Salvadorans migrated to Honduras, Mexico, and the United States, which all had policies equally or more disadvantageous to Salvadorans. I believe it probable that more Salvadorans took refuge in Costa Rica between 1980 and 1982 because those were the worst years of state-sponsored violence in El Salvador (Americas Watch Committee (U.S.) 1991:47). Montes Mozo (1985:82) also argues that this period was associated with higher rates of Salvadoran migration induced by the violence. Deaths, disappearances, and torture were highest in 1980 and 1981. In 1982 they declined dramatically, although the war continued. The violence affected even those who were not the direct targets of threats because corpses were left for others to find and tortured people were released into the community. In 1983 military strategies shifted[4] and in the second half of that year both disappearances and civilian deaths again dropped significantly.[5] The numbers of Salvadorans who went to Costa Rica declined with the violence and before the change in Costa Rican visa policy; sources vary regarding the numbers of Salvadorans who arrived, but do agree on this pattern. Muñoz reports that in both 1980 and 1981 over two thousand Salvadoran refugees went to Costa Rica, while in 1982 this fell to 831 and in 1983 to only 280. The Costa Rican government's Department of Refugees in Migration reported 3,011 Salvadorans in 1980, 1,795 in 1981, 748 in 1982 and 226 in 1983 (Muñoz Jiménez 1985:144; Secretaria Técnica de Población— MIDEPLAN 1988:17). Furthermore, Galván Bonilla and Quintanilla Arévalo (1987:172) report that most Salvadoran refugees in Costa Rica were from the parts of El Salvador most affected by the death squads during those years.

It is difficult to obtain precise demographic information about Salvadorans who were in Costa Rica, but studies provide a generally consistent profile. They were mainly urban in El Salvador (Galván Bonilla and Quintanilla Arévalo 1987): One Costa Rican government source—and other studies give comparable numbers—reports that more than 80 percent of Salvadoran refugees were from the central and para-central regions of El Salvador (DIGEPARE 1989c) where they were concentrated in nonagricultural sectors of the economy (Flores Gamboa 1989). Some contradict this and say that they were as much as 50 percent rural (Vega C. 1984 cited in Basok 1993b:41). I have no other written source for this, but have found that many people have the impression that they were mainly rural. Indirect support for believing the majority of investigations finding they were of urban origin is the fact that most settled in the urban center of Costa Rica, in marked contrast to the mostly rural Nicaraguans who are more widely dispersed in Costa Rica. Several factors, beyond the difficulty of data collection, may help explain this contradiction, although it would be impossible to prove definitively the exact composition of the population.

Those most likely to require the assistance offered by refugee programs were of rural origin and/or female-headed households. This was true among the people I met, and the functionaries of the offices established in Costa Rica by Salvadorans to assist compatriots sometimes said that their objective was to help the rural population.[6] Apart from a desire to be in the country legally, the main reason for obtaining refugee status was to have access to needed economic and subsistence resources available through the government and international aid organizations. Studies of refugees often were done from the population of people receiving emergency assistance and therefore risked being biased toward the neediest sectors of the population. Furthermore, studies of refugees in Costa Rica did not always adequately distinguish between those from different countries. The majority were from El Salvador and Nicaragua, but over time Nicaraguans became increasingly dominant numerically. Often studies of the refugee population gave demographic information for the refugee population as a whole. However, Nicaraguans in Costa Rica were, on average, more rural and even poorer than Salvadorans, in part because they had less distance to travel and a greater history of labor migration to Costa Rica; this sometimes created an impression that most refugees were from rural areas. Finally, some Salvadorans had migrated from rural areas to San Salvador previously for economic reasons (Galván Bonilla and Quintanilla Arévalo 1987:177) and in some ways were consequently both rural and urban.

Salvadorans were so dispersed that it would have been impossible to provide any precise demographic profile of the population, which was not isolable or identifiable, at the time of my study. It is also difficult to provide a simple demographic description of the population because most Salvadorans I met had experienced extremely complex lives. Many had previously migrated within El Salvador. Others, especially men, had also spent time in Honduras, Guatemala, Mexico, Panama, and/or the United States either to work or for refuge during the war. One man who had lived in both rural and urban El Salvador explained to me that in El Salvador it had been necessary to be flexible. It had been so difficult to earn a living that they had developed the ability to look around and find ways to earn a living; whatever one found to do, one did. He had worked buying and selling, as a carpenter, in agriculture, and as an artisan making wood carvings and items out of leather. One man had been a farmer, then a teacher, and was farming again, but he had also worked in construction, sold clothing door-to-door, and sold *tamales*. Another had been an office worker, baker, and carpenter. There was an infinity of such trajectories, making a simple classification of the population by rural or urban or by narrowly defined class position very difficult, perhaps impossible and meaningless. Broadly, however, the population I knew roughly corresponds to the composition of the population described in studies done in the 1980s in terms of when they arrived and class composition.

The people I knew also had a range of experiences of the war and politics, although always to the left or center (to the degree it had existed in El Salvador in the 1980s) politically even though not all had been politically active. Nearly everyone I knew had lost family in the war and some had themselves received death threats before leaving El Salvador. Most of the men I met who were in their thirties had gone to Costa Rica either to avoid serving in the military or to avoid political persecution. Others had been sent out of El Salvador by their families. I met a few urban men who had left because the situation in general had become too difficult, but most had a more direct experience of the violence. Finally, some had accompanied their families to Costa Rica to protect children from the effects of war.

Most Salvadorans in Costa Rica had been what could be described as poor to comfortable before leaving El Salvador. The most destitute segment of society usually could not afford to travel so far. The poorest Salvadorans were either displaced internally in El Salvador or went to Honduras from border areas. Those in Costa Rica included peasant farmers, rural proletarians, and rural semi-proletarians (approximately 20 percent of the population and all commonly called campesinos); artisans and industrial workers (between a quarter and a third); domestic employees, people who had had stands in the markets, teachers, and students. Approximately 14 percent were professionals and 16 percent worked in other services (Galván Bonilla and Quintanilla Arévalo 1987:180–82). Thus they, like the people in my research, span a broad range of class experiences while remaining primarily urban.

The balance of occupations in Costa Rica remained comparable. In Costa Rica they often worked in the informal sector during the years when they could not work legally, and some remained in that sector in the 1990s. In Costa Rica many men worked in construction at some point and many worked as shoemakers. The latter occupation was attractive because they could work at home with less danger that they would get caught working illegally. An important source of employment for women was domestic work. Some men and women also sold things, especially clothing, door-to-door, and some managed to find professional employment. Agriculture, during the harvest season, had also been a common source of employment. Various studies from the early 1980s indicate that approximately one-fifth worked in agriculture, one-tenth as professionals, a third in industry and artisanry, and 40 percent in services: Many people had more than one occupation (Galván Bonilla and Quintanilla Arévalo 1987:344–45). There were approximately equal numbers of males and females and a high percentage of families. Average family size was relatively small. In the 1980s, the majority, approximately 40 percent, were composed of only four members (185–91).[7] Approximately two-thirds of the families were composed of both parents and children, with or without other close relatives (190). The average age was nearly twenty-eight (Pellegrino 1992:cuadro 5).

When they arrived in the early 1980s, Salvadorans did not expect to be long in Costa Rica. Based on the recent experience of the Nicaraguan revolution, they supposed the war would be won quickly and they would return. Many told me they thought they would be away from El Salvador as little as three months; others thought a maximum of one year. The months became years as the war continued, and some people repatriated even before peace accords were signed in 1992. Relatively large numbers returned in 1985 and 1986 (officially 207 and 186 respectively), but it was with the promise of peace that repatriation became a more viable option. In 1991, 205 Salvadorans repatriated through the UNHCR and in 1992, 498 did so.[8] Some resettled in other countries, especially Canada and Australia,[9] which had programs to resettle refugees through the UNHCR. Others went to the United States or Canada independently, sometimes to join family.

In 1993, the year I began my fieldwork, the population had stabilized, although peace was bringing increased visiting between the two countries, and approximately six thousand Salvadorans remained in Costa Rica. Conditions at that time dictated that Salvadorans in Costa Rica choose whether to remain or repatriate. The war had recently ended, aid to refugees was almost completely discontinued, and Costa Rica was encouraging Central American refugees either to repatriate or to apply for residency. Salvadorans who applied normally received permanent residency. Some have naturalized as Costa Rican citizens. Like Alicia, after many years of dreaming of returning home, Salvadorans finally had to make the complex choice of where they would live. Repatriation and national belonging therefore were common topics of conversation. In the following section I review some pertinent literature on these topics in migration studies.

Theories of Migration and Space

Refugee and labor migration have been treated as separate phenomena theoretically despite the fact that in practice they are not always easily separated and the distinctions may be of more political than theoretical importance. In what follows I consider ways in which migration theory that has been applied to labor migration is also pertinent to the study of refugee populations.

Common understandings of migrants, including refugees, have been strongly conditioned by a conception of space that is taken for granted in our culture. This "two dimensional Euclidean space" (Kearney 1995: 549) is a homogenous, continuous, and neutral medium or container. This space is then broken up and organized into contiguous and discrete populations of people, each with a corresponding territory and culture (Gupta and Ferguson 1992). Most often these units are nations and nation-states. In this neatly organized world there is an inextricable link between people, territory, and culture such that people have attachments to only one such complex at a time. This has led people, including policymakers, the general public, and scholars, to divide migrants into two types in a bipolar model of migration in which people move from one autonomous unit of space to another. These contrasting types of migrants are called "sojourners" and "settlers" or, alternatively, "migrants" and "immigrants." In the ideal typical model, the first of these go to another country for a brief period of time, generally as laborers, with the intention of returning home. The second remain in their country of destination and over time reorient their lives to the new country. In either case, people are understood to move from one place to another distinct and distant place, and they are expected to continue to have loyalties to only one country.

Recent academic work on migration has challenged this interpretation by focusing attention on the ways in which it distorts the experiences and social arrangements of many migrants. Migrants, although they can be physically in only one country at a time, may maintain social relations in, and orient their actions toward, two or more countries simultaneously. By documenting transnational fields of social action, scholars have opened up the "field of vision" (Basch et al. 1994:268) in our understandings of migration to other possible social arrangements that cannot be accommodated by the bipolar understandings. This involves a shift to a global perspective on space (Kearney 1995:549). Most importantly, transnationalism in migration is causally linked to the increasingly transnational character of global capitalism since the late 1960s and 1970s. Although migrants to some extent have always retained ties and even political interests in their countries of origin, proponents of transnational perspectives on migration maintain that contemporary conditions are qualitatively different. The material conditions of migration and labor in recent decades have made long-term transnational arrangements increasingly important and often a matter not just of sentiment, but necessity (Basch et al. 1994; Rouse 1989, 1991, 1992).

The growing reliance of capital on flexible accumulation since the late 1960s and 1970s changed the conditions of migration and labor and increased the need for migration by citizens of poorer countries while simultaneously creating greater insecurity within the first-world nations that have usually been studied as the countries of destination. Within developing countries, including El Salvador, that are the main sources of migration, economic change created economic dislocations as export agriculture forced people off land previously devoted to subsistence production and industry drew people into the urban labor market. Economic development created more unemployment and dislocated workers than new jobs, however, and people were forced to migrate from the country-side to the cities and from the periphery to the core countries (Basch et al. 1994:26). Within industrialized countries such as the United States, capital increasingly moved production offshore, creating economic insecurity within those countries also (Sassen 1988). The double insecurity created by economic conditions in both locations encourages migrants to maintain social ties to their families and communities of origin as a type of social security. At the same time, changes in technology have made travel and communication between places cheaper, which facilitates the maintenance of social ties across borders. More specifically, it has made it increasingly possible for people to approximate simultaneous involvement in multiple countries.

This new work on migration is closely related to scholarship on the production of space by capitalism, particularly the work of Lefebvre (1991) as interpreted by Harvey (1990 [1989]) and Jameson (1984). Lefebvre argues that society produces space and ways of experiencing and representing space that are distinctive to the era's mode of production. Therefore, if we are in a new stage of capitalism, "late capitalism," as Mandel (1987 [1972]) convincingly argues, we should expect new ways of experiencing space and time, which Jameson argues is postmodern and Harvey describes as "time-space compression." Transnationalism is a form of experience associated with these developments (Rouse 1991). It is important to note, however, that transnationalism is not a single form produced in an unmediated way by the economic processes of transnational capitalism. Social forms spanning state boundaries have numerous contours. One example is the new ethnicity and political organization Mixtec develop to replace old village identities and loyalties under the conditions of harsh exploitation and prejudice they encounter in migration to northern Mexico and the United States (Kearney 1991; Nagengast and Kearney 1990). Another is transnational circuits connecting locales in a single social space through family and friendship (Rouse 1989). Deterritorialized nation-states that result from combined efforts of states to use migrants (or their descendants) abroad and migrants' involvement in political or development efforts "back home" (Basch et al. 1994) are a third, quite distinct, transnational form. The precise configuration and style of transnational social relations is the result of processes in which people create these social fields, but always in ways influenced by dominant categories and processes. Not only global economic forces, but class transformations, ethnicity or racial ideologies, and national projects influence the forms that these spaces take.

There is a second, implicit, way in which this approach to migration is related to the literature on the social production of space. Both consider the ways in which spatiality is produced through social relations at all levels (e.g., global capitalism and migrant family arrangements) and recognize the fact that multiple styles of space may coexist. Massey's (1994) presentation of space as "social relations stretched out" is a useful way of describing this interpretation of the nature of spatiality or the social production of space. Specific configurations of social relations create localized places as well as the transnational spaces migrants produce. The transnational perspective on migration therefore does more than free us to recognize alternative social arrangements in migration. It has involved a move away from thinking about migration in terms of movement through abstract space to theorizing about the nature and experience of space itself and the ways in which specific spaces are socially produced within a framework of contingent agency. Although I examine a case of migration in which relatively few people had transnational involvements to the degree the literature on transnational migration analyzes, it is this framework in migration studies that has most influenced my thought.

Refugees are, in the terms of traditional migration studies, sojourners who will repatriate as soon as possible. This is a logical consequence of the way in which they are defined as people who leave their country involuntarily, in contrast to other migrants who leave of their own volition. Forced to leave, they are expected to always retain their orientation, hopes, and dreams in their country of origin while the country in which they live in the interim is no more than a temporary haven. This is reflected in refugee policies that define repatriation as the "best solution" (Stein 1986; Warner 1994).[10] The focus of host governments, aid organizations, the UNHCR, and refugees themselves is generally, at least initially, oriented toward that day. Everyone involved assumes that repatriation is what refugees want, without regard for the changes that time brings or the fact that conditions of exile may influence what they come to want. The presumed best solution for the refugee problem continues to be repatriation, despite the fact that so many do not, in fact, go back.

Common understandings of migration maintain that if a person leaves a territory voluntarily, it is possible either to return or to adopt a new country and culture. Refugees are a problem in this scheme because they are forced to migrate. Consequently the best solution is believed to be for everything and everyone to return to an imagined earlier condition when people and territory were united and harmonious. By repatriating and, presumably, taking up their old lives, refugees make both themselves and their countries whole again. The other policy solutions for refugees are deemed less desirable, but have much the same goal. The second solution is their integration into the host society. Finally, some refugees are permanently resettled in third countries as immigrants.

In either of these final two solutions, refugees are expected to become a permanent part of another people/territory/culture complex. Within this framework, refugees can come to be anomalous if they remain as refugees after conditions seem to permit repatriation. Since refugees are almost by definition part of an emergency situation, they are not expected to remain permanently. To continue to be recognizable as such, long-term refugees must maintain their orientation toward their original home by remaining marginal to their host society. When refugees live in camps this is enforced or reinforced spatially. When they successfully integrate into a host society and begin to feel a part of that society, they become less refugee-like. If the UNHCR or host government judges that conditions are such that repatriation is possible, refugees cannot continue to exist as such; at that point they must choose one country or the other.

The questions posed with regard to non-refugee migration focus on the relationships people have to different places. Because refugees are represented as having exerted no volition in leaving and as being solely oriented toward return, they are often represented as placeless and even culture-less (Malkki 1992; 1995b).[11] Yet it is obvious that refugees, as people and not a category, are very much in place—in the world—regardless of whether they eventually repatriate or not. Moreover, regardless of long-term goals, refugees must live in the place where they are through the near future. Therefore it is necessary to consider their relationships to both the place from which they originate and where they find refuge. There has been a tendency in refugee studies to over-generalize about "the refugee experience" based on "an organismic, functionalist view of society that constructs displacement as an anomaly in the life of an otherwise 'whole,' stable, sedentary society" (Malkki 1995b:508). Attention to the different relationships refugees have to different places is one remedy to this homogenization of experience.

Refugees are not so much out-of-place as reemplaced in a space defined by the UNHCR (in most cases) in combination with the multiple nations they inhabit or have inhabited. A complex interaction involving international treaties, politics, economic conditions, nongovernmental organizations, and other national, global, and local forces shapes the rights they can attempt to demand, the resources they can access, and the spaces they can occupy. In the process, refugees encounter new and unexpected spaces and places shaped by political, social, and economic processes and given meaning through culturally defined concepts and social interaction. Thinking about the experiences of refugees in this way has the benefit of making them less radically different from other migrants, just as in real life they are not always as categorically distinct as they seem in theory and law. It also avoids over-generalizing about "the refugee experience" since the exact way in which all these determinants come together varies over time and space just as they do for other migrants and non-migrants.

The case I present contradicts the expectation that refugees necessarily repatriate, although Salvadorans did retain an expectation for many years that they would repatriate. It does largely conform to the situation described by the bipolar interpretation of migration in which some migrants eventually settle and lose their orientation to the country of origin. However, it does so not because this was the inevitable outcome, as some interpretations of migration suggest, but because a particular configuration of political, economic, social, and ideological conditions encouraged it. It was no less produced from configurations of historically specific social relations than other, transnational, forms of migration.

In a more subtle way, however, many Salvadorans who remained in Costa Rica did call into question that bipolar model as well as dominant understandings of space and national belonging. People are expected to orient their lives toward the one country where they belong. However, despite the fact that Salvadorans had reoriented their social relations and lives to be almost exclusively in Costa Rica, they could feel that they belonged in both countries. In the bipolar model, some migrants adapt to the new country, but there is no analysis of ways in which they may feel their lives have been split in half. My analysis of this issue contributes to the study of migration more broadly—regardless of whether the form it takes is that of transnational circuits and communities, settlement, or sojourn. In all the work on migration, people somehow belong to a space in which, in the long run, they orient their social interactions. In this way, the work on transnationalism operates under the same larger paradigm that equates people with a space. The valuable contribution of the transnational perspective is to show that people are able to create other kinds of space that are not contained by state borders. This perspective questions the style of space in which people necessarily belong, but not the manner of belonging. This lacuna in the social sciences has limited our understanding of the experience of migration by obscuring an important source of melancholy and ambiguity.

Salvadorans I knew in Costa Rica recognized, implicitly or explicitly, that people have varied types of attachments to places. Current residence, citizenship, an orientation to a shared legal or cultural code, family and other social relationships, gratitude, loyalty . . . these are all different kinds of attachment. The dominant interpretation of space equates people, territory, and culture and assumes that all forms of attachment are formed with reference to the same triad, but this is not logically necessary. The transnational perspective does not make this same assumption since it emphasizes the way in which attachments form in multiple places, or a discontinuous space, but it does not disentangle the ways in which people are connected to places. People's life experiences may lead these attachments to be in different places and consequently people may even find it undesirable to have them all in one country. Perhaps this is most obvious in those cases of refugees who are forced to leave their country, are unable to maintain sustained contact with their country of origin while in exile, and are permitted to participate with relative freedom in the life of their country of refuge. These conditions impede sustained participation in both countries simultaneously. In these cases it is probable that people find themselves caught between a country they did not wish to leave and one that gave them a home when they most needed it. Over time that latter home becomes important, but the former frequently remains significant. Many Salvadorans in Costa Rica found themselves in just such a position.

Questions of Method

This book is based on nineteen months of fieldwork in the Central Valley of Costa Rica between 1993 and 1995. This fieldwork was informed by preliminary trips in the summers of 1991 and 1992, two month-long visits in the 1980s, and a year as a student in Costa Rica in 1981. The last of these was the same year that many Salvadorans arrived, a fact I found invaluable in thinking about the country as Salvadorans first encountered it. I have also returned for brief visits in the summers of 1999 (when I took a Spanish version of my dissertation, which forms the basis of this book) and 2000.

I first became interested in Salvadoran migration when I was in Costa

Rica in 1981. At that time Costa Rica was receiving large numbers of Salvadoran refugees and they were frequently in the news. My interest was renewed when I began graduate school in 1989. I was struck by the extent of displacement both from and within El Salvador and interested in the effect of this on the country and the people who had not migrated. At the time, however, it was difficult to plan research in El Salvador, which was still at war, so I considered research with refugees. Although I began graduate school with a commitment to work in the United States, I turned my attention to refugees within Central America because intraregional migration had been less studied than migration to the United States and it presented a contrasting set of circumstances. It would not have been possible to do the in-depth participant observation research necessary for ethnography in the Salvadoran refugee camps in Honduras because visitors were permitted in the camps only on a limited basis. In Costa Rica, Central American refugees were an important issue and I could do research freely. These factors reinforced my earlier interest and led me to this research project.

During my preliminary research in Costa Rica, I was impressed by the level of organizing among Salvadorans. In contrast with Nicaraguans in the country, Salvadorans formed numerous organizations that provided assistance in addition to educational and social activities. I was interested in learning more about those associations, the role of class in their organization, and the degree to which they were important to the majority of Salvadorans in the country. Another way in which I formulated this question was to ask whether nationality was an important aspect of social organization. Salvadorans did not live in separate neighborhoods and are not easily distinguished from Costa Ricans; I was therefore unwilling to assume that nationality was central in their lives. Between the time I formulated the research and arrived, the war ended, many Salvadorans repatriated, and most of the organizations ceased to exist. I therefore shifted my attention to the issues I discussed in the Introduction to consider the importance of nationality through their understandings of the experience of settlement and talk about repatriation.

Stereotypically anthropologists do research in a somewhat delimited place with "a people." Much anthropological research has been done in villages or towns where it is possible for the researcher to plop down in the center of things, get to know people, wait for something interesting to happen, and ask questions. Even in relatively large towns this same methodology works, perhaps in conjunction with a select sample of households and survey. When anthropologists work in cities, they have usually chosen a center of activity—a specific neighborhood or market, for example—or an institution. In other cases they have done network analyses by following individual networks of relationships to give shape to the city. In Costa Rica I encountered fieldwork conditions very different from those considered typical in anthropology that are ideally suited to the participant observation method that has long been our hallmark; nor were they conducive to the forms of urban ethnography I have just mentioned. I consequently faced several methodological problems: the lack of a centered and identifiable population, linguistic practices, and distrust. In the following sub-sections I explore these difficulties and discuss how I addressed them. The discussion also serves to provide further background information on the Salvadoran experience in Costa Rica.

An Urban "Field"

It is impossible to get lost in San José, Sergio, a future friend from El Salvador, told me shortly after I began fieldwork. It is small, and just remember north is that way, south is over there, and east, and west. "Great," I thought as he pointed. I know which direction is north only when I already know where I am and I feared that having it pointed out to me once, while in a building in Heredia, was not going to help much. It was true, however, that the city of San José was smallish; I regularly walked the length and breadth of it, although this was an odd habit since there were buses and taxis everywhere. I could not truly get lost since I soon walked my way out of my bewilderment. Even so, it was too large for me to follow some of the advice given in anthropological methods classes. It was much too big for me to map or to do a household survey in order to meet the inhabitants.

The population of San José depends on how one defines it—a surprisingly problematical issue.[12] I was never quite sure when I stopped being in the city. There were named *barrios* and *colonias* (neighborhoods) that ran into other places that old novels indicate had been villages. Now they seemed like suburbs to me, except they melded so completely into the city. These in turn quickly ran into other smaller, calmer cities—each the capital of a province with the same name: Heredia, Cartago, Alajuela. Nestled in pockets and the edges were small agricultural areas and towns that continued to disappear into the city at an astounding rate as *urbanizaciones* (developments) of small, tightly-packed, identical concrete houses sprang out of the ground where once coffee had grown. Census figures from 1989 had the population of the *cantón* ("county") of San José at 284,550, or just under 10 percent of the nation's population, but the urban area was much more extensive. The Area Metropolitana of eleven cantones of the province of San José had a population of 840,698; the population of the Aglomeración Metropolitana, which includes San José, Heredia, Alajuela, and Cartago, was nearly 1.5 million, or over 50 percent of the population of the country (census figures cited in Kutsche 1994:28). Of this area, Kutsche writes:

> The Area Metropolitana does not contain any cantons that are so separated from downtown that they operate as suburbs. One can say unequivocally that 29 percent of Costa Ricans live in the metropolis. The Aglomeración includes cantons in which the centers of population are a little separated from each other and appear like the suburbs of North American cities. It is the Aglomeración, not the Area, that is similar to the metropolitan area familiar to the U.S. census, and here half the nation's population lives. The size ratio of San José to the next largest urban centers in Costa Rica is dramatic—about 1:25. (Kutsche 1994:28)

The Aglomeración functions as a metropolitan area in another sense because the economies of these four cities are interconnected and many people commute from one to another daily. None is more than a fifty-minute bus ride from the center of San José. This concentration of the population occurred in a very small portion of the national territory: the approximately 30 percent of the population that lived in the Area Metropolitana de San José occupied less than 1 percent of the land (Mora Salas and Solano Castro 1994:17). This urbanized Meseta Central[13] was the center of Costa Rica in every sense: geographic, symbolic, and administrative. It was the first area settled by Spaniards and at the time of independence accommodated nearly the entire non-native population. Migration from this area colonized much of the rest of the country.[14] It has only been since the 1950s that this has been reversed and net migration has been to the Central Valley instead of from it (Vargas Cullel and Carvajal 1988: 199). The primacy of this area was both reflected in and reinforced by the centralization of political structures, social services, and infrastructure—for example, all newspapers with national distribution were from San José.

Ninety-five percent of Salvadorans settled in urban or semi-urban areas of Costa Rica (Ramírez Boza 1987:78), mainly in the Central Valley.[15]

Some did so with great determination and a few mentioned resisting pressures from the government, through the refugee programs, to move to more rural areas where the government felt it would be easier to accommodate refugees in projects designed to promote self-sufficiency while avoiding competition with nationals in a context of high unemployment.

Although more Salvadorans settled in the cities of Heredia and San José and the towns associated with these cities than in Alajuela and Cartago, they were not concentrated in neighborhoods. Salvadoran organizations created a sense of community for many, which partially counteracted this dispersion by providing centers of activity in the 1980s. OARS (Oficina de Orientación y Asistencia Social a Refugiados Salvadoreños [Office for Orientation and Social Assistance to Salvadoran Refugees]) was one of these. This office grew out of a shelter *(refugio)* in Heredia created by the parish of Fátima in June of 1980, although OARS was not subsequently associated with the church institutionally. It was one of several refuges that operated as large group homes to assist the most vulnerable of new arrivals under the auspices of the Catholic Church. Other Salvadorans, the majority, lived alone, in family groups, or in groups of young male friends. The church was thus of central importance only in the reception of a minority of Salvadorans, generally the most in need. OARS and other offices (particularly La Coordinadora de Refugiados Salvadoreños [Coordinator of Salvadoran Refugees] in San José) were Salvadoran organizations that supplemented the aid given by the UNHCR and assisted refugees who did not go to the UNHCR out of fear born both from experiences in El Salvador and uncertainty about what to expect in Costa Rica (Oficina de Orientación y Asistencia Social a Refugiados Salvadoreños 1982). Projects these organizations operated included medical and dental services, occupational training, finding financing for productive projects from international sources, legal assistance, psychiatric counseling, and cultural and recreational activities. They cooperated with, but were separate from, the Episcopal Church, Red Cross, and IRC (International Rescue Committee), which at different points administered UNHCR-funded programs. They coordinated with each other, but there were also divisions based in part on political differences within the Salvadoran opposition.

Salvadorans formed a multitude of other associations of students, women, indigenous people, and artisans.[16] During the 1980s there were soccer tournaments of teams of Salvadorans organized by where they lived in Costa Rica, musical and dance groups, and associations of university students. Felipe, a university student and shoemaker, told me there were so many organizations a person could not possibly have taken part in them all. People participated in these organizations and events to varying degrees. Some only went occasionally if there was a service they required, for example access to dental care or loans. Others were more actively involved both with a wider range of services and in social activities. Some claimed to have never been involved at all, although they sometimes followed that claim by saying they had only gone to an occasional party.

By the late 1980s there was far less community activity than there had been in the early years of the decade. When I began my fieldwork in 1993 few of these organizations were active, and those remaining were in the process of disbanding. Salvadorans sometimes bemoaned the loss of community that accompanied the reduction in the Salvadoran population in Costa Rica, the loss of money for refugees as conditions in El Salvador improved, and the fact that Salvadorans developed their own lives and no longer had time for, or an interest in, organizing. Although they missed the sense of community and solidarity, they did not feel a need to organize as they had during the years when they felt Costa Rican xenophobia strongly, were concerned about the war in El Salvador, and had a more difficult time making a living in a climate of economic crisis in Costa Rica. OARS was the main organization still operating, although it had greatly reduced its programs and it finished closing not long after I returned to the United States in 1995. Those few Salvadoran-based or other nongovernmental organizations that had served Salvadoran refugees and survived did so by shifting their focus to a larger population and other issues. In keeping with recent models of development, two began providing loans for micro-businesses regardless of nationality.

Because the Salvadoran population was highly dispersed and despite the comparatively short distances in a country as small as Costa Rica,[17] it was not feasible to choose a residential site as a center of research. There was no central place where people met at the time that I was doing my fieldwork. Nor was there any manner to identify the entire population and choose a random sample. I often felt I had pieces of fieldwork scattered all over the landscape: little pieces connected by busses, bus routes, and bus stops that slowly grew into a webbed map in my mind. Added to this map were the lines I made as I walked: from the stop in front of a bar, up the hill, past the *pulpería* (neighborhood shop), up a little more, onto the dirt road, around the corner another 150 yards, and to Teresa's. From the last bus stop of Desamparados, west 100 meters, and north 250. . . .

From la Santa Teresita east. . . . These lines went from park to park, past churches, to cafes and restaurants in which I wrote notes, to the bank. The lines connected people who knew me and each other and others who were only connected through knowing me or through stories. They and the dispersion they represent meant that I could not stay in one place letting people get to know me as they saw me every day waiting for one of those fortuitous events that anthropologists love and for which we are instructed to watch. I had to put myself in the way of people while still being sensitive to the fact that there was no reason they should wish to talk to me and many reasons they might not. They also create a very different field experience from sites where everyone knows each other and gossip spreads quickly.

I met many of the people I knew through OARS, which provided me with an office and opportunities to participate in social activities, occupational training, and literacy classes, and to meet people who received emergency aid, loans, or low-cost medical treatment. The Coordinadora was in the process of closing when I made my preliminary field trip in the summer of 1992. Through that organization I met a group of Salvadorans who were organizing an association of Salvadoran artisans, and they proved very helpful. Although Salvadorans would not introduce people they did not know very well and with whom they did not feel a high degree of *confianza* (trust), I met other people through friends I encountered in each of these contexts.

Sometimes You Need to Lie

I met Antonio about six months into my fieldwork when I was giving English lessons to a group of his friends and relatives. I had known him about a month on the day I have in mind. We were sitting in one of his favorite hangouts when he asked about my family. I told him of my mother, grandmother, and siblings. How many siblings? He claimed to want to know all about each: age, appearance, residence, studies, job. Long before I got to my eighth sibling, I saw his eyes glaze and tried to abbreviate, but he would not let me. Each time I omitted a piece of information he noticed, despite his evident boredom, and asked: What does he study? Where does she live? When he let me finish, I was pleased about one thing. Ever since I began fieldwork, I had puzzled over Salvadorans' aversion to questions in the face of what I had learned to expect was a researcher's job. I was far from averse to avoiding asking questions, but I was not sure what I ought to be doing instead. "Good," I thought, "a safe question." "How many siblings do you have?" A very irritated look flitted across his face before he answered "two" in a way that precluded further inquiry. I took comfort in Briggs's (1992 [1986]) admonition that we "learn how to ask" in culturally appropriate ways.

In my experience, most Salvadorans rarely asked direct questions. This was most marked in those who had lived in El Salvador at least through their late teens, while those who left as children seemed more like Costa Ricans in their willingness to interrogate me. I also witnessed people teaching children not to be too overtly inquisitive. One woman, caring for young grandchildren whose parents were working in the United States, repeatedly chided her six-year-old granddaughter who was quizzing me on how long I was staying at their house, what I had brought. . . . Her two-year-old brother then asked a question of me and the grandmother burst out in exasperation: "Another one!" Another *metiche* (nosy person)! When a very inquisitive nine-year-old, who had spent part of his life in refuge in Nicaragua, visited from El Salvador, his family in Costa Rica teased him a great deal about how many questions he asked. On a couple of occasions, as a practical joke, the entire family colluded in a lie for much of the day before they let him know the truth because they felt he asked too much.

I was told that "a los metiches hay que mentirles" ("it is necessary to lie to nosy people"). One group of young men, when we discussed how frequently I was asked about boyfriends and when I would marry, said it was not anyone's business and advised me to lie. They suggested I invent a fiancé in Costa Rica and claim that we were planning to marry in January before I returned home. I was once warned, when on my way to a Costa Rican's home, to "be careful" because the woman asked many questions. I was not told why this should be a concern. Family members where I lived sometimes responded to questions among themselves with another question: "Why do you ask?" This was not said defensively or sullenly, and they would immediately answer the original question. In addition, many people habitually answered simple, direct questions vaguely. *Por ahí* (around there) or *por aquí* (around here) might answer the questions "How have you been?" or "Where are you going?" Antonio, in particular, drove me crazy with these nonanswers although he seemed completely oblivious of giving them. When I began answering in the same style, he was irritated. Then he noticed how annoying a habit it could be when taken to an extreme, but he did not stop.

One strategy was to ask questions that left respondents free to interpret them openly and answer with as much, or as little, information as they wished. When I first went to OARS, Marcos asked "¿Y su familia, que?" ("And your family, what?"). I was at a loss to know how to answer because it was not clear to me what he wished to know; I could interpret the question in many ways. Sometimes if people wanted to know something, they would first apologize, surround their question with disclaimers, and say I did not need to answer. Alternatively, they asked questions in the form of a statement. José once asked me a question using both these strategies: He apologized profusely, told me I did not have to answer, and then stated that he had seen that gringas in Costa Rica wore either jeans or very loose, long skirts. That was it. I understood the question, but mischievously pretended not to. I was enjoying his discomfiture and made him ask directly whether I ever wear skirts or dresses.

Apparent distrust of questions bore no relationship to the sensitivity of the information requested and people often volunteered the same information if it was not elicited by a direct question. When I talked to Salvadorans about this, they said it was the simple fact of questions that put them on guard. I was told both that it had always been like that in El Salvador and that it was because of the war—with the war and government repression it had been difficult, even dangerous, for many people to trust almost anyone. It was not just distrust or the ingrained habits of past fear that motivated this mode of asking. It was also a form of politeness and circumspection. I once repeatedly avoided giving a direct answer to Juana's polite inquiries about where I was going to spend the day ("visiting") because I knew she would not approve of the dangerous reputation of the neighborhood I planned to visit. We both understood what the other was doing, so eventually she gave up and asked me directly if I was going there. When I answered yes, she laughed about how she had been trying to be discreet while I avoided telling her precisely what she had suspected.

Months after the conversation about siblings, Antonio raised the issue of lying by recounting an argument he had with a woman about whether all people lie. Unexpectedly he confessed that he had lied when he told me he had two siblings. This did not interest me; I already knew, because it was inconsistent with stories he had told me on other days. What I did want to understand was why, so I asked. By then I had learned that sometimes questions could be asked, especially if the person had already evinced an interest in discussing a topic. He pondered and answered that he did not know: At the time his immediate, instinctual reaction was to wonder who I was and why I wanted to know, and then to lie. He added that he had thought I was lying when I told him about my family; he only believed me when, at his request, I produced photos. Then he proceeded to contradict himself, claiming he had not really lied by redefining his terms. Suddenly *hermanos* became brothers, not siblings, and only the ones living near him, to whom he could turn, counted. In these terms, he had not lied since he had two brothers and one sister in Costa Rica in addition to a brother in El Salvador.[18]

Spies and Ethnographers

Ramón was Alicia's ex-son-in-law. He grew up in rural El Salvador on a family farm. When I knew him in Costa Rica he had a pick-up truck that he used to earn a living. Prior to that he had been in a productive project that made machine-knit sweaters. One day I hired Ramón and his truck to take me to meet people. I was with him when we passed someone walking in the opposite direction on the other side of the street. They waved and shouted cheerful greetings. After we had passed he tugged his earlobe to let me know the man had been an *oreja* (informer/spy, literally an "ear"). He told me that Salvadorans in Costa Rica knew who were orejas from El Salvador and were polite to them. The best way, he told me, to deal with one is to be pleasant. Don't avoid talking to them, but don't tell them anything, either.

This was, I thought, sensible advice. It was also, I realized, one way to deal with a gringa anthropologist. I believe this was what Amalia was doing. I did not know Amalia well. We conversed once in the office during the long wait for her appointment with one of the office employees about a loan she had to buy and resell clothing. She told me about her family, the different ways they had earned a living in Costa Rica, her opinions about Costa Ricans, the contrast she saw between the Salvadoran and Costa Rican economies, why she found the office depressing. She was friendly and seemed quite open, but I noticed that she avoided telling me precisely where she lived when she suggested I should visit her sometime. I found the directions she gave to her house suspiciously vague, despite the apparent sincerity of her unsolicited invitation. Days later the receptionist told me that Amalia had been there again when I was not in the office. She told the receptionist to tell the woman I lived with to be careful because I was a gringa. She had experience with people from my country and we could not be trusted. I also suspect that this was the strategy employed by a few people who invited me to their homes, told me they would stop to get me on a specified date, and never showed up. One man told me to come to his house on a Sunday for an interview with his family; when I arrived they had all gone out for the day.

Yet it was difficult to know when I was being deliberately put off and when it was an accident. This is the brilliance behind that strategy for dealing with people you do not trust. Sometimes people legitimately found themselves busy with other errands and could not meet as arranged; I did not expect meeting me to be the highest priority on anyone's agenda. Other people did not have the same sense of time. Marta, with her daughter and two grandsons, was always late, sometimes so late that the rest of us were leaving when she arrived. I could not take it personally when she did not show up at the bus stop at the specified time. Eugenia invited me to her house to visit multiple times, but gave directions that simply did not get me there. The day we encountered each other on the bus after I had been unable to find her home, she adamantly insisted on taking me out for lunch at McDonald's in San José where we were both going. People fed people they cared about and this was an expense she otherwise did not need to incur. But Marta and Eugenia knew me from other contexts, while I did not know Amalia. The man who went out with his family the day he had told me to visit also did not know me; I met him because he was a client at an office that lent money to refugees, but we did not have any other connection. Other people I met that way were more cooperative, but it was generous of them and I tried to avoid putting people in a position where they would feel obliged to speak with me.

Salvadorans sometimes brought up the issue of trust by asking me how people were treating me. Those who knew me best were particularly concerned about how I was received and often asked if I had been fed on a visit because this indicated how well I had been accepted. Some could get quite upset if I was not fed as well as they thought I should have been. I was told that when people got to know me I would have no problems, but until then people would not trust me. This was particularly true given my government's role in the war in El Salvador, but I was also told that the distrust of strangers was more generalized. Some told me they would distrust any foreigner. Others mentioned that they took care not to speak freely even with other Salvadorans. Many people had learned to be more trusting in Costa Rica, but they recognized the pattern from El Salvador. Most often I met people in groups, almost invariably with someone who already knew me. Under these conditions people unobtrusively observed me, sometimes for a long time, until they decided they wished to speak with me. At that point they would begin a conversation, often by asking me a question—perhaps about my siblings or what I was doing in the country. Some Salvadorans said their compatriots would not talk to me unless they already had decided I was someone they would like to know.

Two other factors were influential in some people's wariness. First, people did not want to remember, and the fact that I was studying refugees implied that I wanted to talk about the past. It was time to live in the present, not the past. It is necessary to leave the bad and learn from the good, I was told by various people both as a general lesson for life and a lesson for my study. Although I believe it is necessary to learn from the bad as well, I respected their need to continue with their lives and did not consider I had the right to ask them to relive painful memories for my benefit. Nor was there an urgent need to tell their stories for people to hear in the United States because the war was over. Second, Salvadorans had been studied by governmental and nongovernmental agencies, students writing undergraduate theses, and foreign scholars. They had never seen any benefits from all these studies, so there was no reason to continue to tolerate investigators disrupting their lives.[19]

This distrust would have made it impossible to conduct a survey or contact people without an introduction by a trusted mutual acquaintance, even if it had been possible to identify and locate the Salvadoran population. Furthermore, linguistic practices would have limited the utility of surveys or many other forms of direct questioning. Some told me, in conversations or the few recorded interviews I did, that in interviews or questionnaires with other researchers, whom they had not known well, they had been uncomfortable and had omitted information about their experiences. In any case, I quickly learned not to ask many questions from those flickers of annoyance and vague and non-serious responses.

I spent more time, nineteen months between 1993 and 1995, with Salvadorans than the authors of these many studies did when they administered surveys; this is appropriate for my emphasis on cultural meanings that can best be understood through actual use. What I learned largely arose either in the stories we told as we got to know each other or because they decided I should know and they wanted to help me. Apart from interviews with people who had worked with refugees through the UNHCR, I did few formal interviews. I did six with Salvadorans, one of whom I knew well and three who were good friends with one of my best friends.

These taped interviews, which were in the form of life histories collected in people's homes, typically lasted several hours, more if I include the time I spent chatting and having coffee and refreshments. Although I had prepared a list of questions and topics, I found that in each case I did not ask more than a few questions because people covered everything I had thought of without prompting. Most either apologized for talking so much or asked me why I had let them continue. These open-ended interviews proved useful in part because they showed that the information and stories I was told under more formal conditions were the same as what I was told in more informal settings. I therefore relied most on informal participant observation because it seemed least intrusive and most appropriate under the conditions I have described. I am convinced that although some Salvadorans would have responded to a more aggressive approach, this was neither necessary nor in most cases desirable, and that many of the people (particularly older women) who trusted me would not have done so. In the chapters that follow any long quotes are from taped interviews, when they are not from printed sources. In all other cases the information comes from untaped conversations I wrote down as soon afterward as I could. Throughout the book, all names are pseudonyms and all translations are my own.

I got to know Salvadorans from as wide a range of backgrounds and experiences as possible within the constraints I have described. I did this by taking advantage of the variety of contexts available. I often went to spend time, talk with friends, attempt to make myself useful, read, or write notes in OARS. Through that office I knew some professional Salvadorans. I also knew the people who received monetary assistance, used the low-cost medical clinic, or attended the weekly literacy and sewing classes. These people, who still needed such forms of assistance, were among the poorest Salvadorans in the country. The preponderance of them had been rural in El Salvador and had received little or no formal education there. The majority of these people were women and their families, although some men also used these services. Most of these women were either domestic servants or older women whose ability to earn a living was limited. The older women depended upon the aid, what they could earn selling homemade foods, and assistance from family. Many of them had suffered a great deal in the war; the women usually had husbands, brothers, or sons who had been killed, and some of them had themselves survived massacres or death threats.

The office also gave loans to people either to begin or expand small businesses or to buy property or clothing they resold. I met other people who had received similar loans through a friend and another organization that had provided such assistance. A much larger proportion of the people who had received loans for productive projects had been urban in El Salvador than those who were receiving aid and they were not as poor. Although all those who received aid or attended classes at OARS knew each other, those I knew with loans did not, for the most part, know each other or the people with aid. Through OARS I also met a group of young men who were university students earning a living as artisans. They had gone to Costa Rica as children with their rural families; some of them studied sociology and they were very generous about sharing their experiences as well as their understandings of Salvadorans in Costa Rica. I met a second group of men through La Coordinadora before it closed. Some of this group had grown up in urban El Salvador and others in a semi-rural area. They had all attended school at least through the sixth grade and almost all had graduated from high school. Some would have gone to the university if conditions had permitted. They had done a variety of things to earn a living in their lives; when I knew them most were artisans and/or salesmen. They did not know the people from OARS although they were acquainted with the other group of young men I knew.

This volume is primarily an ethnography. However, the conditions I have described mean that it has been a difficult one to write. Although I focused on Salvadorans, I did so with the assumption that a common national origin did not necessarily imply that people would share other experiences or values. I knew people from as wide a range of class and educational backgrounds as possible. They came from all over El Salvador and they did not form a residential community in Costa Rica. Often they did not know each other. One way to read the chapters that follow is as my exploration of why the disparate people I knew, living in what was itself a large and heterogeneous metropolitan area, belong in a single manuscript. I do this by identifying discourses, narratives, and concepts that people had in common and then analyzing the ways in which people's experiences and use of those discourses varied. What they shared was the experience of having become refugees (in the broad sense, regardless of legal status) and settled in Costa Rica under a very specific set of historical and politico-economic conditions. When the war ended, they shared a concern with the issues involved in deciding whether or not to repatriate. I organize the book around the themes and narratives I heard from people across the spectrum of class positions and experiences.

However, meaning is always socially situated, and there was no reason to suppose that a common narrative meant an entirely shared experience; so I look for difference and variation within what they had in common. In taking this approach, I am influenced by feminist standpoint theory, which emphasizes the fact that the ways in which we are socially situated in structures of power affect how we understand the world (Hartsock 1987; Scott 1991). Gender, age, rural/urban provenience and experience, class, and education were some of the factors that affected people's experience of Costa Rica and which I discuss in my analysis. In my analyses of the concepts they shared and used in discussing their experiences, I move beyond simply pointing out these differences. Instead, my goal has been to move between analyses of difference and similarity to reach another level of understanding of the concepts. I am also influenced by theoretical approaches to pragmatic meaning in language that emphasize the ways in which meaning is situated. Although there are structures, meaning, in this perspective, is always partially emergent from use and is contextual (Voloshinov 1986 [1973]; Williams, Raymond 1977). This perspective runs contrary to a more simplistic conception of meaning as primarily referential. The main theme that runs through the narrative I develop is the varied meanings of the nation and national belonging or identity for different people and under varying conditions. This perspective on language permits me to examine in detail the ways in which the language of nations and national identity played out in different contexts and the sometimes contradictory ways in which discourses of national identity affected the ways in which Salvadorans settled in Costa Rica.

Half a Life

Salvadorans experienced El Salvador and Costa Rica as very different places, despite the many regional linguistic and cultural similarities. I was often somewhat skeptical of their interpretations of national "idiosyncrasy," as it is often called in Central America. On the one hand, some differences they mentioned were idiosyncratic individual observations and not generalizable. On the other hand, differences that were credible I think can be more interestingly interpreted in terms of the specific political and economic histories of the two countries. However, it is important that social processes and relations made that way of speaking meaningful. *Patria* (nation) was said to be a fundamental unit of society second only to family, and this centrality was reinforced for most Salvadorans through multiple experiences including education, the army, and war. Countries were central to becoming a refugee, and the experience of crossing boundaries, particularly under traumatic circumstances, further marked that importance. The change in countries corresponded to dramatic changes in their lives as they went from a country of danger to one of peace, but also one of discrimination and financial difficulties as well as sociocultural differences, and as they entered new configurations of social relations. In Costa Rica the salience of the nation-state was reinforced through migration and refugee policies and representations.

From this initial experience of difference, many Salvadorans came to have a very different relationship with Costa Rica. I explore how some came to live their lives in that country in such a way that it became the country they were unlikely to leave despite their original intentions to repatriate. Some called it their second patria or said that they felt Costa Rican after so many years. I am interested not only in how this happened, but in their experiences of the process and the cultural concepts they used to interpret those experiences. The core of the text is structured around an elucidation of key spatial concepts Salvadorans used in talking about displacement and reemplacement. By examining these concepts and the relationships among culturally defined spaces, I explore how Salvadorans constructed the experience of settlement and the ways in which social variables, such as gender and age, influenced what happened to them. Nationality was an idiom through which they spoke of their experiences of displacement and reemplacement, so I pay particular attention to the role of national belonging and national difference in the ways they were received and their reactions to their lives in Costa Rica.

In addressing these issues I also contribute to ways of thinking about how it is that people belong to sociocultural spaces, including nation-states. I am interested in two aspects of this issue and the relationship between them: the idea that the world is made up of discrete territories and the idea that people belong to one of these territories. It is in this regard that the experiences of Salvadorans in Costa Rica contribute to social-science understandings of migration. While some Salvadorans remained in and adapted to Costa Rica, many developed a sense of dual belonging that is not explained by models of migration.

There are other examples of multiple national identities that are distinct from that which I consider here. In this case, circumstances meant that relatively few Salvadorans were able to approximate simultaneous involvement in both El Salvador and Costa Rica. Instead, their lives in El Salvador were in the past and perhaps the future, while they lived the present in Costa Rica. They came to feel they had a part of their lives and identity grounded in each country, but not at the same time. Legally they had a different set of rights in each country and they could be citizens of only one, so legal criteria were not entirely isomorphic with their sentiments or experiences of belonging. Their experiences were different, therefore, from those of people who hold dual citizenship or migrants and their descendants in the United States documented as developing multiple national attachments. In the former case the relationship between legal categories and experience is different. In the latter, migrants are said to maintain multiple national ties precisely through their ability to remain involved in two countries at once.

I once thought of calling this book *Half a Life*. This phantom phrase guides my thinking still. The term "half a life" comes from an interview I had with a Salvadoran woman. This woman, whom I will discuss in chapter 5, had a son who was happy in Costa Rica and a daughter who was not. Her daughter had told her mother that she did not even know where she was from because she had half of her life in El Salvador and half in Costa Rica. The mother wished she could tear herself in two so that she could take her daughter home to El Salvador and yet remain with her son in Costa Rica.

I chose this title for two reasons. *Half a Life* reflects the fact that the lives people made in Costa Rica were not the same lives they had previously had in El Salvador. I do not intend to suggest that their lives, when I knew them, were incomplete. Indeed, I admire nearly all the Salvadorans I knew for the strength they had shown in making new lives. They had not forgotten what had happened, but they had learned to live with it and with the good things they found. However, there was a sense of melancholy and loss for nearly all, even those who were most content in Costa Rica. They did not choose to leave their lives in El Salvador. Few were better off economically in Costa Rica than they would have been in El Salvador; many were worse off. They had lost family, careers, and dreams. They made new lives and loves, but those other losses remained. The title also recognizes the limits of what I can know. I tried to understand what Salvadorans spoke of often as well as what they rarely mentioned. It was hard to find a way to make what I thought I understood into a coherent manuscript, and much is missing. Much is missing too, I am certain, in what I learned. Without a doubt there were gaps in what they told me and what I could grasp. I cannot claim to have captured some full truth of their lives; this is my best effort, but it is only half as good as it should be.

The phrase carries a third burden of meaning that I only noticed after I had completed the manuscript: It echoes Roque Dalton's poem "Todos," which I quote in chapter 1. In that poem, Dalton memorializes a massacre that took place in 1932. He says since then all Salvadorans had been born "half dead." The injustice that episode represents continued and eventually led to the war of the 1980s. The melancholy and displacement of the people I knew were but another effect of the repression Dalton decried in his poem. If 1932 meant that Salvadorans after that were born but half alive, the events of the late 1970s and 1980s also split in half many lives and families in ways that were not easily repaired.

Salvadorans in Costa Rica

1

Two
Histories

From Colony to Export-Dependent Agriculture

The fifteenth of September is Independence Day in Central America. In Costa Rica it is also sometimes called the Day of Central American Fraternity. The latter phrasing suggests that it is a day to celebrate the fact that the five Central American republics form one *gran patria*, one large homeland divided into five small countries, while the former lends itself to a focus on the smaller nation-states, despite a shared history. This tension between Central America as a unity and five disparate countries weaves through the history of the region. Under Spanish colonial rule Central America was a single administrative unit, and after it was given independence with Mexico in 1821 it formed a tumultuous union between 1823 and 1838. Since then there have been recurrent efforts to create some form of Central American union. Although the roots of unity are found in the colony and early post-colonial efforts, the origins of the vast social differences between the countries, a constant theme in regional scholarship, are also traced to that period. The distinct economic and political systems, whose roots are found in the colonial period, are then traced through subsequent eras to the events of the 1980s. The contrasts among the countries also had ideological consequences in the way Salvadorans and Costa Ricans thought about themselves and their countries.

In this chapter I trace a history of El Salvador and Costa Rica. It is a partial history, which I present not only to give the reader an overview of the politico-economic history that led to refugee movement from El Salvador to Costa Rica, but also to show the ways in which that history was meaningful in the lives of people I have known. The war and refugee mi-

1

gration of the 1980s were the product of a history of politico-economic conditions and displacements that shaped the lives of Salvadorans and the countries they inhabited. These histories shaped conditions not just in a simple objective sense, however, but also as a result of the ways in which people interpreted them. Historical conditions and their socially constructed interpretation are important for understanding the context in which Costa Rica received Salvadoran refugees and the meanings they attributed to refuge, a topic I take up in chapter 2. Finally, these histories are an integral part of how people understood national identity, and I present them in that light. Considerations that would be important in an objective effort to describe what "really" happened are consequently sometimes set aside in the histories I tell here. Perspectives that are important in their own right are also ignored if they were not important in shaping the lives and experiences of the people I knew. These histories are not untrue, but are partial in both senses of the word.

Many Salvadorans spoke with pride of being "a people that has fought," to quote a friend. Another friend quoted a man who answered the question "How are you?" by saying: "Siempre salvadoreño, rebelde y soñador" ("Always Salvadoran, rebellious and a dreamer"). This is a legacy that was sometimes traced as far back as the conquest, as was the legacy of injustice that justified rebellion. Although none of the Salvadorans I knew would normally call themselves "indios," most would have recognized that they were part indigenous by blood (particularly in contrast with Costa Ricans) although not culturally indigenous. More important, they identified with the indigenous heritage of oppression regardless of questions of ethnicity, which until recently were relatively unimportant in El Salvador since identity revolved around class issues instead. Some people spoke of Spanish as a colonial language and assumed that it was spoken better in Spain because the language belonged to the people there. Some asserted that Salvadorans did not consider the twelfth of October (Columbus Day) a day to celebrate. People sometimes spoke with pride of how the indigenous population of El Salvador had fought against the *conquistadores*. I was told, for example, of a Salvadoran professor who reportedly told her class of Costa Rican students this in a critical manner. She told them that the indios of her country had resisted the Spanish conquerors, while those of Costa Rica had not.[1]

In contrast, the indigenous population of Costa Rica, which was much less densely settled, is nearly completely written out of popular history. Costa Rican distinctiveness, like that of El Salvador, is traced to the colo-

nial period, but to the character of the colonizers (rather than conquistadores) and the colonial society. In a newspaper editorial, Miguel Angel
Rodríguez asks the archetypical question of Costa Rican history and provides the elements of the dominant historiography: "What were the reasons for our progress? What was it that allowed us during the first decades of independent life, to pass from being the most backward of the
colonies in the Capitanía General to be the most advanced of the Republics in Central America?" (Rodríguez E. 1994).

Rodríguez mentions the poverty and isolation of the province in the
colonial period and writes of "50,000 poor and illiterate mountain people
who found themselves with independence in 1821" (ibid.). In this single
sentence, he powerfully summons a memory of the poverty of colonial
Costa Rica. The reference to *montañeses* (mountain people)[2] reminds us of
both the hardships faced as a result of the almost impassable mountains
and the fact that the country, named for its coast, began in the mountainous center. It also reminds us of a consequence of that geography that
is a key characteristic in explanations of the country's history: the isolation that was frequently illustrated, often with apparent pride, by the
fact that Costa Ricans did not learn they had been given independence
from Spain until a month after the fact, when the mail arrived. Popular
memory and official historiography recounted that because of these factors Costa Rica was so poor that everyone had to work, even the elite, and
thus a country of yeoman farmers was born and sustained in an egalitarian ethic that treats all people as worthy of respect and no one as above
work. This theme runs through histories of Costa Rica, which are punctuated by ways in which this legacy has been either strengthened or threatened. Salvadoran history, in contrast, is punctuated by reenactments of
the conquest and the colonial search for wealth.

When the elite of Central America began attempting the work of building nations after independence, they concentrated on the development of
export economies to generate much needed revenue. Coffee quickly became, for much of Central America, the export of choice. Coffee production began first in Costa Rica: By the 1830s, approximately four decades
before the rest of the region, the country was exporting coffee to Great
Britain. Ironically, this early dominance was facilitated by the country's
previous isolation and poverty. It was the province most distant from the
colonial center of power in Guatemala and the least developed economically. El Salvador was better integrated into the colonial economy, but in
a way that made it dependent upon Guatemala, while Costa Ricans had

no major export product. The lack of viable alternative investment opportunities helped encourage coffee production in the southern country. In contrast, El Salvador was the center of indigo production, although Guatemala was the financial and marketing center for that production. Although El Salvador came to be a major coffee producer very quickly, it did not begin intensive encouragement of coffee production until the 1850s when a crisis in the indigo trade dramatized the need for export diversification.[3]

Soon the two countries were similar in their near complete dependence on coffee production, but their relations of production could not have been more different. Land tenure and availability of labor varied widely among the countries of Central America and each consequently faced remarkably different problems in developing an export-agriculture economy. Population density was low in Costa Rica[4] and concentrated in the central highlands, as was the land best suited to coffee production. Land was largely held by smallholders and there was a large frontier.[5] The larger landholders and richer citizens might have made efforts to dispossess the smaller producers, but the latter could move to the frontier areas either to avoid wage labor or if they became dissatisfied with labor conditions. Consequently, in Costa Rica it would not have been possible to create the large free labor force necessary for large coffee plantations to dominate production. Instead, municipal, and later national, policies encouraged smallholders to plant coffee.[6]

As smallholders began planting coffee in Costa Rica, they financed it largely through deferred consumption (Gudmundson and Lindo Fuentes 1995), rather than credit, while the coffee agro-export elite made most of its money in processing. A mutual dependence developed between the two classes: Small producers needed to sell their product to the processors, but the larger producers/processors could not fill the growing European demand for their product without the smaller producers. This mutual dependence limited the ways in which the wealthier planters could exercise their power.

Geographical, demographic, and social conditions were markedly different in El Salvador, where the entire territory was more densely occupied and there was no significant frontier. At 11.9 people per square kilometer, the population density was much higher in El Salvador at the time of independence than in any of the other four provinces and nearly ten times that of Costa Rica. As in Costa Rica, the prime land for coffee production was the most densely populated, but in El Salvador much of this land was held either communally or in *ejidos*.[7] The government of El Salvador first attempted to encourage production of coffee on these communal and smallholdings, but this quickly changed under liberal ideology. Coffee requires three to five years growth before it can be harvested and it was difficult for people without capital to plant coffee as quickly as was desired by Salvadoran modernizers, who soon came to feel that communal lands were a hindrance to economic development. As a result, policies encouraging small producers were reversed in favor of policies to privatize the land. The change in land tenure was accomplished very quickly, largely between 1858 and 1890, with the most strenuous efforts beginning with the abolition of communal lands in February 1881 and March 1882.

Salvadorans who, in more recent decades, thought of themselves as rebels against economic injustice and a political system that upheld the rights of capitalists at the expense of farmers and workers and saw in this characteristic a moral link to an indigenous past could find support in events during this period of rapid primitive accumulation. There were major peasant uprisings in 1832, 1872, 1875, 1880, 1885, and 1898.[8] To resolve the problems of rural unrest and insufficient labor on Salvadoran plantations, anti-vagrancy laws were passed that gave agrarian justices in each village the authority to ensure coffee growers a labor force. A rural police force was created to enforce these laws in 1884 and by 1895 it was effective throughout El Salvador. Because El Salvador was so highly populated, once the change in land tenure was accomplished there was a plentiful supply of labor. As a consequence the landowners were able to depend upon low wages to increase their levels of profits and competitiveness.

Costa Rica, with its low population density, had significant labor shortages, higher wages, and generally better labor relations.[9] Wages for rural laborers in that country doubled between 1847 and 1856 (Hall 1978:55). The contrast in labor relations remains true today, as evidenced by the relatively high rates of labor migration to Costa Rica from Nicaragua in particular, but also from El Salvador, Guatemala, and Honduras—from the latter three countries at least, in part the result of active recruitment of workers by Costa Rican employers. Costa Ricans, in contrast, migrate either within the country or to the United States.

The Great Depression

By the first decades of the twentieth century, coffee was well established in the economies of both countries. In 1850 coffee accounted for about 90 percent of Costa Rican exports. This declined precipitously at the end of the century when banana production began on land ceded to U.S. entrepreneur Minor Keith in an agreement to complete the railroad to the Atlantic coast, so that during the 1920s coffee comprised between 50 and 60 percent of exports despite the fact that the total area planted in coffee had increased (Hall 1978:15–16). El Salvador, lacking an Atlantic coast, did not become a site for the United States-based transnational banana companies that have been prominent in the region and, without competition, coffee comprised 88 percent of Salvadoran exports between 1922 and 1935 (Burns 1984:306).

The Great Depression extended through World War II in Central America and brought drastically lowered prices for coffee. In El Salvador the price of coffee fell from twenty-five (U.S.) cents per pound in 1925 to just nine cents in 1935; it reached twenty cents again only after 1945. Costa Rican coffee prices were both higher and relatively protected because of the quality of coffee produced, but in Costa Rica prices in 1935 were just half what they had been in 1929 (Dunkerley 1988:90). This created a crisis, particularly for the lower classes, handled in typically different ways by the ruling elites in the two countries.

1932: El Salvador

> Todos nacimos medio muertos en 1932
> sobrevivimos pero medio vivos
> cada uno con una cuenta de treinta mil muertos enteros
> que se puso a engordar sus intereses
> sus réditos
> y que hoy alcanza para untar de muerte a los que siguen naciendo
>
> We all were born half dead in 1932
> we survive but half alive
> each one with an account of thirty thousand dead
> that began to fatten their interests
> their returns
> and that today manages to anoint with death those who continue being
>   born
> Roque Dalton, "Todos" (1983:505–6)

El Salvador had the highest unemployment in the region during the interwar depression, and government revenues were halved between 1928 and

1932 (Burns 1984:308). In this period of economic crisis the Salvadoran president, Pio Romeo Bosque, held free elections in 1931 rather than name his own successor as had been customary. The winning candidate, Arturo Araujo, promised major reforms, to be funded through cuts to the military budget, that would guarantee the population a minimum standard of living and land reform. But he was unable to implement his programs because of budgetary problems and an inability to reconcile differences among social sectors. In December of that year the military installed his vice-president, Maximilio Hernández Martínez, as president.

This coup was followed by the massacre of January 1932, memorialized in Dalton's poem. The Communist Party and peasant leaders had been organizing an uprising, but when they learned that the government had uncovered the plot, the party attempted to stop it. Even so, in rural areas, particularly in the largely indigenous region of Sonsonante, people carried through with the revolt. They were countered with massive repression. Within days between ten and forty-five thousand people were killed[10] when the total population of El Salvador was approximately 1.5 million. It is said that almost overnight it appeared that the indigenous population had disappeared—either killed or incognito as they changed their style of clothing and language to be less visible and escape the repercussions of being associated with the uprising. The event remains seared in the history of the country and the memories of many Salvadorans. It was commemorated in the name of the 1980s revolutionary guerrilla force and current political party FMLN (Frente Farabundo Martí de Liberación Nacional): Farabundo Martí was one of the martyred leaders. Throughout the period after Martínez there were coups and counter coups as a result of conflict among the ruling elite, but none of this became of great symbolic importance historically. Nor did the political maneuvering affect the population in the traumatically direct and large-scale manner of the events of 1932.

1948: Costa Rica

The economic crisis of 1930–35 was less severe in Costa Rica than the rest of the region. Costa Rica experienced zero economic growth during that period—but the other four countries had negative growth. Despite the relative strength of the Costa Rican economy, there was increased discontent with the standard of living of the majority of Costa Ricans and consequently with laissez-faire liberalism, but more far-reaching reforms

were enacted in this country than in El Salvador. In the banana plantations of the Atlantic coast, there was a strike in 1934 against the United
Fruit Company that involved approximately ten thousand workers [11] and
was led by the Communist Party. [12] This strike is the most celebrated instance of class conflict in Costa Rican history, but it is one that has been
absorbed into a nationalist discourse. The conflict was not just between
classes; it was also largely between Costa Ricans and foreigners—United
States plantation owners and administrators—and it has been subsumed
within a discourse of Costa Rican anti-imperialism, rather than class.

The worst of the economic crisis of this period occurred in Costa Rica
during 1940–44, and it was at this time that more serious social reforms
were initiated. Rafael Angel Calderón Guardia was elected at the beginning of the decade and began reforms that were opposed by his upper-
class backers. This led him into a three-way alliance with the Communist Party and the Catholic Church. A socialized health-insurance system
was instituted in 1941, in 1943 the country's first labor code was enacted,
and in that same year social guarantees were added to the constitution.
Despite the economic crisis and problems caused by dependence on two
export crops, Calderón did not enact economic changes that would have
undermined the coffee elite, but could have helped other economic sectors and reduced coffee-dependence. As a result the government encountered opposition among the rising class of small-business owners, professionals, and the old planter/processing elite alike.

In the 1948 elections, the various opposition groups joined forces—despite their disparate interests—in support of Otilio Ulate, a conservative.
Ulate is believed to have won the elections, but the governing party an-
nulled the results and civil war erupted, with the opposition represented
by José Figueres. In April Figueres's forces had control of much of the
country, but Vanguardia Popular (the Communist Party) controlled the
capital. A peace agreement was negotiated and signed on the nineteenth
of April after slightly more than one month of fighting. In May Figueres
and Ulate signed a new pact. Figueres was made the head of a junta that
would rule for an interim period of eighteen months and subsequently
turn power over to Ulate as the legitimate winner of the elections.

During his interim rule, Figueres instituted a number of reforms that
built on those of the first half of the decade. He abolished the army [13] and
nationalized the banks, which created opportunities for a new middle
class by opening up credit. Citizenship rights were expanded as women
were given the right to vote. Laws affecting blacks in the country were

changed, many claim, to give them greater rights. It is often said in Costa Rica that it was after this that they were permitted in the Central Valley. This is not true, but they had been forbidden to work in the banana plantations on the Pacific coast and this was changed.[14]

The 1948 revolution, not the 1934 strike against the United Fruit Company, is the moment considered decisive in shaping recent Costa Rican history. Furthermore, the strike is primarily remembered for its anti-imperialist and nationalist potential, while the revolution is presented as a moment in which reforms and social rights were defended and expanded to permit greater democratic participation and equity. In contrast, in El Salvador the most memorable moment is one of unresolved internal class conflict in the massacre of 1932.

1932 Revisited

Julia, who was taken to Costa Rica with her family as a child in 1981, told me that she had believed that the problems in El Salvador started recently with the violence of the late seventies and early eighties, until she started talking to some of the Salvadorans who were organizing the community of Salvadorans in Costa Rica. They told her about the more distant history of her country. They told her about 1932. Nineteen thirty-two: Antonio talked about it to me a few times because his mother had taught him about it. She and her family had fled their rural home during that massacre to live in a different, safer region where he was born thirty years later. He believed that most Salvadorans did not know about 1932 unless they had family who were affected and told them as his mother had told him. He attributed the discontent that he and most of his family felt with the system to the influence of his mother and grandmother: They taught him and his brother "to think."

Dalton, in the poem "Todos," continued:

Unámonos medio muertos que somos la patria
para hijos suyos podernos llamar
en nombre de los asesinados
unámonos contra los asesinos de todos
contra los asesinos de los muertos y de los mediomuertos

todos juntos tenemos más muerte que ellos
pero todos juntos
tenemos más vida que ellos.

Let us unite half dead that are the patria
in order to be able to call ourselves its children
in name of the assassinated
let us unite against the assassins of everyone
against the assassins of the dead and of the half dead

all together we have more death than they
but all together
we have more life than they.

Dalton (1983:505–6)

As Dalton suggested it should, 1932 has been a rallying point for organization and discontent in the country—another link in a chain of exploitative and repressive relations between oligarchy and workers. It was also a reference point for the elite: with it they had won—or stolen—fifty years of apparent calm. In Costa Rica, Figueres, in the minds of many, won for Costa Ricans the democracy and peace they have enjoyed in the intervening fifty years—peace and democracy that came to exemplify what it meant to be Costa Rica (Gólcher 1993). Although the social reforms that have underwritten the distinctiveness of Costa Rica were begun before he came to power, he and his party were given credit for their continuation. The party that he founded, Liberación Nacional, remained associated with a strong public sector and social programs, although it more recently has been obliged to support the International Monetary Fund's austerity programs.

After World War II

Central America after World War II became even more intensively tied to global developments. Import Substitution Industrialization was promoted, especially with the Central American Common Market beginning in the 1960s. Originally the United Nations Economic Commission on Latin America (ECLA) recommended a common market to permit economies of scale and a larger market for Central American goods. As envisioned by ECLA under Raúl Prebisch, foreign investment was to be limited to a minority share of any enterprise, and a planning commission would have ensured that each country had an allocation of new industries. Both these features were eliminated, however, under the influence of the United States. This meant that much of the industrialization occurred through multinational (often United States-based) corporations and was dependent on advanced technology and inputs from the developed countries. This capital-intensive industrialization created relatively few jobs. Local financing and repatriation of profits by multinationals diverted capital away from more socially productive economic development and contributed to balance of payment problems.[15]

During the same decades the United States-funded Green Revolution brought advanced technology to agriculture in an effort to raise production. Export agriculture was encouraged both through export-crop diversification and the increased use of chemicals. Consequently the agricultural sector is now not only dependent on the global economy for export markets and prices, but also for the cost of inputs to production. This growth in export production led to increased consolidation of land and a need to import basic foods for domestic consumption as production of those crops was pushed off the best land.

The combined industrial and agricultural development efforts did lead to economic growth, but not always to improved conditions for all of the population. Even so, the postwar years of growth prior to the oil crises of the 1970s did help create a larger middle class and did permit increased social spending by countries.

El Salvador

In 1950 a new constitution was promulgated in El Salvador that guaranteed "liberty, health, and culture, economic well-being and social justice." The workweek was limited and women were given the right to vote. The government granted urban workers, but not rural labor, the right to strike. The constitution also included an anti-sedition provision and the government actively, and violently, suppressed dissent. The decades of economic growth that followed were similar in their mix of minor reforms, small political openings, and repression of dissent.

Expansion of export agriculture was facilitated by the use of new chemical fertilizers and pesticides, and new areas of the country were incorporated into export production. This precipitated a new generation of land consolidation as new technologies made old crops practical. Cotton was first when pesticides made it possible to bring more land into producing this crop in the 1950s and 1960s. In the 1970s beef production in El Salvador expanded as the United States raised its quotas and approved packing plants in El Salvador in 1972 and 1973. Rural landlessness concomitantly increased dramatically: In 1961, 12 percent of rural households were landless, in 1971 it was 29 percent, and in 1980, 65 percent (Dunkerley 1982:63; Williams, Robert 1986:170).

Landlessness and unemployment were exacerbated in 1969 when war broke out between El Salvador and Honduras and the latter country forced 130,000 Salvadorans to return home from Honduras where they had been living and, mainly, farming in an area near the border.[16] High levels of rural unemployment (in 1963 the rural labor supply was 57.7 percent higher than demand [Dunkerley 1988:185]) meant that planters did not need to improve labor relations, and most were unlikely to perceive reasons to do so.

The displacement of the rural population by the growth of export agriculture caused increased migration to the capital and abroad. Between 1961 and 1971 all departments (provinces) of El Salvador had net migration away from the rural areas, with only La Unión as a mild exception. San Salvador and the exterior were the main destinations of these migrants (CSUCA, Programa Centroamericano de Ciencias Sociales 1978). This is reflected in the life experiences of many Salvadorans I met in Costa Rica who had moved to San Salvador either to work as young adults, or with their families in their childhood and early teens.

In the industrial sector, El Salvador did well in the regional common market by many economic measures. Industry grew rapidly (24 percent between 1961 and 1971), but it was unable to absorb the displaced rural workers. Investment in capital-intensive industry meant employment did not rise as much as industrial production: Employment in manufacturing in El Salvador rose only 6 percent in that same period (Armstrong and Shenk 1982:47). The percentage of the population employed in this sector actually decreased from 12.8 percent in 1961 to 9.8 percent in 1971 (Russell 1984:54). The oligarchs of El Salvador continued to rely on inexpensive labor to compete and create profits in industrial production, just as they did in agriculture.

Social protest and repression both increased in El Salvador during the late 1970s as the economy was affected by the worldwide economic crisis. The state in El Salvador had been the guarantor of labor relations ever since it formed a police force to ensure labor for coffee production; consequently all labor problems were transferred to the state (Guidos Vejar 1980). There was no way to protest economic conditions without protesting the political situation; any opposition could be interpreted as antipatriotic. As protests became more organized and serious, state violence increased.

The size of the armed forces, with United States funding and training,[17] expanded from ten thousand to twenty-four thousand between 1979 and 1982 and to fifty-six thousand in 1987. This was reflected in the experiences of nearly all the men I knew who would have been in their late teens and early twenties at the turn of the decade. Military service was obligatory, but in practice this had not always been enforced. During that period this changed and young men were conscripted from the streets and outside of schools. Men commented that "it was a crime" or "a sin" to be a man then.[18]

Under President Carter the United States made weak moves to encourage respect for human rights and even cut military assistance, cuts that were compensated by unprotested aid from Israel. The true message, or at least the most consistent one, sent by United States foreign policy might be estimated by the words of Carter's ambassador to El Salvador, Frank Devine, who wrote in his memoirs (quoted in Montgomery 1995:73): "[Human rights] was an appropriate emphasis . . . [but] there is . . . a difference between doing this in one's own country and asserting the right or duty to impose our human rights standards upon other countries, which may or may not be ready for them."

Perhaps many among the ruling class of El Salvador were not ready for human rights, but the fact that much of the population was is evidenced by the increasing levels of opposition. In the late 1970s popular organizations "could consistently put 100,000 to 200,000 people on the streets in demonstrations" (Lungo Uclés 1995:154), although the total population of the country was only about five million. The opposition continued organizing and unifying. By 1980, the FMLN, a coalition of five major opposition groups, had consolidated. Earlier that year the government had killed Monseñor Romero, the archbishop in San Salvador and a vocal voice for moderation and against state violence, as he gave mass. By 1981 a full civil war had erupted.

Some of the stories Salvadorans told me about the second half of the 1970s were hopeful and hinted at a time of excitement and possibility created by the intensive level of popular organizing and Monseñor Romero's weekly radio-broadcast mass in which he denounced human rights abuses. It was also a period of economic difficulty, reflected in the violence of everyday life from high unemployment, low wages, and increasing police brutality. During the war in the 1980s, these problems only grew worse. In 1984, real working class wages were just 57 percent what they had been in 1973 (Booth and Walker 1989:150). In 1980, 68 percent of the population lived in poverty (García and Gomáriz 1989–90:108).

It is estimated that over seventy-five thousand people were killed during the war, but in some ways it was during the early years of the 1980s that the violence was most intense. In each year between 1980 and 1982 over twelve thousand people were killed and nearly one thousand disappeared or were detained. These were the years during which most Salvadorans went to Costa Rica and nearly everyone I knew had been directly affected by either the state violence or the massive buildup of military forces. On December 31, 1991, peace accords were signed.

Costa Rica

Costa Rica was affected by the same global forces as El Salvador. Despite the fact that the country presented itself as one of yeoman farmers based on the availability of an agricultural frontier,[19] landlessness grew to be comparable to that of El Salvador: In 1971, 22 percent of the rural labor force was landless (Seligson 1989:170) (compared to 29 percent in El Salvador), although a larger percentage of the land was in medium-sized farms in Costa Rica and less in micro parcels.[20] Income distribution also was less skewed; the bottom 20 percent of the population in Costa Rica received twice the share of income that they did in El Salvador.[21]

As opportunities declined in rural Costa Rica, the combined result of the expansion of export agriculture and the shrinking of the frontier, the urban middle class expanded through education and the remarkable growth of the public sector in the decades after the 1948 revolution. Between 1950 and 1966 the government doubled the percentage of the work force that it employed (Denton L. 1971:18). The Costa Rican state steadily extended social benefits (including education, retirement pensions, and health services) to more of the population. This contributed to the growth of the middle class and a strong belief that it was possible to get ahead through education. It also improved the overall welfare of the population and the country attained impressive indices of social welfare and development. In 1997 the United Nations Development Programme ranked the country as having "high human development" and 33rd of 175 countries in human development; El Salvador ranked 112th (United Nations Development Programme 1997).

Industry grew to contribute just over 20 percent of the gross national product in 1976 from 12.5 percent in 1952, while the relative importance of agriculture fell a corresponding amount (Soto Badilla 1982 [1979]:133). Unlike El Salvador, there was a corresponding rise in the percentage of the population employed in industry (Fernández Pacheco 1988:70). Between 1960 and 1980 the proportion of the economically active population employed in agriculture in Costa Rica fell from 51 to 29 percent while in El Salvador it declined only 12 percent; in 1980, 50 percent of the Salvadoran workforce was still in agriculture (Booth and Walker 1989:148). In Costa Rica, most of this growth was in the Central Valley: In 1975 only 15 percent of industry was in the provinces of Limón, Guanacaste, and Puntarenas (ibid. pp. 236–38). This reinforced the dominance of the urbanized Central Valley in the country.[22]

Although the extensive social programs Costa Rica developed improved the quality of life in the country and helped create a climate of social unanimity, they were expensive and largely funded through public debt. Before the economic crises of the 1970s this seemed sustainable, but the economic pressures of that decade changed the situation. The consumer price index had risen by about 5 percent a year in the late sixties and early seventies, but in 1973 inflation rose to 15 percent and in 1974 to 30 percent. This clearly reflected the effects of the oil crisis on a dependent economy. During this first crisis, the government adjusted wages, giving the greatest relief to the lowest-wage workers (Williams, Robert 1986:184). It also raised spending on social programs at a rate exceeding that of inflation[23] and increased national control of businesses vital to the public sector, including transportation facilities and infrastructure and petroleum refining and distribution.

The oil crisis at the end of the decade was accompanied by an ill-timed fall in coffee prices in 1978. The government initially responded by again increasing social spending. This became increasingly difficult to sustain under the combined effect of rising import prices and the depressed value of coffee. The government had maintained a fixed rate of exchange with the U.S. dollar, but in 1981 Costa Rica was forced to devalue the national currency; it went from approximately twelve (U.S.) cents to two cents before it stabilized late in 1982 (Williams, Robert 1986:185). In August of that year the country ceased debt payments (Edelman and Kenen 1989:187). In 1982 inflation was between 90 (Dunkerley 1988:631) and 100 percent (Williams, Robert 1986:86). The gross national product nearly halved; even adjusted for the phenomenally high inflation it fell: Measured in 1970 U.S. dollars, GDP per capita was 996 in 1979 and 834 in 1983 (Dunkerley 1988:631). Open unemployment rose dramatically from about 4 percent in 1979 to nearly 10 percent in 1982; in the latter year underemployment was 22 percent.

In macroeconomic terms the country recovered quickly, in part through assistance from the United States.[24] In 1983 a portion of the debt was renegotiated and an International Monetary Fund austerity program agreed upon to end subsidies to basic foods, continue budget cuts, privatize state-owned enterprises, and raise rates on utilities. Inflation was reduced to just 11 percent in 1983. Yet the effects on the lives of people living in Costa Rica could not be ameliorated as quickly as for macroeconomic indicators, particularly given the nature of the cure, although the effects were not as deep as had been feared. Even so, inequality increased. The share of national income that went to the richest 10 percent of the urban population rose from 23.2 percent in 1981 to 26.9 percent in 1992, while that of the poorest 25 percent fell from 9.5 to 7.9 percent (United Nations, ECLAC 1995). It was this Costa Rica that refugees entered in unprecedented numbers: In 1983, between 8 and 10 percent of the population of the country was foreign-born, while just ten years earlier it had only been 2.5 percent (Zúñiga S. 1989:22).

One way to interpret Salvadoran history is as a series of episodes where repression and rebellion faced off. At key moments, when the elite could have instigated reforms to create a more equitable society, more moderate forces were defeated and reactionary approaches were used instead. In this way the oligarchy managed to appropriate great wealth for itself, but at the cost of governing far more through force than by consent. In this reading, the most salient episodes of Salvadoran history involve the contestation of that rule and attempts to institute a more popularly-legitimated form of government and economy. Unlike Costa Rica, Salvadoran history is primarily one of class conflict. Although they identified with an indigenous past, until quite recently an indigenous present was obscured in the country.

Costa Rican history contains many of the same tensions and went through the same globally-induced crises, but in marked contrast to El Salvador the moderate and reformist voices nearly always prevailed over more repressive ones. The key events emphasized by Costa Ricans tend to exemplify either national unity against foreign forces or the rapid reconciliation of conflicting interests rather than interclass conflict. This can be interpreted as a defeat for peasants and proletarian Costa Ricans. In this interpretation, Costa Ricans were co-opted by a government and ruling class into accepting token reforms and promises over structural change that might have created real equality. However, it also led to a tradition of which the country is justly proud: Inequality is not as great and living standards are higher than in the rest of the region. It also created a norm that the government must make some attempt to meet in order to retain legitimacy.

The crisis in the 1980s in Costa Rica is significant beyond the fact that people's lives were made more difficult because of the way it articulated with national identity. Costa Rica had presented itself as fundamentally egalitarian, yet this condition, or even the appearance of it, was increasingly difficult to sustain with the economic crisis. The interpretation of Costa Rican history I have presented in this chapter was articulated into a nationalist discourse that in large part depended upon a contrast between a peaceful, socially developed, and egalitarian Costa Rica and the rest of Central America.[25] But the economic crisis threatened to make Costa Rica more like the rest of Central America in poverty and social inequality. Refugees from that region arrived at the same time as the political and economic threats, and this was important in how refugees were represented and treated by Costa Ricans. The coincidence of these developments had a significant effect on refugee policy in Costa Rica and, more generally, on the experiences of the refugees themselves. I turn to these issues in the next chapter.

2
Meanings of Refuge

People Pigeonhole You

"Yes, people generally pigeonhole *(encasillar)* one. Perhaps for the way of speaking we seem like Nicaraguans or the others, Hondurans and Guatemalans." Lucrecia, a Salvadoran woman who had lived in Costa Rica since 1981, explained to me in these words the way in which Costa Ricans tried to identify people they suspected were foreign, despite the difficulties this posed since the subtle characteristics that might have marked them as Salvadorans could be confused with the differences between Costa Ricans and Nicaraguans or other Central Americans. Salvadorans were also sometimes mistaken for *guanacastecos*, people from the Costa Rican province of Guanacaste, which borders on Nicaragua.[1] Lucrecia and her husband, Guillermo, then spoke of the discrimination many Salvadorans had experienced in Costa Rica. They had not, however, and they attributed their good fortune in this regard to the fact that they had taken care not to be known as refugees among their neighbors, although they had made no effort to hide the fact that they were Salvadoran. "Salvadorans yes, refugees no," they told me.

Most Salvadorans commented on the issue of rejection and the precariousness of their position, either as foreigners or as a consequence of their migratory status, regardless of their personal experiences or how their own relationship with Costa Ricans had changed over time. Some, like Guillermo and Lucrecia, had not experienced rejection directly, but commented on this and theorized why they had not when others were less fortunate. Some were embittered over slights they had experienced. A few attributed the problems they had encountered to their own behavior and the psychological effects of having lived under a violent dictatorship. Some felt Costa Rican rejection of Salvadorans was past or a problem only for those who spent time disreputably in the street. Others felt that xenophobia was ongoing, although perhaps more muted for them than it had been before Nicaraguans became the focus of public attention. Many thought it a latent possibility even while they lived their lives peacefully for the moment. Regardless of personal experience, the issue remained for all.

Reflecting on Lucrecia's comment that Costa Ricans tried to pigeonhole them and the importance that many Salvadorans placed on how they were categorized by Costa Ricans, I begin by considering the importance of processes of classification for the study of refugees. I then discuss the shifting legal system for identifying refugees in Costa Rica during the 1980s as this emerged through the interaction among national, regional, and international processes and systems of meaning. We will see that the United Nations introduced a new legal category, but the meanings that category came to have in Costa Rica were not the same as elsewhere because of the ways in which it became inflected with class and national connotations as it was reconfigured as part of a new system. This case demonstrates the need to examine how different systems of classification interact under specific politico-economic conditions to give substance to categories of migration in people's daily lives. The chapter ends with a consideration of ways in which Salvadorans worked with, through, and around the categories of migration and citizenship used to pigeonhole, and stigmatize, them.

Kearney (1986), in a review of anthropological studies of migration, points out that "in a strict sense, migration is the movement of people through geographic space" and as such its study pertains to demography. In anthropology, he argues, the study of migration is generally the study of "migration and . . ." something else. When he wrote this article, the something else typically was development; more recently it is identity. Although it seems logically true that migration is about movement through space it is plausible to argue that migration is instead about the ways in which people are categorized with relation to space. The truth of this alternative formulation is revealed when we remember the amount of effort expended in differentiating among types of migration or consider the forms of movement that typically are not called migration at all. Societies define types of movement and classify people within an elaborate series of categories accorded different values in the social landscape.

These systems of classification, which mark who is from where and who has what rights in which places, are crucially important in our lives. They are important even for those of us who either do not wander far from where we were born or do so in such a way and space that it is typically called a move rather than migration. For refugees and foreign labor migrants, of course, the repercussions of their places in this system of classification can be more detrimental.

> Refugees are constituted, in Douglas' sense (1966), as a dangerous category because they blur national (read: natural) boundaries, and challenge "time-honoured distinctions between nationals and foreigners" (Arendt 1973:286). At this level, they represent an attack on the categorical order of nations which so often ends up being perceived as natural and, therefore, as inherently legitimate. (Malkki 1995a:8)

In her classic work *Purity and Danger*, Mary Douglas (1984 [1966]) analyzes how anomalies and ambiguities in a system of classification may create a sense of unease and become a source of either danger and pollution or latent power. Lissa Malkki (1990, 1995a) draws on Douglas in her analysis of refugees as people out of place in what she memorably calls "the national order of things." She argues that in a world dominated by the idea that we all have a nation (or at least a country) in and to which we belong, refugees are anomalous. One way this is evidenced is in the frequent representation of refugees as people without a country—or even without a culture. Their anomalous position, she persuasively argues with evidence from practices and discourses that commonly surround refugees, also means that they are perceived as a danger to national security and borders. They are represented as a problem to be solved. One complicating factor in applying Douglas's framework to people, Malkki notes, is that people, unlike dirt and other matter out of place in a socially and culturally defined order, can and do categorize in addition to being categorized by others. In her ethnographic work, Malkki analyzes the conditions within which Hutu refugees living in Tanzania "categorized back" and how historically specific political, economic, and social contexts conditioned the ways in which they interpreted, identified with, and used the category of "refugee." However, she is somewhat less careful in distinguishing between an international discourse about refugees and the ways in which refugees are categorized by national and international authorities in specific cases.

Although we tend to think of classification as rigid and uncompromising, Douglas emphasizes the contextual nature of the process. Anomalies may be positively or negatively valued and people's tolerance of them varies. She illustrates this point early in *Purity and Danger* with the example of people's different tolerance for a dirty or untidy house even within a single society. If we apply Douglas's framework to migration, this is clearly true; however we can also see that the difference in people's tolerance of migrants (and in this category I include documented and undocumented, political and economic, refugee and non-refugee) is not innocent in the way that a tolerance for dirty laundry on the bedroom floor is. People's attitudes toward those individuals who are, to follow Malkki, anomalous in the national order are political attitudes influenced by various discourses, experiences, and ideologies.

Anomalies also must be interpreted, Douglas argues, not only in relation to the system of categorization that creates the anomaly, but within the cultural and social context that gives the whole system meaning. For refugees, this needs to be done not just with how people categorize back, but also with how they are categorized by others. This means that we must pay attention to two aspects of how the category "refugee" gains meaning in any given situation. First, we must consider the place of this category in relation to not just the national order, but also other ways of classifying people within that order. "Refugee" is not a leftover category for all people who are outside the national order. The category is in fact created and subsidized by that order. It is also only one status within a system for classifying all those people who cross state borders—a system that includes tourists, temporary residents, and undocumented workers, among others. Second, we must consider other aspects of the social and cultural context as these inflect the meanings of the migratory categories. It may be true that many people find migrants, including refugees, anomalous in the national order, and for that reason, as Malkki and others have argued, easy scapegoats for social problems. Yet this does not fully explain specific cases of discrimination or negative representation. We must consider the context within which refugees and other migrants live and the places different nations occupy in the national order. Although ideologically all nations may be equal in "the family of nations," in practice they are not. Countries are experienced in different ways, have different statuses in the international order, and different symbolic values within the nationalist discourses of their counterpart states—values that adhere to citizens. The system of classifying refugees in Costa Rica in the 1980s was further complicated by the ways in which national and international legal systems interlocked and interacted with national, regional, and international politics during a period of crisis. By the end of this period, a new legal framework had evolved that did not correspond to the prior systems of classification.

Shifting Categories of Refuge

Prior to the late 1970s, Costa Rica had no *refugiados*, "refugees." The term "refugiado" was introduced into the Costa Rican legal system with the UNHCR. In 1977, Costa Rica signed the United Nations treaties governing refugee affairs and the UNHCR set up its regional offices in San José, the capital of Costa Rica. These two events began a process in which the Latin American category of *asilado* was partially supplanted with the UN "refugiado." In 1978 refugiados first became a prominent part of Costa Rican life with the arrival of Nicaraguans fleeing the war in their country. They were given *prima facie* (as a group) refugee status in Costa Rica, but by the UNHCR. They were in the country only a few months and remained on the border; when the Sandinistas won the revolution in Nicaragua in 1979, these refugees returned home. As a consequence, this first cohort of Nicaraguan refugees had no significant impact on Costa Rica's legal or migration system. Neither before nor immediately after this episode did Costa Rica have internal legislation or bureaucratic organization to deal with refugees. It was not until Salvadorans began arriving in appreciable numbers in the early 1980s that the country began developing policies governing refugee affairs, and these early efforts were pervaded by a sense of crisis and emergency. This fact combined with the severe effects in Costa Rica of the world economic crisis of the early 1980s and the fact that Costa Rica is a small, relatively poor country to ensure that the country depended greatly on international assistance with the refugees.

In 1979, official figures had fifty thousand Nicaraguan refugees in Costa Rica and only 254 Salvadorans. In the following year this changed dramatically; over two thousand Salvadorans were officially registered and only eighty-six Nicaraguans. In 1981 a similar pattern was observed, although the number of Nicaraguans began to rise. In 1982 the balance shifted as 748 Salvadorans and 1,043 Nicaraguans were registered. In the following year, it was 279 Salvadorans and 5,731 Nicaraguans. During the rest of the decade, the numbers of Nicaraguans remained elevated and Salvadorans low [Office of Refugee Migration cited in Wiley (1991)]. The numbers from countries other than El Salvador and Nicaragua were not large enough to concern us—or the Costa Ricans. Note that most Salvadorans arrived between 1980 and 1982; these were also the worst years of the economic crisis in Costa Rica: In 1982 inflation was between 90 and 100 percent.

In October of 1980, in response to the unprecedented number of Salvadorans arriving, the Costa Rican government passed its first refugee bill, which put the UNHCR in charge of receiving applications for refugee status. These applications were to be reviewed by a government commission known by the acronym CONAPARE (Comisión Nacional para los Refugiados), which began meeting in May of the following year. By then there were already six thousand applicants whose cases would need to be reviewed and, apparently to expedite such a daunting task, Salvadorans were also given prima facie refugee status. This was replaced with individual evaluation of cases in December of 1981. CONAPARE was first assigned directly to the Presidency but, within days, it was moved to the Ministry of Public Security (Barthel 1987:47). It included representatives from the government, the UNHCR, and the Red Cross (then administrator of UNHCR-funded assistance) and mainly discussed problems of coordination between these entities (Muñoz Jiménez 1985:46), although it was in charge of determining and documenting refugee status. In 1982 the government, under President Luís Alberto Monge, restructured CONAPARE, more fully defined its functions, and provided the commission with offices. It was put under the Ministry of Justice and voting rights were taken away from the UNHCR representative.

The criteria for, and manner of, determining immigration status changed on various occasions, as did the policies toward work and aid.[2] In 1982, just six months after it was reformed, CONAPARE was reduced to executor of policies devised by the National Security Council. Less than one year later, in 1983, the latter was replaced by the Office of Refugee Migration in the Ministry of Governance and Police. Two years later CONAPARE was replaced by DIGEPARE (Dirección General para Refugiados) under the jurisdiction of the Presidency. There was a similar flux in the UNHCR-funded nongovernmental programs.[3] In May of 1980 the Episcopal Church came to an agreement with the UNHCR to assist all refugees, and in that year the Red Cross began work with Salvadorans. In 1982 all programs passed to the Red Cross after a disagreement between the UNHCR and the Episcopal Church when the latter refused to assist Nicaraguans in the belief that they were not true refugees but Contras or ex-National Guards from the Somoza regime. When Monge was elected in

1982, the government wished to have control of programs and in 1983 they were passed to the Instituto Mixto de Ayuda Social, a governmental social assistance program. In 1985 programs were transferred back to another NGO, CASP/Re (Centro de Atención Social para Refugiados). CASP/Re and the UNHCR disagreed and programs were passed to the Asociación Centro-Integral Atención a Refugiados, another NGO, in 1989. Finally, IRC (International Rescue Committee), which had been operating the Costa Rican government's refugee camps for Nicaraguans, took responsibility for all refugee programs. Most programs were terminated by December of 1993.

For our purposes the details are less important than the rapid and constant changes. New government agencies were created and old ones supplanted. Administration of programs switched from the government to one NGO and then another. This instability reflected a constant attempt to respond to the changing social, economic, and political conditions of the country, the number of people who were arriving, and changing perceptions of the refugee crisis. They show Costa Rica's attempts to gain control over the situation while depending on the UNHCR and international assistance. The shifting policies also give indications of how new and confusing it was for Costa Rica to deal with large numbers of refugees and glimpses into the severe sense of crisis that pervaded the country; note, for example, that refugee affairs were placed under the ministries of the Presidency, Justice, and Public Security.

The changes also reflect changes in the government. Ramírez Boza (1989) and Larson (1992) identify four stages in government policies: 1978–82, which ended with the decreasing power of the UNHCR vis-à-vis the government; 1982–85, when policy was oriented toward national security and control of the labor market; 1985–86, in which neutrality was reaffirmed with regard to the Central American conflicts; and post 1987, during which negotiations brought an end to the wars and created the possibilities for repatriation. The first period corresponded to the presidency of Rodrigo Carazo; the second, Luís Alberto Monge (1982–86); the third and fourth, Oscar Arias (1986–90). The first stage was one of confusion as the country attempted to deal with the unprecedented crisis. In the second, Monge had promised a total crackdown on refugees; Salvadorans told me they were afraid they would be deported when he was elected. They were not, but his presidency was less conciliatory and more repressive than other administrations, not only with refugees but also other sectors of society that made popular demands as a result of the eco-

nomic crisis (Valverde R. and Trejos Paris 1993). During that period, refugee policies were particularly oriented toward national security and economic concerns, reflecting the problems the country was facing. Finally,
Arias campaigned on the issue of peace in Central America and reoriented
the country's politics toward conciliation both internally and externally.
The fact that the mutating policies were reactions to specific domestic
and foreign conditions does not controvert the fact that this represented
a new and confusing experience for Costa Rica, one to which no one was
quite sure how to react.

Although Costa Rica had not previously received refugiados or developed well-defined procedures for dealing with refugees, it did have
a history of giving refuge, which was frequently referenced in discussions of the refugees of the 1980s and 1990s (e.g., Flores Gamboa 1989:
181). Evaluations of refugee policies and programs and theses on refugees always began with this history. These antecedents included an in-
ventory of well-known, elite Latin Americans who had been given asylum at some time. During the 1970s a slightly larger number of South
Americans with asylum in Costa Rica included professionals, authors,
and scholars. Even so, it remained a relatively elite status and the number of people with it in Costa Rica was always small. The recitation of this
history laid the ground for pleas by Costa Rica for help from the international community based on the contrast between past and present populations seeking refuge in the country. This history also formed part of a
discourse that promoted the acceptance of refugees into national society
by appealing to the nation's better nature to counteract xenophobia. For
example, one social scientist argued that it was necessary to study the
economic and political implications of migration "in a country of 'open
doors' for migrants and refugees such as Costa Rica is, which is now a
tradition that forms part of the idiosyncrasy of the Costa Rican people"
(Zúñiga S. 1989:26). The appeal to a tradition of hospitality to those in
need in a society that made justice, regardless of citizenship, a top priority validated acceptance of refugees and attempts to treat them fairly,
while rhetorically giving the country a position of moral superiority in
the global arena (cf. Barboza Chavarría 1988). The juxtaposition of this
discourse of solidarity with repeated calls of alarm indicates the double
bind many Costa Rican officials felt. The country was incapable of dealing
with the refugees, but obligated to take them. It wished to uphold ideals
of democracy and justice, which were the bedrock of the country, needed
to avoid antagonizing international organizations that provided the funds

to maintain refugee programs, and realistically could do little to stop the arrival of Central Americans across the Nicaraguan border. At the same time, domestic economic and political pressures were daunting and it was feared that refugees could potentially make those problems worse.

However, and this fact was not noted, the refugees cited in that tradition of welcome and tolerance were asilados, not refugiados. "Asilado" was a legal category based in Latin American treaties.[4] The *Convención sobre asilo y refugio políticos*, signed in Montevideo in 1939, and the *Convención sobre asilo territorial* and *Convención sobre asilo diplomático*, both signed in Caracas in 1954, define two types of asylum (*asilo*) (reprinted in ACNUR—División de Protección Internacional 1984). Under these agreements, diplomatic asylum is given to petitioners outside of the host country's borders (for example, in an embassy) and territorial asylum—sometimes referred to as "refuge" (refugio)—is given from within the host country. In both cases the individual is an asylee (asilado) and someone who needs asylum as the result of his or her political activities.[5] This distinction is based solely on the location in which the request for protection is made and does not refer to the reasons a person is in danger.

This geographical distinction based on where one applies is not part of the United Nations' Protocol regarding refugees and was not maintained in Costa Rica after the UNHCR began working with the Costa Rican government on refugee affairs. The United Nations defines refugees more broadly to include not only those who would qualify as a Latin American asilado, but people who are outside of their country for specific reasons:

> any person who . . . owing to a well-founded fear of being persecuted for reasons of race, religion, nationality, membership of a particular social group or political opinion, is outside the country of his nationality and is unable or, owing to such fear, is unwilling to avail himself of the protection of that country, or who, not having a nationality and being outside the country of his former habitual residence, is unable or, owing to such fear, is unwilling to return to it. (Cited in Malkki 1995b:501)

This definition is much broader than that of asilado and it has been reinterpreted over time by the United Nations and international legal experts to be more inclusive. Thus, for example, the United Nations has intervened on behalf of refugees who did not leave their country of residence, victims of famine, and groups of people given refugee status on a prima facie basis rather than as individuals. However, this de facto extension of the UNHCR mandate does not dictate that signatory countries extend the definition in a similar manner, although the Latin American countries followed Africa in amending this definition in 1984 in Cartagena to include those who flee from generalized violence.

The Costa Rican constitution stipulates that signed international treaties have the force of law. So for some years after the country signed the United Nations Protocol in 1979 the two systems of refuge co-existed. In 1986 Costa Rica changed its legal code to include both categories in a single system of classification. At that time, asilados were defined as those with a political reason for taking refuge. Their cases were examined directly by the president's office. Refugiados were defined as people who have any other reason to fear for their lives in their home country. In the context of Central America in the 1980s, this meant the victims of war. This codification of the two categories into a single system of classification changed the legal meaning of the terms by bringing them into a direct relationship. In particular, the term "refugiado" was de-politicized.[6] The distinction between political and nonpolitical refugees, which Costa Rica has normalized as a contrast between asilado and refugiado, is not part of the United Nations protocol which in practice the UNHCR uses to include both Costa Rican categories although, if read literally, it would only cover asilados. This was a new distinction that does not correspond exactly to any of the international treaties. The Costa Rican woman in the UNHCR who explained it to me was proud because she believed that Costa Rica was the only Latin American country to have the category "refugiado" in law. This was another example of Costa Rican progressivist distinctiveness and the country's continued commitment to social justice and consequent difference from the rest of the region.

This distinction between refugiado and asilado was not in place when most Salvadorans arrived. Even after the legal system was changed in 1986, they were not considered for asylum—political—status regardless of what they did before going to Costa Rica. Salvadorans were granted refugee, rather than asylee, status neither because of where they applied (the Latin American system) nor because of the basis for their fear (the current Costa Rican system), but because the country needed the United Nations to care for them. There was a clear class bias in the use of these terms. Asylees had always been relatively elite. Salvadorans and Nicaraguans in Costa Rica were almost entirely, to borrow the words of a Costa Rican UNHCR official in my interview with her, *común y corriente* (common and ordinary) people, even when they had been doing extraordinary things. Most were relatively poor, and even those who had not been poor in El Salvador had left their property and livelihoods behind. Many needed some form of assistance, at least initially, because they arrived with nothing and because they were not permitted to work legally in the early years of their time in Costa Rica. Although some were middle-class, Central American refugees were not perceived by Costa Ricans as middle-class and even many Salvadorans associated the legal status with need and dependency. The class biases of the terms were facilitated by the fact that one applied for the two statuses through different channels.

The Costa Rican distinction is a result of the prior existence of the mainly elite category of "asilo" in Latin America, but it also reflects, and was made more meaningful by, the contrast between a few elite and professional asylees and the masses of Salvadoran and Nicaraguan refugees who came to exemplify the category "refugiado" for Costa Ricans. To understand the meanings attached to the word "refugiado" in practice as they affected Salvadorans, we need to remind ourselves of the dominant representation of Costa Rican history as well as the politico-economic conditions of the 1980s. The fact that the category of "refugiado" was new meant that there could not have been an easy discourse already available to explain refugees, just as there was not initially any bureaucratic infrastructure or procedures to deal with the volume of immigration occasioned by the wars in Central America. Consequently the word took on connotations within the national context of the time—a context of economic and political crisis throughout the region that seemed to threaten the most fundamental aspects of Costa Rican existence. "Refugiado" came to mean, for most Costa Ricans, the stereotypes they had about the Central Americans who were the majority of refugiados. The Costa Rican government encouraged the consequent prejudice against refugees by subtly using refugee policy to deflect criticism against the state for worsening social conditions toward an outside cause.

Refugees in a Metaphorical Island

"We have lived the illusion that our small nation could isolate itself from the world. It could be a paradisiacal island in a troubled world and a nation that through its respect for the principle of nonintervention in the political affairs of other countries, through that simple fact, uncontaminated by all the political realities that surround it" (Lic. Rodrigo Fournier quoted in Sánchez P. 1982). "A paradisiacal island"; Salvadorans used the same metaphor when they told me, as many did, that "in those years arriving in Costa Rica was like arriving in paradise." In a newspaper editorial, Echeverria Esquivel (1994) called the country "almost an anomaly in the world" in his description of a monument at the University for Peace. The island metaphor gains meaning from this sense of being an anomaly, because an island is set off from the rest of the world of continents. Costa Rica was set off from the rest of Central America and even the world. Its anomalous position gave the country a sense of power through moral superiority. It gave the country a sense of security, as if its difference were an amulet. The arrival of large numbers of Central American refugees, perhaps more than any other event, convinced Costa Ricans like Fournier and Lopez that the country was not an isolated paradise, but a part of Central America with a related fate. The country in the 1980s became "contaminated," as Fournier suggests, "by all the political realities that surround[ed] it." That "contamination" suddenly made it clear that the country might not be as anomalous or autonomous as it had believed; suddenly it was "surrounded" by dangers to its distinctiveness.

"A thousand Salvadorans enter per month," announced a newspaper headline in July 1982 (La República 1982a). In a short article replete with the phrase *se informó* (was informed), which leaves us totally uninformed about the source of the article's data, we learn that seventeen thousand Salvadorans entered Costa Rica in the eighteen months prior to July 1982 and that by the end of the year there could be twenty-four thousand. We are told that these Salvadorans were taking work from Costa Ricans in agriculture, artisanry, and construction. After this alarm, the article elaborates on the problem of Salvadorans in the country: "LA REPUBLICA was informed that the Salvadorans come in complete families, most without economic resources that 'they work in anything to subsist.'" After two sentences of general information about refugees in the country, the article continues: "It was said too that 'among the Salvadoran refugees are mixed some delinquents, whose trace is lost' within the national territory." The next sentence informs us that the government was going to begin a study of the Salvadorans, one assumes to compensate for lost traces, and then: "There are many complaints from Costa Ricans because, above all in the area of construction, the 'Salvadorans work for whatever and they displace them [the Costa Ricans], which increases the level of unemployment in the country.'" This article conveys a sense of panic and loss of control. Many people were entering the country and no one knew where they were or what they were doing. Another article from the same year carries the headline "11 thousand Salvadoran refugees disappeared" (La República 1982b). They could be working, displacing Costa Rican labor during a period of economic crisis, training as *guerrillas*, or committing crimes; these were the fears most repeated in the newspapers in addition to "psychosomatic and pathological deviations"[7] (Ramírez Boza 1989:12). No explanation was given for these problems, nor were solutions offered in the papers (ibid., 14).

Refugees were only the most visible agents of incursion. Fournier's statement is from the news coverage of a panel in 1982, sponsored by the Colegio de Abogados (Association of Lawyers), on "terrorism, organized crime, the security of citizens, the problem of refugees, and the relations of Costa Rica with the rest of the region" (Sánchez P. 1982). The format of the panel illustrates the connection often drawn, at some level, between refugees and the various dangers Costa Rica was thought to be facing during the crisis.[8] These dangers, as presented in news articles and by public officials, to the political and social stability of the country conform to the distinctions drawn between Central America and Costa Rica. Of particular importance were the country's relative economic equality, peace, and healthcare. Education and race or ethnicity were also sometimes raised, but in the context of the 1980s were relatively muted in comparison to the first set of issues.

Importing Inequality

Salvadorans arrived during the worst years of the crisis and therefore it is not surprising to find that economic issues were an important part of how they were received and perceived. It was widely reported that the refugees were in direct competition with Costa Ricans for jobs and that they brought down wages; this came up often in newspaper and policy writing of the early 1980s.[9] Economic complaints are common with migration, but in Costa Rica, in addition to the fear over job competition during a period of expanded national unemployment, the concern took a distinctive form as a result of the ways in which classlessness had been part of the dominant representation of the country. Refugees could seem to put that in question, and perhaps it was easier to focus attention on the refugees than on the fact that, in dollar terms, the per capita income in Costa Rica had been halved. Prejudice against refugees was exacerbated by a belief that the country was taking care of them. Refugees did receive assistance in the form of money and goods (particularly food and school supplies), but many Costa Ricans did not realize that this was paid for by money from abroad (Campos V. et al. 1985:94–95).

In a 1986 introduction to a study for CASP/Re the authors drew connections between the influx of foreign retirees and the refugees. Both, they argued, were caused by the global crisis that led people to leave their own countries in an effort "to maintain their personal or familial patrimony whether that be a great material fortune or the great fortune to continue materially with life" (Fernandez et al. 1986:3). The implications of this for Costa Rica were important:

> The most profound consequence of all this, and perhaps the least visible, is that we are importing social inequality, this ingredient that the traditional historiography denies in Costa Rican society. Although even superficial empirical evidence destroys the thesis of social, economic, and cultural egalitarianism, it is not less certain that the degree of inequality grows with increased socio-economic distance and thus increases the subjective and objective possibilities that ghettos, ethnic minorities, and new situations of social and economic marginality will arise. (Fernandez et al. 1986:3)

Costa Rica was in danger of losing even the appearance of middle-class character because refugees could form an underclass[10] and the retirees an upper class. A great deal of the concern over refugees, and the goals of refugee policies, swung between two contradictory issues both related to class: the fear that they could be a force for revolution if they became a segregated lower class and the fear of their taking Costa Rican jobs.[11] This ignored the fact that much of the inequality resulted directly from the economic crisis and not migration, but even considering those broader issues it was still a problem since refugees could make inequality more visible by increasing the numbers of poor. This could have created situations of increased marginality and caused social unrest. For the same reason, rural settlement of refugees was theoretically preferred by the government (Arguedas C. 1984). It was believed that in a rural area they would be less likely either to form a marginal population or to compete with Costa Ricans.

Policies regarding refugees and work paralleled changes in the economy, although policy changes were justified in pragmatic terms. Refugees in the first years of the decade, when the economic crisis was worst, were not permitted to work legally. In 1983, the year that the country made dramatic economic improvement, headlines still referred to the "refugee problem," but there was increased recognition that they must be permitted to work. One headline reads: "The only solution is to put the refugees to work" (La República 1983a). That was the year that work permits were first available to refugees—although few were granted—and the government first began proposing productive projects as a way to incorporate refugees into the economy without displacing Costa Rican labor. The explanation I have heard and seen is that it became obvious that the refugees were continuing to arrive and would not return soon, but it also coincided with an improvement in the economy. By 1988 refugees were heralded as the solution to a labor shortage in manufacturing and agriculture (La Nación 1988).

Health

> The rural person suffers from many diseases, product of the contamination that the refugees bring us, in addition to the lack of vaccination from the Ministry of Health.
>
>   There is no preventive medicine, this has diminished. . . . [Other illnesses] result from chemical products, on not having the orientation from the companies that sell them telling the correct use of them. (Central de Trabajadores Costarricenses 1989:17)

In these excerpts from a presentation of rural workers, there is a rapid jump from the initial reference to (Nicaraguan) refugees to other more systemic problems: lack of services and education. It was often suggested that refugees were less healthy than Costa Ricans as a result of being from poorer countries. Although there may have been some basis for this perception,[12] it was little documented and cannot explain the full extent of problems in the country's health care system. Morgan (1987) discusses many other factors that led to problems in the system. The growth in poverty created by the economic crisis led to increased medical problems for much of the population. Furthermore, the country's socialized medical system (Caja Costarricense de Seguro Social, aka "La Caja") had financial trouble. The economic crisis increased the cost of imported supplies and slowed the growth of needed infrastructure and expanded care. The system had relied on foreign assistance and this was reduced as priorities abroad changed, the country became too healthy for USAID monies, and austerity programs forced budgetary cuts. None of these facts was raised in the news coverage on refugees and health. A study of news articles in three newspapers between 1984 and 1987 found that 13 percent of the negative information published about refugees came from the Ministry of Health (Ramírez Boza 1989:13–14), so it appears likely that refugees were being used to draw attention away from other problems in the health care system. This is particularly striking given the importance of that system for the social achievements so central to predominant representations of Costa Rican national identity.

Porras, in a study done for the Ministry of Health, provides an example of concern with health issues and refugees. In "Deterioration of Health in Costa Rica as a Result of Migration from Nicaragua," she lists health problems. Diseases like malaria, tuberculosis, and meningitis that had been either eliminated or almost eradicated in the country had reappeared and she provided the number of cases for every imaginable illness among Nicaraguans in Costa Rica (Porras Zúniga 1987). Porras then proceeded to give elaborate statistics on every conceivable crime, also among Nicaraguans: the number of cases and a breakdown of each by age and sex of the perpetrator. She did not elaborate on the relevance this had, if any, to health issues. The only connection I could find is that both were problems attributed to refugees—at that point usually assumed to be Nicaraguans—that seemed to threaten Costa Rican society. The various forms of pathology attributed to refugees, Salvadoran or Nicaraguan, were sometimes conflated.

Violence and Subversion

"It is known that some people [Salvadorans] who enter as refugees, later go to Nicaragua to train there with the guerrillas" (La República 1982b). Salvadorans were often assumed to be sympathizers of the guerrilla movement in their country because they had left El Salvador. In the article quoted, the author claims that it was "known" that they entered Costa Rica in order to return to train in Nicaragua. There was also concern that the guerrillas might be training in Costa Rica.[13] The fear that the country could become a military training ground was comprehensible in the context of a border shared with Nicaragua, United States pressure on Costa Rica to cooperate in the Contra war in return for economic assistance, and the use of Honduras by the United States and the Contras. However, the quote from the 1982 article that opens this section indicates how little of the fear was based in a rational consideration of the situation. The "fact" that Salvadorans entered Costa Rica to return to Nicaragua to train as guerrillas makes no logical sense. Geography dictates that there would have been no reason to go to Costa Rica from El Salvador to get to Nicaragua; most people went through Nicaragua to get to Costa Rica. Furthermore, the Salvadoran and Nicaraguan guerrilla forces (in the case of Nicaragua, the Contras) were ideologically opposed while the Nicaraguan government was sympathetic to the Salvadoran guerrillas. This is another reason members of the Salvadoran opposition would not have gone to Costa Rica to sneak back into Nicaragua. In fact, some Salvadoran men told me they were harassed by Nicaraguan border officials, when they passed through the latter country en route to Costa Rica, for leaving El Salvador rather than remaining and fighting with the guerrillas.

When Salvadorans were most visible, the term "refugiado" carried the weight of anticommunism and fear of subversion in Costa Rica. Even in the 1990s, when remembering their years in Costa Rica, many Salvadorans spontaneously told me they knew nothing about Marxism. When those who were sympathetic with, or had participated in, the FMLN said this, they told me that they had learned their politics in their own lives. I never asked about politics and this declaration seemed like a non sequitur until I realized how strongly the anticommunist sentiment had been directed against them during the early 1980s. Some Salvadoran homes were searched by Costa Rican authorities for Marxist literature despite the fact that such books were both legal and for sale in Costa Rica.[14] Government officials cited in newspaper accounts accused the only refugee camp for Salvadorans (Los Angeles in Guanacaste) of being a training camp for guerrillas, although no evidence was ever offered to support this allegation. On a few occasions when the government knew that Salvadorans would be congregated in a particular place, migration officers went to check people's identification papers. Migration officers also watched for Salvadorans at the main post office of San José. One family told me this was not a problem for them because it was not true at any other post office; they lived near another town, so they simply avoided the San José office. However, I knew one woman who, with a Costa Rican friend, was arrested at the post office because they did not have their identity cards with them; both were accused of being undocumented migrants.

When the numbers of Salvadorans decreased relative to Nicaraguans a new dynamic was introduced as the latter came to be equated with refugees. Salvadorans speaking about the mid-eighties said that the two terms "refugiado" and "nica" (Nicaraguan) came to mean the same thing. One written example I found of this conflation of national and migratory statuses was in a government document in the National Library in

San José. Throughout the entire volume, an "emergency plan" for the arrival of refugees, the word *nicaragüenses* had been penciled out by someone who replaced it with the correction "refugiados" (DIGEPARE: División de Ingresos 1987). Relatedly, "refugiado" was often used colloquially for undocumented migrants, who were mainly Nicaraguan. Government agencies appealing for foreign assistance with refugees included undocumented migrants in a third category, "externally displaced," as a type of refugee. A 1986 survey of the Costa Rican public found that 45 percent of respondents did not know the difference between undocumented migrants and documented refugees (Flores Gamboa 1989:152); by the mid-1980s both were commonly assumed to be Nicaraguan.

It seems from newspaper clippings and the stories that Salvadorans told that anticommunist actions diminished as Nicaraguans, who had left Sandinista Nicaragua, came to stand for all refugees. I have never heard a Costa Rican say anything nice about Nicaraguans, except that they are good workers. Even this is contradicted, since people also call them lazy. I was told by Costa Ricans that this antipathy has always existed and long predates the refugee crisis.[15] Even some Costa Ricans I met who were politically progressive and had worked in refugee offices said things like "I am not xenophobic but . . ." and spoke badly of Nicaraguans in my interviews with them. A Costa Rican friend of a group of Salvadoran artisans I knew said that some Nicaraguans might be good, but a person does not have time to get to know every one of them to find out, so it is easier to assume they are not. Although in the first few years of the 1980s when most refugees were Salvadoran they did suffer from great discrimination, the large numbers of Nicaraguans who went to Costa Rica after them deflected Costa Rican attention to that national group. Then it was better, less stigmatized, to be Salvadoran than a refugee because of the association between Nicaraguans and refugiados and the belief that refugees were receiving aid from the government. A characteristic frequently attributed to Nicaraguans was violence, rather than subversiveness. This made them, and by extension refugees, dangerous to Costa Rica: They were often perceived as bringing crime. Just as the assumption that Salvadorans were communist had meant they might be plotting to overthrow democracy, Nicaraguan violence was a threat to the peacefulness of Costa Rican life. During the late 1980s and early 1990s crime in Costa Rica often was attributed to Nicaraguans in the newspapers, even though no one could possibly have known who the culprit was.[16] Again, there was a notable displacement of problems onto refugees.

Costa Rican nationalist discourse interacted with the dangers that the economic and political crises of the 1980s posed for Costa Rican distinctiveness to shape representations of Central American refugees. Nearly all refugees were Central American. It is therefore understandable that the two kinds of classification, national and migratory, became conflated. This had important repercussions for how Salvadorans felt they were received by Costa Rica. Although they settled freely in the country and many eventually adopted it as a home, they also retained the memory of rejection. In subsequent chapters we will see ways in which Salvadorans successfully integrated into Costa Rican society; the tension between rejection and acceptance, however, was always present even many years after Costa Ricans had stopped thinking about Salvadorans or El Salvador and turned their attention exclusively to Nicaraguans.

Salvadoran Reactions

The way in which the category of "refugee" carried these connotations for Costa Ricans affected Salvadorans and their experience of displacement. Although they were grateful to Costa Rica for the protection they had received and appreciated the positive aspects of the country, they resented the discrimination and rejection they had felt. That resentment did not, however, lead them to propose an alternative, more positive, representation of refugees. Instead, they de-emphasized their association with the category even as they used it for their own ends. They worked with and against it in their daily efforts to live with dignity and survive poverty. They treated refugee status as one more resource, not a personal characteristic. When Salvadorans arrived, they were not sent through any processing center and no one directed them to apply for recognition as refugees. In fact, most started life in Costa Rica on tourist visas that they periodically renewed. It was up to them to learn of the possibility, and benefits, of becoming recognized refugees and to search out the appropriate office to apply. Many told me they did not know of this possibility until they met a compatriot who informed them about it as a means of solving some pressing difficulty. This has an important implication: It was the Salvadoran who actively chose that status.

Despite the prejudice I have briefly described, there were significant reasons to opt for refugee status and people mentioned these when they spoke with me. Registered refugees could receive monthly monetary assistance for rent and other basic needs, monthly allotments of internationally donated foods, school supplies, medical care, technical training, and the equipment and money necessary to start small productive projects, or micro-businesses. They also had legal permission to be in the country and did not have to spend significant amounts of time in lines at the migration office renewing their visas each month. Official recognition as a refugee therefore was a pragmatic reaction to resource accessibility and not purely a consequence of leaving home.

The stigma of being a refugee among Costa Ricans was not solely based on nationalist prejudices. In the context of economic crisis, Costa Ricans believed that their government funded refugee aid. Some resented the assistance that refugees received because they perceived it both as an advantage they did not have and as siphoning resources from nationals. It is, therefore, not surprising that Salvadorans de-emphasized the aid they had received. Invariably, people told me that they had not received aid . . . *except* for some food, *except* for the monetary assistance, *except* for some loans to start a micro-business. People who did not need any of these forms of assistance could choose not to become refugees, a status that for many implied dependence. Even so, Salvadorans who had received it also emphasized that the aid was by rights theirs. They knew that the money was donated for them by international agencies and foreign governments. In emphasizing this fact, they attempted to redefine the nature of the assistance and make it less stigmatizing.

Salvadorans generally did not attempt to disguise the fact that they were foreign, although they did not make a point of telling people. In contrast, many did tell me of efforts to avoid recognition as refugees. Women were the ones who told me most of these stories—although men did tell of hiding from migration authorities who came to homes to make sure registered refugees were not working. Men, who could spend more time in the relative freedom of the street, were more free to establish their own networks of relationships either with other Salvadorans or with Costa Ricans who did not need to know their migratory status. Because women were more responsible for the home and family, they were in some ways significantly less able to avoid the stigma of refugee aid than were men. They were generally the ones who went to the aid offices to pick up emergency aid and monthly food allocations. These, especially the latter, potentially required a very public form of identification as refugees. One woman described to me the ways in which she managed this. Food was given out once a month. She had a relatively large family, so the allowance was fairly hefty. This meant that she took one of the children with her to help, and they took a taxi home because it was too much to carry on the bus. The neighbors were likely to inquire when they saw the family using a taxi, not an ordinary expense, with large quantities of groceries. Rather than explain that they were refugees, the woman told them that she bought all their food at the supermarket once a month to save money. Children also were unable to escape the stigma of being refugees because of their responsibility to be in a circumscribed space in which their belongings could be examined and questioned. They had to go to school in donated uniforms that were, as charity often is, of a lower quality than the uniforms of their classmates. They had to use book bags that all looked alike and were a style not shared by classmates, whose parents bought them bags. Those bags were called "refugee bags" in some schools. Costa Rican school children are required to have a set of colored pencils. Refugee children had the boxes of six colors and looked longingly at the larger boxes of twelve or twenty-four.

Men had a slightly different relationship to the aid given. First, they usually were not the ones who picked up subsistence aid from the offices. Second, they were more likely than women to receive a second form of assistance. Once it became apparent that refugees would be in the country for years rather than months, agencies attempted to foster self-sufficiency by helping them set up small productive businesses. Men were more likely than women to receive this assistance. This form of help increased the independence of the receiver and did not publicly mark a person as a refugee in the ways the direct subsistence aid did. It is not surprising, therefore, that woman were more likely than men to emphasize necessity in speaking of refugee aid. Men more often emphasized their clever ability to take advantage of the system or ingratiate themselves with officials who could facilitate things for them in the aid offices. The independence men could exhibit was further strengthened by their ability to freely use public space where they could develop new social networks. On the other hand, there was one realm in which the spatial norms made being a refugee easier for women. Although women tend to earn less than men, their dependence on informal and domestic employment meant that they could more easily find work without a legal work permit. Men's more public forms of employment meant it was more difficult for them to hide employment from migration authorities. In response, when they worked, many relied on forms of self-employment that could be done at home and easily hidden, for example shoe-making and other artisanry. In these cases this often meant that they could care for children while the women worked outside the house.[17]

Although they attempted to avoid being known as refugees in some settings, in others Salvadorans used their status and some would say abused it. Some collected assistance from multiple sources and even referred to this as their job. Although aid organizations did not approve of this, they did not share information so as to prevent it. None of the aid by itself was sufficient to live, so in fact refugees were faced with few options if they were not incorporated into one of the productive projects, the beneficiary of a work permit, or receiving money from family elsewhere. They could work illegally or they could collect aid from as many sources as possible.

Finally, Salvadorans worked against the category in another way. Just as there were contexts in which some Salvadorans used the fact that they were refugees, they created contexts for refugees that could be used by anyone. They formed organizations that provided solidarity and assistance for Salvadoran refugees. These organizations provided a range of activities and services that were mainly used by Salvadorans. But they made these available to all Salvadorans, regardless of legal status; all refugees, regardless of nationality; and indeed to Costa Ricans who were equally poor and in need. In doing so, they exemplified an approach to identity that can be summarized with the phrase they often used: "identify with." They identified with people in similar structural conditions regardless of nationality or migratory status, even as they also used those two forms of identificatory classification. This called into question those categories while simultaneously recognizing their importance.

Much effort has been expended in academic work on refugees in refining systems of classification to distinguish refugees from other migrants. There are valid political reasons to do this. However, in refugee studies this predilection toward classification has led to vast generalizations regarding "the refugee experience." Malkki's study of the national order as a system of classification provides us with important insights into the ideologically charged representations of refugees and the assumptions behind refugee policies. However, her analysis of how individuals and societies react to refugees largely remains at the abstract level of the ideology of "a family of nations" in which nations are equal and autonomous units. My research illustrates that while it is true that there are ways in which refugees are excluded from that order, they are at the same time a part of that order. First, as Malkki also recognizes, they are created and maintained by it. Second, they are received by host countries not just as refugees, but as nationals.

The experiences of Salvadorans in Costa Rica demonstrate that the category of "refugee" must be understood in its social context of use. It is not just that the conditions of reception shape refugees' attitudes toward and use of national and migratory categories by creating conditions in which particular social relations are possible and different categories of social identification are useful. It is also the case that attitudes toward national categories and nationalist ideologies inform the meaning of refuge. The category of "refugee" is interpreted in light of attitudes toward specific nations. The interanimation of the two systems of classification affected the Costa Rican legal system in a permanent way. The category of "refugiado" began as a bureaucratic necessity because the country needed international assistance to deal with the unexpected and unprecedented numbers of Central American refugees who arrived in the 1980s. The way to obtain that assistance was through the United Nations and international NGOs, and this required using the legal categories those entities recognized. Therefore the UNHCR refugee regime supplemented a Latin American system of refuge that was already in Costa Rican law and migration policy. Costa Rica eventually created its own legal definitions of asylum and refuge, which do not wholly correspond to either the United Nations or the Latin American traditions of refuge.

The way in which Costa Rica defined itself in opposition to the rest of Central America informed the meaning of the term "refugee." It did this within a historically specific politico-economic moment that made some issues more important than others as the crisis threatened the fundamental bases of Costa Rican distinctiveness. The Costa Rican state facilitated this process by focusing on refugees as the problem in ways that deflected attention from the economic crisis, growing poverty, or a less easily monitored undocumented population. All of this shaped the context in which most Salvadorans went to Costa Rica, in addition to creating a sense of possible rejection. In particular, ideologies of national difference affected the ways in which they were received and inflected the ways in which they understood the changes they experienced. The forces I have described in this chapter created an environment in which nationally defined differences were important and to a large extent superseded both the similarities between the two Central American countries and other possible explanations for those differences. In the following chapters, we will see not only how culturally defined spaces were interpreted in terms of national belonging, but also how feelings of rejection gave way to belonging.

3
In the Street

Mujeres Liberadas

Upon arrival, Salvadorans interpreted their experience of migration to Costa Rica in part through contrasting sets of social values expressed in terms of gender and space. The contrast they perceived between the two countries in this regard is important for understanding their experience of national difference. Use of space is often highly gendered and is one of the ways in which we become gendered people. Space, like gender, is associated with basic values and social structure; as daMatta (1991 [1985]) notes in a discussion of house and street in Brazil, space does not exist independently from values that permit people to orient themselves in society more generally. Changes in ubication, either geographic or social, may therefore be experienced in terms of changes in the use of space. In subsequent chapters an understanding of the relationship between gender and space also will help us to appreciate how the experience of arrival in a new country may vary by gender, age, and class.

Salvadorans I met in Costa Rica, regardless of class or whether they were of urban or rural extraction, made interrelated observations about contrasts in gendered behavior between the two countries. Their comments were themselves gendered, since men remarked on behavior in the street and women on that of the home. Men said that Costa Rican women were more *liberadas* ("liberated"). Women said that Salvadoran men were more *machista*.[1] Together they presented an image of greater gender equality in keeping with the general tranquility of Costa Rican social relations. Many people told me that Costa Ricans had a nice culture (*una cultura bonita*) because of the greater equality and harmony they per-

41

ceived in interpersonal relations by both class and gender. Despite this positive aspect, their observations could also be made as a form of critique of Costa Rican customs, since gender norms are among the most basic expressions of what we value and who we are.

Salvadoran men often commented on the behavior of women in public when they contrasted the two countries, and their observations demonstrate the close relationship between (perceived) sexuality and women's "liberation." Miguel, a Salvadoran artisan shoemaker, told me that many men in El Salvador had thought Costa Rica would be wonderful because their impression, based on reports of men who had been to Costa Rica before them, was that there would be many sexually available women and men. This turned out to be another instance of the unreliable information available to them about Costa Rica, but it is interesting to think about why some men had that impression. I will return, briefly, to his innuendo on the sexuality of Costa Rican men after first discussing the beliefs many men initially had about Costa Rican women. Miguel and other men told me that in El Salvador they would have thought that any woman who smoked or drank in public was a prostitute. Costa Rican women, it seemed, were in "the street" more freely and could be seen smoking and drinking. From this they often initially extrapolated that the women would also be freer sexually. In Costa Rica they had to become accustomed to the fact that this was not true. Some men, who either had arrived in Costa Rica earlier or married Costa Ricans, told me that they had warned other Salvadoran men not to impugn Costa Rican women and that these "liberated" ways of acting were not signs of moral turpitude. Ironically, some men told me that they found their expectations about the sexual mores of Costa Rican women frustrated by demands of marriage— Salvadoran women were said by some Salvadoran men to be easier in this regard. These men found a bemusing contradiction between their interpretation of the use of space and the conclusions they could draw about the women they saw.

Men had to adjust to this situation, and some Costa Rican women also compromised, albeit within patterns that were already available to them in Costa Rican society. Some Salvadoran men told me they had felt pressured by women and their families to marry their Costa Rican *compañeras* after the women became pregnant. It is plausible that working-class Costa Rican women and their families pressured men to marry more than in El Salvador. Costa Rica had a very high rate of formal marriage in comparison with the more northern country. Although people over age fifteen

were almost equally likely to be in stable marital relationships, in El Salvador approximately half of all such relationships were free-union while
in Costa Rica only about 15 percent were free-union rather than formally
sanctioned marriage.[2] I am not sure why so many Salvadoran men seemed
to resist marriage, but it appeared to make them feel trapped and too responsible.[3]

While some Salvadoran men felt that Costa Rican women were too
insistent on marriage, many Salvadoran women commented to me on
what they perceived as Salvadoran men's reluctance to commit to women
and children. Alicia told me that in El Salvador children only had their
mothers because men left for other women. Costa Rican men were
thought more likely to be responsible husbands and fathers and more
oriented toward the home. The observations of Salvadoran women find
possible support in statistical evidence, without denying that many Salvadoran men are in fact responsible fathers. In El Salvador 69 percent of
children were not legally recognized by their fathers (García and Gomáriz 1989–90:149). There is no comparable statistic for Costa Rica, but the
same source estimates that one third of Costa Rican children might have
been born outside of legally sanctioned unions (408).[4] Another indirect
indicator of the family irresponsibility many Salvadoran women attributed to Salvadoran men was the incidence of women-headed households.
Twenty-seven percent of Salvadoran women in El Salvador were heads of
households in 1985 (110); this was the highest rate in Central America. In
contrast, only 7.5 percent of Costa Rican women were household heads in
1984 (44).[5]

In general, family structure is related to access to resources, although
it is never completely determined by economic factors (Hareven 1978:
456). High levels of female-headed households and relatively low rates of
formal marriage, such as were found in El Salvador, are common in situations of poverty in the Americas and Caribbean (c.f. Brown 1975; Stack
1975 [1974]). They are also more common in the poorer sectors of both
Costa Rica and El Salvador, although the nuclear family predominates
across all classes in Costa Rica (García and Gomáriz 1989–90:113; Vega R.
1992:29). Based on a comparative study of family structure and poverty
in different cultural regions of the world, Blumberg (1978) argues that
only particular types of poverty are associated with female-headed households. The conditions conducive to this family form are the following:
individuals are the unit of labor power, females have equal access to subsistence opportunities, opportunities for women can be reconciled with

child-care responsibilities, and all the resources available to a woman (including the labor of children and welfare) are not "drastically less than those of the men of her class" (Blumberg 1978:529). Blumberg suggests that "the Conditions are fulfilled most frequently among groups which are not only poor, but also constitute a surplus labor population in the context of a larger political economy" (528). The high rates of unemployment and labor migration, which I described in chapter 1, are just two symptoms of the fact that this was the case in El Salvador. Costa Rica, in contrast, is more often characterized by a shortage of labor, particularly in the rural sector.

Blumberg's conditions thus describe the Salvadoran case very well (cf. Tripp 1983). Consequently, it is not surprising to find higher levels of female-headed households and children without fathers in El Salvador.[6] From some men's point of view, this was experienced in the ability to maintain relationships with women without necessity of marriage. For some women, it could be better not to marry in situations of extreme poverty, such as existed in El Salvador, because men could provide little while dominating much (Brown 1975). Although marriage could provide stability to women and their children when men had access to more resources and employment opportunities, the very poorest, especially rural, of the Salvadoran women I knew explained to me that they had thought it better not to marry because men could be abusive and it was harder to leave a husband than an informal relationship. They described how they had chosen fathers for their children, but did not discuss husbands for themselves.

Costa Rica provided a strong contrast to El Salvador. The poverty rate was much lower. In Costa Rica prospects for supporting a family were better, as were chances for improving one's economic position (or that of one's children) through education.[7] Historically, landownership was more widespread in Costa Rica and an agricultural frontier provided the possibility of colonizing new lands until relatively recently. Elsewhere in Latin America, patriarchal, neolocal, nuclear families have been more common among peasants where resources were available to support new families as children grew up and married (Deere 1978).[8] Therefore it is not surprising to learn that in Costa Rica the nuclear family has been the predominant form of family organization since the colonial period, although other forms, including extended families and women-headed families, have always been present to a lesser degree (Acuña M. and Denton L. 1979). The predominance of male-headed nuclear families in

Costa Rica continued in recent decades despite the fact that the availability of land diminished. During this period the possibilities for education and occupational mobility have increased with the expansion of the public and industrial sectors and consequent urbanization (González 1983). This gave children (including daughters) expanded opportunities that liberated them from the strict authority of fathers and husbands. Economic opportunities in general were better in Costa Rica for both sexes, and wages were higher than in El Salvador. These conditions, conducive to the growth of the middle class and middle-class aspirations, were also more favorable to marriage than those of El Salvador.

Salvadoran men and women also said that Costa Rican men were less machista in other ways. I am uncertain about the meaning of Miguel's innuendo about the sexual availability of Costa Rican men, nor did anyone else comment on this to me, although another friend who was with us during this conversation did not dispute the statement. It did generally seem to be that the more "liberada" women were thought to be, the less "machista" their men were believed to be. The same behaviors that were criticized as machista were often associated with "the way men are." For example, demanding food or coffee was a not uncommon, and, some felt, machista habit. Some men told me that it was a way to assert dominance or to let other men know that one was in charge. It was also, I was told many times by women who neither liked it nor fought it, "the way men are." Perhaps, given the frequent conflation of sexuality with other aspects of gendered behavior, some Salvadoran men initially would have taken contrasts they noted in men's behavior more generally to mean less "manly" in the same way they had misinterpreted the Costa Rican women to be more promiscuous on the circumstantial evidence of other public behavior.[9] If so, I expect that this would have been most true among those, mainly working-class and artisan, men with the least invested in "house."

If women are "liberated," are men less "machista"? Salvadoran men who spoke with me on the topic saw the affirmative proven in a particular instance of male public behavior. Men in Costa Rica may go to the market and carry bags of vegetables home, either on their own or for their wives. Salvadoran men told me that they would never have done that in their patria. Sergio, an accountant, told me that if they had gone to the market in El Salvador, they would have been very abrupt, acted uninterested, asked prices, but not bargained. Through these mannerisms they would have distanced themselves from the act of marketing. Nestor, a shoemaker from urban El Salvador, opined that this was just "machismo" because he would think nothing about carrying a big bundle of leather down the street. So, he observed, the problem was not that he was ashamed to carry things in public. Leather was related to work; vegetables were clearly domestic for him. He also volunteered that he would not do housework despite the fact that he felt sorry for his wife, who worked all day and came home to do housework at night. In keeping with a common pattern, the eldest of his children, a boy, helped with some household chores during the day while his mother was at work. I saw him doing a cursory job on the floor one day while I visited. Men did women's work if it was absolutely necessary, just as women did men's work if it was necessary. A child, with less power, was more likely to get stuck with that necessity than a grown man.

Unlike the men, Salvadoran women commented more on home than street behavior when they compared the two countries.[10] They asserted not only that Salvadoran men were more machista and less responsible to family, but also that Costa Rican men were more likely to help in the home.[11] Sofía noted the contrast when she went to Costa Rica from rural El Salvador. She told me that this made her see that things could be different for women and she therefore decided to teach her son and grandsons to do housework. I watched Sofía's grandson clean the floor one day as she and I talked. He did an admirable job; she was clearly a good teacher. She also had her grandsons do their own laundry and help prepare dinner. She had put a great deal of thought and care into this: She explained to me how she decided what to require and taught them each according to his abilities. She described how unjust it had been in El Salvador, especially in the countryside, where women never finished working, but men could come home expecting dinner and relaxation. She commented on how it did not need to be like that for other women if sons would learn to do a share of housework. She praised her son-in-law in Canada, a Salvadoran, for the ways in which he participated in housework and child-rearing. Sofía was the only person I knew who put this level of effort into practical measures to fight women's oppression, but other women made similar observations. Women told me that Salvadoran men, especially those who married Costa Ricans, had learned to be less machista in Costa Rica. When Salvadoran men were known to do housework in Costa Rica, it was assumed that they had changed and not that they might have helped in El Salvador.

It is not so simple to determine relative degrees of women's domination because there are many dimensions to inequality that make it im-

possible to construct a linear scale. I therefore do not want to argue that
Costa Rican women were really more "liberated" and Salvadoran women
more restricted. In fact Salvadoran men sometimes said that their women
were less easily dominated, more likely to stand up for themselves and
more in charge in the home. It is also important to consider the meaning of behaviors in context and not in contrast with our own preconcep-
tions—whether these be social scientific, gringo, or Salvadoran. For example, Chant (1991) notes that Costa Rican men in Guanacaste helped
with marketing, but she adds that men did not participate very much
in other household tasks. This has been my experience in other parts of
Costa Rica; generally the men I have known only did housework if they
did not live with their wives or mothers. Chant observes that going to
the market was a highly visible way of helping that could simultaneously
serve as a way for men to have greater control over household finances.
Her warning is well taken. It would be interesting, however, if men in fact
benefited from being seen helping, since this contrasts with a situation in
which men could feel demeaned by being observed helping with domestic chores.[12] It would also be important to consider the motives behind
such help: Some men in Costa Rica might have helped with marketing
because of a belief that women should not have to do heavy lifting, but
neither to share domestic work more evenly nor to control the domestic finances. It was also the case that the market was at once public space
and domestic chore. Therefore different people could interpret it differently, or it could mean different things in different societies. It is equally
necessary to consider more closely the meaning of the Salvadoran men's
observations. They said that women smoked and drank in public more in
Costa Rica; they did not say that women were in public more. They only
commented on the way in which (some, not all) women were out. Salvadoran women never told me that women could be in the street more
freely in Costa Rica or were expected to be at home more in El Salvador.
So the difference was not necessarily where women or men were or even
where they were expected to be, but in the types of behaviors some people
engaged in and the contrasting meanings attributed to those behaviors.

　　Despite the differences perceived by Salvadorans, the same discourse
of gendered expectations was used in both countries. People had a variety
of interrelated ways of talking about these shared expectations, but these
met in a language of space crystallized in the spatial terms "house" *(casa)*
and "street" *(calle)*. The former was associated with women and family
and the latter largely with men. Each space also corresponded to, and

metaphorically represented, a series of interrelated values and behaviors. This model of space was fundamental for understanding social relations and values in Central America.

House and Street

House and street were parts of an apparently widespread Latin American cultural model of space in which a series of values and gendered associations, or ways of being, formed a "geography of honor" (Beattie 1996:440) that organized what people did when and where and how others interpreted those actions. The terms of this model have been described in various Latin American countries including, to cite only a few cases, Mexico (Rouse 1989, 1992), the Dominican Republic (Simonson 1994), Nicaragua (Montoya 1997), and Brazil (Beattie 1996; daMatta 1991 [1979], 1991 [1985]; Lauderdale Graham 1992 [1988]). The model is central to discussions of gender in the region, even when it is not the focus of the analysis. Although the values associated with each space are remarkably consistent in the abstract descriptions, the rigidity of the gendered division of space in actual practice, and the articulation between the model and politico-economic conditions vary greatly. We can assume, also, that the behaviors associated with the values may vary as may the values that are most emphasized in interpreting behavior. I will not explore the details of how the abstract model was instantiated, and therefore changed, in different historically specific settings in Latin America. Here I only present the decontextualized values of this general Latin American model, which I later explore in greater specificity in the context of urban Costa Rica. The reader should therefore take care not to assume too rigid a differentiation in actual practice throughout the region; much of the rest of the chapter implicitly demonstrates that greater flexibility of action is often possible despite, or even because of, the ideological content of the model.

In Latin America, women are widely associated with home or house and men with street. House is associated with family, the basic unit of social order, while street is the domain of extra-familial relationships, both economic and sexual. House signifies safety and street, danger. House is the domain of order. House is respectable and responsible, street is not. House is associated with respectable use of time, while street implies vagrancy and/or freedom—depending on one's point of view. These connotations in turn reinforce the gendered dimensions of space, since men are presumed better able to negotiate the dangers of street, and women are thought to be naturally more responsible and familial.

There have been two independent theoretical moves in interpreting this cultural framework, one developed in work on Spanish Latin America and the other on Brazil. In the first framework, the fact that men are associated with the street and its activities while women are associated with house, family, and domestic activities is of central theoretical importance. As developed in the early 1970s in feminist anthropology by Rosaldo, Ortner, and Chodorow (Rosaldo and Lamphere 1989 [1974]), and presented by Rosaldo (Rosaldo 1989 [1974], 1980), the public/domestic distinction was an effort to explain the apparent universality of male dominance in human societies without reducing social forms to an effect of a deterministic biology. They argued that "in all human societies sexual asymmetry might be seen to correspond to a rough institutional division between domestic and public spheres of activity, the one built around reproduction, affective, and familial bonds, and particularly constraining to women; the other, providing for collectivity, jural order, and social cooperation, organized primarily by men" (Rosaldo 1980:397). In this perspective, house/street can be seen as a culturally specific example of this more abstract social-scientific model (cf. Rouse 1989, 1992).

Although Rosaldo intended the public/domestic as one of functional domains, in practice many analysts have used it and the related public/ private contrast to refer to physical spaces. The conflation is itself intriguing, but I feel that the most interesting insights of this analytical model are often precisely when the physical spaces of public and private do not correspond to the functional domains of public and domestic. It is this disjunction that women potentially use to their personal or familial advantage—for example when a woman works in the fields or in paid employment and is praised for it because it is on behalf of her family, despite the fact that it takes her from her home. Another example of the power of this ambiguity is women's involvement in political protests in Latin America. Women could protest against military regimes more effectively by mobilizing their domestic roles in the public realm (Franco 1985; Radcliffe 1993). Other scholars note that women are more likely to organize for political ends that are related to their domestic roles (Jelin 1994 [1990]).

The second body of work on house/street considers Brazil and has been inspired by daMatta (1991 [1979], 1991 [1985]). He treats these two spaces as distinct realms of meaning ("esferas de significação social") and values that organize social relations and behavior. House and street are associated with fundamentally different, and contrasting, forms of social organization that together form a spatial and temporal "grammar"

(1991 [1985]:41) for society. The values and style of social relations in each sphere give shape to what Brazilians do where, when, and how. In Brazil, daMatta argues, the house is a space of hierarchical familial and friendship relations. House involves a "traditional" and "personalistic" form of social organization that places each person in relation to other people. Street, in contrast, is organized around impersonal and individualistic relationships governed by (potentially arbitrary) political authority. The public realm of the street is ordered by a more abstract, "universal" logic of capitalist work and state power. Similarly, he argues that the two spaces are governed by different forms of time. House has a cyclical time of family events. Street has a linear and cumulative historical time typical of the "West." DaMatta draws on Weber in describing these two ethics, but argues that the two forms coexist in Brazil instead of being stages in a historical shift in society. This framework of contrasting spheres exemplifying different ethics is central to daMatta's interpretation of the distinctiveness of Brazil, which he calls "the Brazilian dilemma" (daMatta 1991 [1979]). It distinguishes Brazil, he argues, from other industrialized, but Protestant, Western societies, like the United States, which are governed by a single, individualistic ethic in both the public and private realms. One implication of this part of his argument is that in his analysis "house" and "street" are both spaces and styles of interaction. Hypothetically the two realms are equal. However, he notes that the logic of either may be valued more under particular social circumstances.

He and some scholars working in his theoretical framework use the tension between house and street as physical spaces and ethical realms to explore occasions when the logic of "house" invades "street," or vice versa (e.g., Prado 1995). Thus, daMatta analyzes the relationship between house and street by looking for times and places in which the two are connected or when ritual mediates between them. Some spaces in the street have the potential to take on a house-like character or value. For example, this happens at work when employee-employer relations are modeled on the family, and in the market, which has a domestic aspect. Some house spaces (e.g., a parlor) take on street-like functions by mediating between relationships of the house and street. Rituals also mediate between the two spaces in varied ways. Some rituals open the house to the street; some open the street to the house. Apart from these occasions, the two remain, for daMatta, self-contained and internally consistent realms that dictate what people can even consider talking about and how they relate to others.

Other scholars have built more directly on his observations regarding the gendering of public and private space without emphasizing this larger framework for understanding Brazilian society (e.g., Beattie 1996; Lauderdale Graham 1992 [1988]). These scholars pay close attention to the politics of gender in everyday life as they explore specific cases. In my own understanding of Central America, I adopt this selective appropriation of daMatta. I am not convinced that the style of social relations in the two "realms" are as absolutely distinct in the urban context I know in Central America as his framework implies. More important, I believe that his manner of describing the two spaces obscures the fact that relations in the street can be qualitatively different for men and women.

We can take as our point of departure daMatta's suggestion that the spaces of house and street are realms of social meanings. These are not neutral spaces; they are realms of moral meaning fundamental to the constitution of society and individuals. The street, as people I knew used the term, was a much less homogeneous space than his model suggests. It is not simply that women are associated with one space and men with the other, but that the ways in which women can use the public sphere may be different from the ways available to men. I explain this more fully by paying theoretical attention to daMatta's observation that house/street is a private/public, or domestic/public, division of space. Women's association with the "private" means that they often must use a variety of strategies for comfortably negotiating public space, or the street, dominated by men, not that they do not use those spaces at all. To simplify my discussion, and because it was the space most important to how Salvadorans oriented themselves upon arrival in Costa Rica, I focus on the street in the following section to show, ethnographically, how it was produced, as a meaningful space, through social action informed by the values associated with it. My discussion, like the space, will be dominated by men. I was also more likely to spend time with men in public and with women in domestic spaces. The following ethnographic discussion of the ways in which use of space is negotiated through the play of values not only provides a more complex understanding of the model I have just outlined, but also an understanding of how Salvadorans and Costa Ricans could have different interpretations of behavior within a "single" cultural model. The examples that follow are of Salvadorans in Costa Rica. However, the meanings and strategies that they illustrate were common, in my experience, to both nationalities. Despite the differences Salvadorans discerned between the countries, there were no observable differences in their behavior in the country and no one suggested they had altered their use of space in Costa Rica. In my interpretation, the difference is not strictly speaking one of national cultural difference, but rather of access to resources by people operating within what was essentially one framework.

Competing Values

Los Muchachos

Juana, a middle-aged mother originally from a family farm in El Salvador, was critical of many *amigos callejeros*[13] although she knew them only by reputation. She generally criticized people who spent considerable time out if they had families. She would say she could not understand how, having a family, so-and-so (male or female) could spend so much time in the street. They were my friends, so I defended them by emphasizing the things they did to be good fathers. Juana, drawing on the perception that men in El Salvador often were not good fathers, approved but said they must have learned it in Costa Rica. Then she agreed with my suggestion that people would talk about these men without knowing all the facts. People would assume that they were irresponsible because they were often in the street, she assented.

The group Juana and I were discussing included Miguel, Enrique, and Antonio, among others. Brothers, uncles, cousins, nephews, and friends: the core members of the group, in the configuration I knew best, were artisans from semi-urban and urban El Salvador. Like most of the Salvadorans I knew, they had all worked in a variety of other jobs including agricultural labor and selling. Some had worked in factories; Enrique had once owned a *soda* or small restaurant. Sometimes they worked for other people, sometimes for themselves either as a group or alone. Most of them were in their mid-thirties and had gone to Costa Rica in their late teens or early twenties in the early 1980s. When I knew them, they sold their work in the plaza in San José and by commission at stores catering to tourists. When one of the organizations that worked with Salvadoran refugees closed, they, with others, had taken over the lease, phone line, and mailbox to form an association of artisans. There were many places men could go, including a range of restaurants and bars from the very respectable (and increasingly expensive) to *cantinas*, which were for serious, and much less costly, drinking and where women were probably never seen.

Even so, this group liked having their own place to drink and socialize, although they also went to bars and restaurants. Despite the fact that it was a private spot, they could still be considered morally in the street because they were neither at home nor working.

Although they sometimes had a beer with me, they behaved impeccably. They told me on various occasions that they would make sure nothing bad happened when I was with them. Sometimes they had parties about which I was told with few details. Antonio advised I not go (although Miguel told me other women did); when I asked why, he said, without elaboration, that he did not think I'd be interested in talking about "those topics." He also sustained that if I were there the party would be more constrained. I asked why, and he said it was because they respected me. This did not mean I did not hear about or see some of what some of them were concerned to avoid doing in my company, just as, on a couple of occasions, I witnessed efforts by men to woo women other than their girlfriends and compañeras. When I was not with them they occasionally got in fights with Costa Ricans, Nicaraguans, and, once, an off-duty policeman. I would hear about these episodes later because fighting was another thing they would not do when I was present. These men clearly protected me from the moral and social connotations of being perceived as callejera, in the street excessively, even as they occasionally accompanied me for beer in locales where few women were to be seen. They did so through their own relative abstemiousness while with me; making it clear that I was with them in a variety of implicit and explicit, verbal and non-verbal, ways; and treating me with respect.

It is clear that there was sometimes a basis for the association of men, drink, illicit sex (or talk of it), and potential violence with the street. This group of men knew that many people, like Juana, would disapprove of their choice to be there. A young Costa Rican woman worked in an office in the building they rented. One day José and Miguel puzzled over the fact that she called them "don." Don and doña, the feminine form of the title, were terms of respect used before a person's first name. In some countries they are used more selectively, but in Costa Rica, a country in which the *tu*, or informal "you," form was almost completely unused,[14] most people were called don or doña at some point in their lives. It was used with people from all classes as a token of respect earned with age and the responsibilities and demeanor of adulthood. These men had been in the country long enough to know this, but still they wondered why she used it with them. One finally concluded that it was out of "buena educación"—she was brought up well and polite—because he could think of "no other reason."

Not all men I knew spent significant amounts of time in the street. Men recognized the desirability and respectability of house. Sergio, an accountant who never spent time in the street, noted approvingly how nicely dressed Alberto was the day we ran into him as we went for the mail: "bien formal" with his tie. Sergio liked seeing him this way. He remembered when Alberto was not so *formal* (serious and reliable in addition to formal) and in the street . . . either drinking or on marijuana, Sergio was not sure which. Being *informal* was a common critique of individuals and groups that were too disorganized, casual, or unreliable. Alberto now sold books on commission, had five children to care for, and often felt very pressured by all the responsibility. Despite the fact that his work often kept him physically in the street, he was no longer callejero and can't be described as "in the street." He had a legitimate motive for being there and was not out at night without reason; in the evening he usually went home to his family.

While some were quite pleased to be in the street with as little "formality" as possible, other men, like Alberto, felt they could not to the same degree as they had in the past. Some occasionally joined the group and left early to rejoin family. Some men spent more time in the street at one point in their lives than another or more time from month to month with changes in their personal circumstances. They could *formalizarse* (become "serious") for some reason—health, love, or God—that made house more appealing than it previously had been. They recognized that if they wanted to keep a family and home, they had to respect their wives' desires to have them there more regularly. Working class and artisan men sometimes spent more time in the street if problems at home, either financial or personal, made the street more attractive. Some men disapproved of anyone in the street as irresponsible. Yet others were like another friend, Mauricio. He said of *callejeando*[15] "no me nace" (it did not appeal to him) despite the fact that he was single, in his twenties, of the same class position as others who were out, and without family responsibilities. Occasionally he went to places like cantinas to see what it was like; this was an option that was more open to him as a man than it would have been to a woman. He granted me this point grudgingly. Men *se orientan* (get their bearings) more easily in the street than women, he conceded. He also recognized that there were places in the street that a woman would have had a hard time entering, especially cantinas, which were the cheapest and least reputable places to drink.

Men had greater access to street than women, who were more closely associated with home responsibilities. However, many people disapproved of both men and women who were in the street excessively. There was room to disagree over how much was too much because family responsibility was a vague criterion which could be fulfilled in varied ways. Although it was harder for women to spend time in the street than men, the degree to which this was gendered varied for different people.[16] For example, one day Juana and her husband were criticizing a professional family for permitting the teenage son and daughter to spend too much time playing "in the street" (i.e., not at home) with friends. Diego made no distinction between the boy and girl and criticized the parents for not giving the children some source of diversion at home. He felt they were in the street because they were justifiably bored at home. His wife made a clear distinction and said that although it was bad for both children, it was worse for the daughter. One danger often in people's minds was that young women ran the risk of pregnancy if in the street too much. The repercussions of unsanctioned sex, presumed more likely when "in the street" than at home, would have been worse for women than men, again because it was harder for women to avoid family responsibilities.

There was disagreement over how bad it was to be in the street for whom and under what conditions based on what was best for the individual or family. I was told of a few families in which women and children were not permitted to go out freely, even at the expense of the physical or economic well-being of the family, among both Salvadorans and Costa Ricans. Other people criticized men who did this as harshly as they criticized men, women, and children whom they thought were in the street to the detriment of family. Even so, I occasionally heard women give the fact that their husband wouldn't "let them" as an excuse not to participate in something that would take them away from their house. It was an entirely plausible excuse since other women accepted it without question — even without seeming to expect the husband to be asked before the excuse was proffered. I was not always convinced that the women I heard use this excuse were not doing so only to avoid explaining that they did not want to do something. Using another person as an excuse obviates any need to argue and makes saying no easier, if the excuse is culturally believable.

Women did spend time in public and the women I knew were critical of any man who wouldn't let other women do so. They walked there, they met people, they went shopping, they worked, they went out for recreational purposes. I knew a few who sold things door-to-door. The men I knew with daughters all wanted them to have an occupation so that they could take care of themselves. Some told me that women needed to be financially independent from men in order to protect themselves from abuse or domination. In their plans and hopes for their daughters, they recognized that some men could be abusive and that the ability of men to control women was related to women's ability to use public space independently. Even so, some men, Costa Rican and Salvadoran, did not want their wives to work outside of the home either ever or after children were born.

Men were more likely to exert this direct control over the use of space of others. They also influenced the use of space by women unrelated to them by making the street uncomfortable through looks and comments if women walked alone, seemed to loiter, were dressed "provocatively," or for no apparent reason other than gender. Even so, I occasionally heard men use their wives as excuses or explanations for not doing something. Once I was with a group of men when two of them said they had to leave because they did not have permission from their wives to be out with us. Another man tried to make fun of them for needing permission from women, but one of the two calmly replied that he believed it was necessary to take the woman into account if you wished to have a home. Everyone accepted the explanation.

Both men and women could use the wishes of spouses as an excuse, but when any commentary was offered to these two types of situation the reactions were tellingly different and similar. The idea that men might tell women what to do often was greeted with indignation toward the men but acceptance and belief. The idea that women might order men was accepted with a suggestion of ridicule—unless the men were able to assert that they were only being responsible to family. Men clearly had more authority over others and more autonomy. However, in both cases people made the argument that all members of a household should be considered in the actions of any one member. Women and men were both open to criticism if either their behavior or their control over others was thought to be to the detriment of other members of the family. Although the street was potentially associated with varied forms of irresponsibility (particularly violence, illicit sexual encounters, drinking, and marijuana), it was the fact of being out at the expense of family that seemed most reprehensible. Family responsibility was thus the central and dominant value of the constellation of values associated with space.

The social evaluation of street as irresponsible was countered by positive values; freedom was one of these. If this had not been so, there would have been no reason for disagreement over what people did. It was not just the men who were most in the street who recognized these other values, but also people who were more committed to the effort required by house. If street was escape from family responsibility, it was also freedom in contrast to the boredom and constraints of house and the demands of work. In the street, Antonio and his friends avoided discipline. They were free *(libre)*.

To Be Killed by a Schedule

On Sundays nearly everything in San José was closed, but the city filled with families regardless. On Sundays San José had a very different feel from any other day of the week. On other days the sidewalks were crowded with individuals working, shopping, doing errands. It was hectic. The streets clogged with cars and buses all spewing fumes into the air, and nearly everyone seemed to be trying to get somewhere else as quickly as possible. Some people, those who did not spend very much time in the street, told me that the city gave them a feeling of "desperation." Many feared the center of San José because crime was supposed to be worse there than elsewhere in the country. On Sunday it was different; tranquility reigned. There was more room for people with less traffic. Most stores were closed, so a person's attention could be focused more fully on one's companions. Public space became family space.

As we drank our fruit shakes, Antonio looked enviously at the apparently happy families and wished he could "do that," despite the fact that he wanted to be "free." In the street he was free, he claimed. "Free from what?" I asked. He was free from worries, free to do as he pleased. He complained about how the woman with whom he had lived for ten years had wanted him to tell her what he wanted for dinner and wanted him to eat it when it was ready. He wanted to eat or not eat when he felt like it. He wanted to be free to regulate his own schedule, to be free from time constraints. Another potential problem with home life was the pressure of having people depend on you under difficult circumstances that made your ability to fulfill their needs uncertain. During one particularly difficult period Antonio had nieces, nephews, his own children, and an unrelated child whose parents had temporarily left him with Antonio —he thought perhaps the child had been abandoned—all living in his home. His mother was ill and lived with him too. His ex-compañera (companion/partner) was pressuring him into getting back together. Then he spoke more than usual of leaving; at the very least, he wanted to go camping for a weekend to be "alone." Unfortunately, he could not do this because no one would go with him.[17]

Antonio also needed people—family and a compañera—and claimed that he wished for a family that would make him want to stay at home. His mother told him that he would never have that because he spent too much time in the street. No woman would marry him unless she were *una de aquellas* ("one of those ones") who, he said she said, were on the street corner smoking marijuana or drinking. She wanted him to meet someone to marry and take care of him after she died, and the women he could meet in the street were not good candidates. He dreamed about being free to travel, to wander around South America. He would go, he claimed, when his children grew up and did not need him anymore. Then again, he would brood and ask me how he could do that if he could not be alone.

Antonio only wanted a break from his increased responsibilities, but many working-class and artisan men dreamed of leaving most when things were difficult. Nestor, a Salvadoran shoemaker, told me that was the first thing men thought to do under difficult circumstances. Women could not leave so easily, he said, because they were more constrained by their responsibilities to children. The conflict between freedom and family might have been equally strong for both, but it was more difficult for women to choose the former and more difficult for people to imagine them doing it. A few did, but there were far fewer single fathers than mothers; I only knew one. Men under these kinds of economic pressures often did not leave; another, less drastic, option was to spend more time in the street in the company of male friends. The street took them away from the worries and interpersonal tensions of households with too many problems and not enough money.

People who accepted the value of home and the constraints imposed by family responsibility did not always enjoy it. Some women who criticized men for spending too much time in the street at the expense of their families also complained about never having time to be out. They made this complaint even as they professed not to understand why men would rather be in the street than at home. Women, if they were able to escape house responsibilities, sometimes went out to the street to alleviate boredom. One Sunday in San José, walking between bus stops, I came across a grandmother originally from rural El Salvador. She looked as if she had some errand, and I asked what she was doing. She answered "nothing." She was bored at home, she said, and had gone to the center of San José to get out of the house. Boredom at home was something women understood even if they did criticize it in men. Many men in turn understood why women would be bored. Just as there were both women and men who managed to be at home without undue boredom, men who spent much of their time in the street sometimes were bored there. Once Enrique, Antonio's brother, confessed to me that he was bored with San José and the *plaza* where they sold. Then he grinned at me and said that was the price of his freedom to be in the street all day.

One way in which Antonio and his friends were free was in their work as artisans and selling. They had no time schedules or supervisors telling them what to do when. They also had relatively light constraints on their freedom from the form of self-employment they had chosen. Enrique had previously been self-employed in a different occupation when he owned and operated a soda (small restaurant) with his wife. He used the same word to describe it and why he quit as another family used to describe the work of the dairy farm they had left: *esclavizante* ("enslaving"). Those were ways of earning a living in which the work was never-ending, could not be rescheduled, and shaped everything people could do. These friends liked earning a living making and selling artisanry in part because they could earn the amount they felt they needed—no more and, hopefully, no less—in less time than they would have working for someone else and without being told what to do. At the same time, there was always the danger of being too undisciplined while enjoying this freedom. Miguel, a shoemaker and leatherworker, once told me how he had felt himself losing that discipline a person needs. He briefly took a job in a factory to get his discipline back. Prior to that he had been in a workshop with others who left him with nothing.[18] During that period, he told me, he had been embarrassed to go home to his compañera and children because he could not take anything toward the family's support. If these men were too lacking in self-discipline, given their avoidance of the discipline of others, they ran the risk of not earning enough. Earning too little put some part of their lives in danger: time in the street, home life, or both. However, one benefit of the time the men spent in the street was that, when possible, they helped each other during difficult economic times.

Other people also avoided discipline in the street. One evening, while I was with some of these men, I met a Costa Rican boy who looked about eight years old and was living in the street. Miguel, who had been getting to know the child, told us about him. The boy said his mother hit him at home and his Nicaraguan father was in the United States. Miguel asked the boy why he did not go to PANI (Patronato Nacional para la Infancia), the child welfare office. The boy replied that there they wanted to "kill" *(matar)* him with their *horarios* (schedules). There was an hour to get up, to eat, to be back in the evening . . . hours for everything, he said. Antonio called him "callejero por derecho"—naturally callejero. Like them, the boy did not want to be told what to do and when to do it. In this case, it was the state, rather than family and work, that threatened to imprison him in its orderliness. If the state succeeded he would be well prepared to become a good worker and family man someday in the future. In the meantime, we bought him some dinner and worried about the fact that he was shivering-cold in the cool San José night and that the men thought the city too dangerous a place for a child to be in the street.

One thing they valued in addition to freedom was "goodness" *(ser bueno)*, which largely seemed to encompass solidarity with others and a sense of equality and justice. Few of them had been more than marginally active in political or community organizing, but they had been sympathetic to the FMLN and critical of the system in El Salvador. One day the two brothers, Enrique and Antonio, argued about the possibilities of being good. Enrique maintained that it is possible to be good, to practice solidarity, and not act solely in one's own narrowly defined interests. His brother argued that no, "ganó el billete" (money won): The world works on the principles of capitalism and self-interest. At first we all debated; very soon all of us except those two became quiet because they were passionately getting louder and louder. Finally Enrique left the room, but Antonio continued arguing alone. He repeatedly and belligerently asked us if it was not true that money had won. We all silently looked at him in wonder. I asked him, as others nodded, why he was being so argumentative since we were not contradicting him. He emphatically responded: "Porque me da cólera" ("Because it makes me angry")! He had seen the cold war end and the apparent victory of capitalism. This meant the end of dreams of a different kind of social order for many Latin Americans. The end of the dream was reflected in the difficulty of living in a way that was true to their ideals within a capitalist system, a topic that Antonio raised in other conversations with me.

Even without this uncommon level of political awareness, the act of refusing to be responsibly at home at appropriate times was implicitly a renunciation of not only the discipline, but also the values required by capitalist development even by individuals who were not consciously critical of the system. One of the criticisms of, and assumptions about, men in the street "too much" was that they were not providing adequately for their families or accumulating property and consumer goods that the family, in some sense, also needed. The assumption that these men were irresponsible mirrored the assumption that they were drinking or smoking marijuana when in the street. Either or both of these assumptions may or may not have been true, but there was no necessary connection between these activities and being out. Nor was there a necessary connection between being out and irresponsibility. However, even as they were practicing and enforcing values like solidarity with those less well-off and within the group, others could see them and judge them as irresponsible toward home and family—sometimes regardless of the facts. This judgment was made even by people who valued such solidarity . . . when it was practiced in other venues where positive values were not obscured by negative ones or when it was not practiced to the detriment of family needs.

In other historical contexts, the value of social responsibility and solidarity with others could compete with family as an alternative framework for evaluating action. This was the case when people chose between working for change in El Salvador and family responsibility. Social responsibility as an alternative value to family responsibility was less accepted by Salvadorans living in Costa Rica, at least after the war ended, because people no longer perceived a need for the level of solidarity and political mobilization, which had been necessary under more difficult politico-economic conditions. People told me that in El Salvador solidarity had been necessary because it was the only way to survive. To a degree, solidarity had also been necessary during the 1980s when life had been more difficult in Costa Rica than it now was. When I was there, the consensus, with few exceptions, seemed to be that people could, and therefore should, manage on their own in Costa Rica. The men I knew who spent the most time in the street did not justify their time there with reference to social values. They did not attempt to assert that their time in the street should be interpreted primarily in terms of the solidarity they practiced or even expect that people who did not spend time in the street would recognize that value in their practices. They valued the street for freedom and friendship, but accepted that this could make them less "respectable" to some other people. This was reflected, for example, in their mystification over why the Costa Rican woman called them "don."

The street meant freedom to these friends even as it continued to mean irresponsibility and illicit activity for others, like Antonio's mother, who criticized him and, in her worry, told him no respectable woman would want him. In fact, it was not just any freedom. It was freedom from the responsibility and discipline of both house and capitalism since a capitalist work discipline was necessary for maintaining most families. At the same time, it was the difficulty of actually fulfilling the demands of family responsibility that made the street more appealing for some men. Under conditions in which earning a living was difficult, they were likely to invest less in a respect for capitalist discipline and some may even have needed the street to earn a living because the relationships they made there could benefit them with knowledge or economic opportunities.[19] This had been particularly true in El Salvador, where salaried work had been very difficult to obtain.[20] In Costa Rica far fewer people were in as precarious an economic position as in El Salvador. In 1980, 68 percent of Salvadorans lived in poverty. Costa Rica was relatively less poor with 25 percent poverty in that same year (García and Gomáriz 1989-90:438). This helps explain the perception Salvadoran women had that men from their country were likely to be less responsible to family. It was in fact much more difficult in El Salvador for the majority of the population to earn enough to fulfill that level of responsibility than in Costa Rica. Unable to sustain a home economically, it is little wonder if some men, in El Salvador or Costa Rica, were disposed to spend more time in the street.

The position of women workers in the two countries clarifies the contrast in how Salvadoran men observed women practicing public leisure in the two countries. Although women were somewhat more likely to work outside the home in El Salvador than in Costa Rica,[21] there were significant differences in their work. The contrast is not so much in the occupations they filled as in the meanings their work had, on average, for families. Women, as we have seen, in El Salvador were more likely to be the primary source of support for dependents than their counterparts in Costa Rica. Most fulfilled this responsibility in conditions of poverty with work that was very insecure. In 1984, 90 percent of working Costa Rican women were salaried while, in 1985, only 43 percent of employed Salvadoran women were salaried and 41 percent were self-employed in the industrial and service sectors (García and Gomáriz 1989-90:78, 160).[22] This reflects a much higher reliance on the informal sector for women in El Salvador. Unemployment in Costa Rica was three times lower than in the northern country (6 versus 18 percent [ibid., 418]). Unemployment and informal work would have entailed a high degree of economic inse-

curity for many Salvadoran women and is symptomatic of the more difficult economic climate in El Salvador for both men and women, particularly the working class. The kinds of employment that many Costa Rican
women had gave them not only spending money, but also the social relationships necessary to go out respectably accompanied by people they
knew. Formal and professional employment, especially in the public sector, have been particularly important for women in Costa Rica. These
formal workplaces provided bounded and reputable places within which
coworkers got to know each other.

The economic conditions I have described for Costa Rica were also
more conducive to a consumer economy that encouraged the acquisition
of goods for the home and "appropriate" forms of public entertainment,
that is, forms that did not threaten family or work responsibility within
this model, across most social sectors and not just in the middle and upper
classes. On average, Costa Ricans could afford more than Salvadorans and
the country not only consumed more but distributed it somewhat more
equitably through higher (albeit still low) wages and social programs; the
impoverished are a much smaller portion of the population.[23] This was
reflected in the fact that Salvadorans considered Costa Ricans more con-
sumerist than people were in El Salvador. Salvadorans claimed that in
their country food was first, but in their adopted country people would
go hungry and take on debt in order to buy nice clothing or better fur-
nishings for their living rooms.[24] Under these conditions, it is plausible
that women workers in Costa Rica (who were less likely to be the head of
their household, more likely to have access to formal work and education,
and lived in a more affluent economy)[25] were often able to use a portion
of their time and money "in the street" in reputable ways.[26] Those who
could do so were the women Salvadorans observed in the street, and it
was their behavior that was interpreted in a language of national difference and morals.

Practiced Place

DeCerteau makes a distinction between space and place in his book *The
Practice of Everyday Life*. "A space," he writes, "exists when one takes into
consideration vectors of direction, velocities, and time variables. Thus
space is composed of intersections of mobile elements. It is in a sense
actuated by the ensemble of movements deployed within it" (1988 [1984]:
117). In his framework, place is a static structure imposed upon us while

space is formed through use; it is what he also calls "practiced places." Drawing in particular on speech act theory, deCerteau is interested in practice, or the ways in which "the ordinary man" plays or improvises with imposed systems. "A practice of the order constructed by others redistributes its space; it creates at least a certain play in that order, a space for maneuvers of unequal forces and for utopian points of reference" (18). Where deCerteau fails us is in not exploring where either these practices or the systems come from or how they are reproduced, and in ignoring the relationships among those "mobile elements" otherwise known as people. Doreen Massey, in contrast, is most interested in the way in which we produce space and place out of social relationships. In her framework, places are "articulated moments in networks of social relations and understandings" (1994:154–55). She uses this insight to analyze the ways in which places (in her sense of the term, which is closer to the colloquial usage than is deCerteau's) are in fact connected to wider social processes, like global capitalism. Although she pays less attention to the micro-level of interpersonal relationships and processes, the model works at that level as well. It is fruitful to combine these two theorists' insights in considering how "the street" can be a single place but multiple spaces in deCerteau's sense of the terms, and in thinking about how people, especially women, can manage to be in the street physically without suffering the reputation of being there morally. To do so, we must also take seriously daMatta's observation that house and street are spheres of social meaning or signification.

A space made of social relations takes on different meanings for people as contexts change even while the overall language remains the same; the standard gender associations of the places are no longer sufficient since thinking of space in this way precludes assuming a simple determination of space by cultural ideology. A space made of social relations must also be negotiable because relationships are. This "negotiation," either in the sense of people vying over meaning or in the sense in which we cope with or navigate a situation, occurs through the ways in which people "practice" the system and manipulate meaning through behavior. Within a model that limited women's use of "the street" by closely associating them with home responsibilities, use of space, and the very meaning of "street," was negotiated for both men and women in both countries. This occurred most through the overlap between related discourses, especially those of gendered space and family responsibility, which meant that there could never be an absolute division of space by gender. Reference to these discourses was made not only through actual behavior, but the context of that behavior: how, when, where, why, and with whom.

The fact that house and street were at once physical spaces and realms of meaning complicated the gendered use of space. This fact meant that "street" could have seemingly incommensurate physical and social referents, and this created ambiguity. The street was a moral space of potential danger, morally suspect behavior (or its potential), and irresponsibility. It was also a public arena of legitimate release from the tensions of work, a place where some people had legitimate ways of earning a living, and a place where people did necessary errands. Each of these uses of street was marked by different behaviors and forms of social relations. Most importantly, it was extended and apparently unnecessary time in the street that was most criticized, most likely to be evaluated as morally suspect, and most difficult for women. It was this manner of being in the street that epitomized the space. More necessary, respectable or transitory uses were not always described as "in the street." I distinguish between these through the distinction between being morally and physically in the street.

The values associated with each space were interrelated but not inextricably linked. For theoretical reasons it is necessary to recognize the potential disjunction between the varied meanings analytically, although there may be historically specific conditions when they coincide neatly. The fact that the street was said to be dangerous is related to, but not identical with, the fact that it was a space of freedom or irresponsibility. It differs, too, from the fact that the street was a space where people made new, extra-familial, social connections. Similarly, "house" was safe and respectable, but also boring and constraining. We do not need to assume that a person simultaneously references all the meanings associated with a space when they use it. If this is so, then the spatial model becomes much more complex than most discussions have recognized, with more possibilities for people to interpret behaviors in varied ways. It also becomes easier to see how the same discourse can be practiced in very different ways in different countries or regions and times characterized by different socio-economic or politico-economic conditions. Finally, it means that different values theoretically may be more meaningful or more feasible under different politico-economic conditions while other aspects of the model would be less noted. For example, I would expect that among the upper and upper-middle class the value of freedom or sociality might be more strongly associated with "street," which may then be less strongly gendered, since they have more resources to be out respectably.

However, despite the varying and overlapping values that permitted this fluidity, I make a qualitative distinction between the association of house with family and the other values associated with each space among the Costa Ricans and Salvadorans I knew in Costa Rica. Family, not the individual, was considered the basic unit of society in Central America,[27] and the use of street was ultimately evaluated through reference to house in the form of family responsibility. In practice, this meant that people with less family responsibility were less tied to the house and more able respectably to spend time in the street. This reinforces the utility of the public/domestic model in understanding these spaces. Women were more closely associated with family responsibilities and consequently more constrained in their use of the street and the extra-familial forms of cooperation that took place there. The same factor means that younger, unmarried people often had more freedom than older people, particularly if they were in school or work and consequently had legitimate access to spaces and social relations that could be translated into a respectable use of the street.

In the following chapters, we will see that this gendered space was not only a way of interpreting the changes experienced in migration, but an important aspect of the conditions people found upon arrival and how they could adapt to the new country.

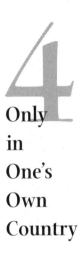

4
Only in One's Own Country

Variations on Some Themes

We were making tortillas over the wood fire behind the house when Victoria asked me if I like to dance. She had gone dancing often in El Salvador, but never in Costa Rica. I asked why. She paused and said she did not know; "Some things one can only do in one's own country." In one's own country one could do as one wanted, but in another country it was different. Her father had not liked to dance, but her grandfather had very much; dancing was a family tradition I heard about from various family members. Her nieces said that both she and their other aunt had liked to dance in El Salvador; as children the nieces had accompanied their aunts when they went to community dances. Neither aunt danced in public in Costa Rica and neither married or had children, although they were in their mid to late forties when I knew them.

I avoid dancing in any country; still, I found Victoria's story poignant. I heard about many losses, but this one affected me in its own way because it was the one I least understood while remaining small enough for me to wrap my mind around. I could comprehend other losses. I understood and empathized with people who had plans to go to the university when the campus was closed by the army. I sympathized with men who were forced either to leave everything they knew and loved or to serve in the army for a system they hated in a war with which they disagreed. I thought him reasonable when one man told me he sometimes still resented the fact that he had to learn a manual trade instead of a profession when his education was interrupted.

Other losses were too large to understand completely: At first they

threatened to overwhelm me with fear and horror until somehow they became a part of my own sadness, despite the fact that none of it happened
to me. I could only admire people's strength and ability to continue. I believed Sofía, who had lost much of her family in a massacre, when she said
it always seemed like yesterday. I respected her all the more for her cour-
age, her care and thoughtfulness in raising her son and grandsons, and
the resolute effort she put into learning to read in Costa Rica. But it took
all my imagination to think through what it would be like to love dancing and to give it up without even being able fully to explain why. It must
have still bothered Victoria sometimes; she, not I, was the one who raised
the topic. For a moment I idly wonder what her life would have been if
she had remained dancing in El Salvador. Most of all I wonder about the
answer. How is it that there are things one can only do in one's own country, things that affect one's life in such profound yet subtle ways?

Why should a person stop dancing? Antonio did not seem to understand either, although he stopped telling me it does not matter in what
country one lives. He too was from El Salvador. One Sunday on his day
off from the army, into which he had been inducted, he sold his gun on
a street corner in San Salvador. He added the proceeds to the money the
army had given him for drinks and prostitutes on his day off and left for
Mexico. He hated it; he missed his family, earning a living was difficult,
and it was all much too hard. So he returned home despite the danger:
He told me that the worst thing a person could be was a deserter; you
could murder a person and get away with it, but not desert. He tired of
hiding from the army in El Salvador and went to Costa Rica. He was *buscando al sur* (heading south) in the same way that he had earlier been
buscando al norte (heading north toward the United States). Many years
later—still in Costa Rica but now with children, his mother, two brothers,
a sister, nieces, and nephews—he said it really did not matter where one
was; a person could adapt to any country. Ignoring the fact that on a previous occasion he had told me the story in which he had not adapted to
Mexico, I suggested that maybe it was different if one were a woman. He
answered no. I mentioned a woman who never danced again; he replied
with thoughtful silence.

Victoria's nieces sometimes went dancing with friends after classes
and work or on the weekends. So it was not that one could not dance
in Costa Rica. Many times I heard Costa Ricans claim that *ticos* (Costa
Ricans) liked to dance all too much; this supposedly indicated that they
did not take anything seriously and were unwilling to work hard. This,

they said, was an attitude that held the country back. Ostensibly it should have been easier for a woman to dance in Costa Rica than in El Salvador. I was often told how much more "liberated" Costa Rican women were than Salvadorans, and many people, men and women, experienced Costa Rica as a place where there was more freedom than there had been in the wartime El Salvador they had left.

Although Antonio was noncommittal regarding the contrast between men and women, when I spoke with one couple about their experiences, the husband quietly stated that it would be more difficult for women to go to a new country than men. He said this not as if it were a profound insight, but as a commonsense statement of fact. My discussion in chapter 3 of house/street as a cultural model of space, social relations, and values explains why that would be true. I therefore organize my discussion around the experiences of men and women. I simultaneously examine differences among men and among women through other social variables: age, education, and degree of urban experience. The contrast between Victoria and Antonio's understandings of the possibilities of new countries and the differences between Victoria and her dancing niece suggest the need for this approach. Why would she have intuited, even after fourteen years, that some things were only done in one's own country, while he came to feel that it was possible to adapt to any country despite one failed attempt in Mexico? Why would one woman in a family dance and another not? Clearly the new country was not the same for each of these people despite their many common experiences. In the following subsections, I consider varied ways in which access to social relations and space came together for men and women to create their sense of what was possible in Costa Rica. This chapter also introduces the concept of *ambiente*, which I will define and discuss more explicitly later in the chapter, as a way of thinking about how our ability to do things is conditioned by social relations and space.

Alone

Javier was a shoemaker who operated a small workshop and had a loan at OARS. He employed two other shoemakers while he occupied much of his time finding clients to increase his business. One day he spoke to me about ambiente: how he had had to find it in Costa Rica, whether I had yet found mine, that if he repatriated he would have to *ambientarse* again. One Monday in August of 1993, I accompanied Julia to visit him at his workshop when she went to see how his business was progressing. He was living with his "grandmother"[1] in the home of a Nicaraguan woman, a single mother, from whom he rented space for his workshop and to live. His grandmother was the closest he had to family in Costa Rica. He was young, perhaps in his early thirties, and single. He had lived in San Salvador before going to Costa Rica in 1981.

The day we visited he was not there, but the brother of the owner of the house was. Alvaro took us to the tiny patio where Javier's two quiet and shy-acting Nicaraguan employees were working. The brother, who had lived in Costa Rica twenty years, spoke with us at length in a wide-ranging conversation that covered naturalization, the attitudes of Costa Ricans, his life in that country, the business affairs of Javier, and his sister's situation. The house had been his until he sold it to her. Some of his siblings disapproved of the fact that she took in boarders and sold meals, but he felt it was fine because that was how she earned a living. It was her affair *(asunto)* anyway, he added. Javier had originally met her when he ate lunches with other construction workers, before he became a shoemaker. The brother told Javier that we had visited. A few days later he went to the office and stayed a while, well over an hour, I believe, talking to me. It was on this occasion that we spoke of ambiente.

He told me life in Costa Rica was difficult, but with great effort one could get ahead. I asked why it was so hard. He answered that it was because the ambiente was different. I wondered how it was different, and he told me "in everything." For a moment I thought he was only contrasting the two countries at an abstract level; they would be different for anyone. Then he continued with an explanation more personal and specific to the situation of Central American refugees, particularly those who were *solo*, "alone," although still within the context of Costa Rica in general. It seemed from his discussion that while it was possible to describe the structures that made Costa Rica different, the important fact about the ambiente of that country was that people held different positions within it.

Javier told me that in El Salvador one knew how to do things, how to get ahead; in Costa Rica, no. Life was harder for a foreigner because the Costa Rican had his family—his brothers, his uncles, his cousins—and his lifelong friends from childhood. It was more difficult, he told me, for those who came alone than for people with family. He said wistfully that, from what he had seen, families (of Salvadorans in Costa Rica together) helped one another.

There were also, he felt, many other obstacles for the foreigner, although he speculated that might change with the possibility of naturalization. He said that Costa Ricans gave preference to other Costa Ricans; housing was hard to find and they did not rent to foreigners. A foreigner could inquire, and perhaps the landlord would "take all the facts" as if considering renting, but he or she would not do it. If there were two people and one was tico, they would rent to the Costa Rican.[2] He believed this was logical: They had to take care of people from their own country first. He felt it was almost impossible for foreigners to obtain their own house. There had been an organization that helped refugees to do so, but the aid was too little. He spoke at length about the difficulties of being foreign. So I asked, following up on his earlier comment regarding naturalization, if it would be easier if he naturalized. This time he thought and said perhaps a bit, but he did not believe the situation would improve very much because he would always be a foreigner regardless.

He spoke with great feeling of his love for El Salvador. He still felt Salvadoran and he would never renounce that. I asked him why he did not repatriate. He had been to visit in 1991 and had felt a strong emotion on arrival; even so, he did not want to repatriate. He would have had to return to find his ambiente again in the same way he had in Costa Rica. He had no means of earning a living there. He did not know anyone in El Salvador anymore. He had family in Canada—Toronto and Montreal—but not El Salvador or Costa Rica. Either I did not think to ask why he did not move to Canada or the question did not fit into our conversation easily, but I believe he would not have left Costa Rica because of his grandmother. She could not have obtained permission to immigrate, and he could not have abandoned her at her advanced age.

Javier's conversation was the most extended and explicit discussion of ambiente I had. In the conversation I have summarized, when I asked him how the ambiente of Costa Rica was different and more difficult than that of El Salvador, he considered a range of interrelated factors. He commented on structural conditions, such as institutions providing access to needed resources, that had affected him. His position as a foreigner and a refugee meant that he had a different relationship to those institutions than did Costa Ricans. He spoke of the knowledge a person has of how to go about getting things done in a place. This kind of practical knowledge in part involves knowing people who can help, and he considered the importance of social relationships developed over a lifetime. Events in El Salvador had disrupted those relationships when he became a refugee. In his assumption that it was natural for compatriots to help each other first, he further underscored the vulnerability of foreigners whose social networks were limited. The importance of countries as the locus of his ambiente was an effect of the experience of migration; previously, in El Salvador, his ambiente had been in San Salvador. With international migration the relevant level of contrast became national, and nationally defined structures affecting ambiente became the salient level of comparison as lower levels of difference were partially effaced.

Javier said it was harder for him in Costa Rica than it was for some Salvadorans and Nicaraguans because he was solo. As with the English word, "solo" (masculine) or "sola" (feminine) can refer to a state of being physically alone or isolated. However, and the English word carries this overtone also, although perhaps to a lesser degree, it could carry connotations of being unprotected and abandoned. Even people who were not "alone" in a strict physical interpretation of the word said they were solo if they felt that there was no one they could trust, no one who could help them in difficult periods of their lives. Javier was solo because he did not have people to help, while he had his elderly grandmother who depended on him completely. His isolation from the assistance family could have provided seemed to make him feel more vulnerable to the other disadvantages of being a foreigner and a refugee.

Family, Friends, Street

It is important that Javier mentioned family, including extended family, and friends from childhood when he explained how the ambiente was different for him because he was alone. In Central America these were often the strongest relationships, and people expected them to be most important. For many people their best and most reliable friendships were among relatives; some people told me that it was only relatives who were true friends. Siblings and parents were particularly important, although uncles, aunts, and cousins were also often central relationships. Don Eugenio was in his sixties and had been a baker in Costa Rica, an office worker in El Salvador, and a furniture maker in the United States. He warned me that people were lucky to have just a few true friends, other than family, in the course of their lives. He told me about his youth in El Salvador, which had been made more difficult when he was left without family at a young age and by "friends" who betrayed him at work. The next most important category of friendship was childhood friends;

it was in childhood that people, perhaps particularly the working class, were most free to develop close friendships because it was then that they had the fewest responsibilities and constraints on their time. The two groups of male friends I knew were composed of brothers, cousins, and childhood friends with an occasional newcomer, sometimes described as "almost like a brother." Coworkers and university students also became friends because they were legitimately together on a regular basis.

In the rest of this section, I discuss the ways in which some men used relationships with family and friends in making their lives. First Ramón and, at the end of the section, Alfredo provide examples of men who used the street most extensively. Sergio, Antonio, and Raúl provide three contrasting configurations of relations in the street, friendship, and family. The point is not that these men exemplify particular strategies, but that they illustrate how men could draw on these kinds of social relations, as their own situations permitted, to find the kind of *ambiente* in which they were comfortable.

Ramón was from rural El Salvador where he grew up on a family farm that had been large enough for his family to live comfortably without being wealthy. In Costa Rica he had been in a group productive project that made machine-knit sweaters. Eventually the project disbanded. He used the proceeds from his portion of the group's capital to buy a pickup truck. He earned a living transporting people and things with this truck when I knew him. This manner of earning a living took him all over, and he knew many people. The day he took me to meet doña Elena, I saw his networking ability in action as he used it to benefit both himself and others. She had a small *bazar*[3] in front of her home. Her husband, Arturo, reupholstered furniture at home; he had learned this skill in a course at one of the refugee assistance programs. Ramón knew that Romelio, another Salvadoran, needed some chairs refinished. He asked if Arturo, who did not know Romelio himself, could do it at a good price. Arturo said yes, so Ramón said he would mention the possibility to Romelio and bring the two men together. Before leaving he also bought a few items from doña Elena and promised to buy two towels on another day.

Sergio was studying medicine in El Salvador when the army closed the school, so he began studying political science. Then a professor warned him and some other students to leave the country. He went to Mexico, where he became involved with a group of students organizing solidarity for the Salvadoran opposition and subsequently was obliged to leave the country. From Mexico he went to Costa Rica. On two occasions a year apart Sergio recounted to me similar versions of his arrival. In one version he arrived with some dollars, a bottle of rum, and the address of a doctor he had met while they were both students in Mexico. In the other version it was the dollars, two bottles of whiskey and a letter of introduction. Either made a good story, as he indubitably intended, and foregrounded the fact that he arrived with very few resources, prospects, or social connections. On his first day in Costa Rica he ran into a Salvadoran friend he had not realized was there. That friend was involved in organizing the first refugee aid office and asked him to get involved, too.[4] He did well and was given gradually increasing responsibilities until he had a career as an accountant, for which he had never studied, for nongovernmental organizations. In retrospect, he felt he had been fortunate to fall so quickly into that first job because it integrated him into Costa Rican society immediately. It quickly gave him an advantageous *ambiente* despite having arrived by himself.

Although he told me that in the first years he was in Costa Rica he went out more, when I knew him he did not spend time in the street. He had a few friends close enough to visit, but he did not see them often—possibly once a month. He was more likely to visit his wife's family. He did not know the people in his neighborhood well, although they were friendly. There were a few families there that he could turn to for favors and one man with whom he sometimes talked about soccer. Even so, he told me that people in the neighborhood did not know him. This seemed common in the urban Meseta Central of Costa Rica: Neighbors often did not know one another's names, although they usually did recognize one another and had some limited interactions (cf. Biesanz et al. 1988 [1982]: 42–46). In these ways Sergio conformed to a model of responsible and respectable family behavior for men, as discussed in the previous chapter.

In Costa Rica most socializing was in the family and visiting outside the family was discouraged (cf. Biesanz et al. 1988 [1982]:161–62). A common way to emphasize the extremely close nature of a friendship was to say that you visited each other's homes. Many people told me with whom they were on such terms and how few such friends they had, often only one or two families. Even among very good friends it was rare to visit more than about once a month; most people considered visiting more often to be excessive. Victoria told me of one woman who lost all her friends from visiting more often than that. This was especially true for women, but men also avoided frequent visiting. The main exception was men who spent time together in the street, if that can be considered a form of visiting. I heard both men and women praise others, male and female, who did not go out very much. There were occasionally other exceptions to this; I knew one neighborhood where people visited more often, both because some of the women worked together feeding nearby construction workers and because a pulpería served as a kind of community center.

Antonio's story of arrival was strikingly similar to Sergio's despite class-based differences. Both first went to Mexico. Both emphasized the absence of other people they could rely on upon arrival in Costa Rica and how quickly they settled into the country. Antonio returned to El Salvador after a year in Mexico and then went to Costa Rica. He arrived in San José with fifteen (U.S.) dollars in his pocket. He found a hotel room that cost between two and three dollars a night. He told me that there was a room for one dollar, but it did not seem safe to him; others also included this detail in their stories. The bus from El Salvador arrived in San José at night, so the first thing people had to do was find a place to stay. The compromise between affordability and safety was an issue for people who arrived with almost nothing, nowhere to go, and no prospects. Antonio was bored by himself in the hotel room. To alleviate the boredom, he went for a beer, and another, and another . . . until he was left with five dollars, which he somehow made last a week. He, too, told a good story with precisely the right details.

Talking to men in the street, Antonio made friends who told him where to go for help and of a woman who rented rooms in her house in San José. Later he found the place where he first lived in Cartago when one of these friends invited Antonio to move in with him. With each move, in which he gradually became more situated in Costa Rica, he also became more enmeshed in social relationships. Antonio met men in the street who directed him to the Red Cross, which was then administering refugee programs. He persuaded that organization to give him a sewing machine to make things of leather. In telling this he emphasized his own cleverness at obtaining the assistance, as if he had not truly needed help. He could do this, he maintained, because in Costa Rica there were no artisans since there had been no lack of work. In El Salvador they had needed to be more creative in finding ways to earn a living. He reported to me that within three months he was financially secure; within three years he had a house. He had motivation to save for a house: His mother wanted to join him in Costa Rica, but she would not unless he could provide her with a house and security. People more commonly reported that they had avoided the acquisition of houses, or even smaller goods like televisions, in the expectation of soon returning to El Salvador.

Another aspect of Antonio's ambiente was family. At one point he worked for a brother who was a furniture maker. When he began to sell things, a second brother assisted him in finding clients. The use of these ties and others like them was fluid. One month a man would work with a brother or an uncle; later he would pick up a different trade or job out of boredom, to help a friend, or in hopes of better pay or opportunities. For example, Felipe was a shoemaker and a university student. When he injured himself at work, he went to work in his brother's printing shop. Later, he began working for a shoemaker in the neighborhood where he lived; then he began repairing shoes at home because he could earn more if he kept the profit for himself. This followed a pattern also used in El Salvador. In El Salvador Raúl's family had been rural, but one by one the siblings had gone to San Salvador, each helping those who followed. Since Raúl was one of the youngest, he had benefited from what his older siblings had achieved through migration and hard work before him. This continued with the family's second round of migration from San Salvador to Costa Rica. One of his older brothers had been a printer in San Salvador, and in Costa Rica gradually built up a printing business. When Raúl went to Costa Rica his brother was able to employ him. Later Raúl learned shoemaking from Nestor, another Salvadoran whom he met while hanging out with men in the workshop of a shoemaker. All these relationships of both friendship and kinship were available as resources to be used creatively in the art of living. The fact that Javier was without family in Costa Rica made his life more difficult because he lacked one of the primary types of relationships.

Alfredo had been in Costa Rica since the 1970s and was in his forties. He was one of Antonio's friends and part of a group that sometimes drank together and sometimes worked together. Everyone else in that group had family in Costa Rica. Most had compañeras or ex-compañeras and children in addition to other family. Alfredo seemed only to have the street. He commented to me how much he enjoyed spending time in the plaza. When I asked why, he said it was because he knew people there. One night he chivalrously walked me across San José to my bus stop. En route, he told me how he had previously worked in a factory. He worked in it by day and was also the night watchman. The chemicals from the paint thinner in the factory made him ill, so he quit when the factory burned down and was going to move to another location. Then his Salvadoran friends from the plaza helped him by giving him work selling; they liked to help another Salvadoran when they could, he said. Alfredo was fortunate to have their help because, despite the fact that he had been in the country longer than they, he seemed to have fewer resources to fall back upon when he lost his job. This was largely because he did not have family in the country as they did. Nor had he invested the time and effort necessary to create and keep a family; other men who initially had been by themselves formed families. They, like Sergio and others, found women, had children, bought or rented houses, and created homes. Alfredo found his ambiente in the street. His story shows how this particular ambiente gave him not only freedom, but also insecurity that was compensated for by the help friends he made there could give.

Like Ramón, Sergio, and Antonio, other men also found places to live, jobs, information "in the street." Many of the stories told by men were of arriving by themselves and feeling disoriented, trying to find an address of some contact from El Salvador, and running into someone in the street. Alternatively, they did not have a contact address, stayed in an inexpensive hotel, and began meeting men in the street who oriented them to other options. Often they found a group of men to hang out with and one of these men would teach them to make shoes, tell them about a job, or even give them employment. This is not surprising since it was a space men could easily access and one where men could network and visit. As we saw in chapter 3, some men were there a great deal, but even those who were rarely in the street often made their first social contacts in Costa Rica there.

It is not surprising that the street figured prominently in the stories most men told me about their first days in Costa Rica and how they found places to live or ways of making a living—in other words how they began finding their ambiente. They arrived without knowing many people and did not have access to other defined places. How did women, with less access to the street, find out about things? How did they orient themselves and find an ambiente? I have a hard time imagining most women getting a useful (and respectable) connection in the street in the way so many men described. Certainly they could not rely on this to the extent that many men did. I next explore the stories of some women that contrast with those of the men we have just met. The contrast is most striking in the more limited ability of women to meet people in the street, the consequently greater reliance on family and/or bounded and legitimate spaces as sites of social relations, and the unequal impact of family responsibilities.

Street

Women used a variety of types of relationships and venues in varied combinations. Few, however, used the street to the extent that many men did. I knew one woman who did in some ways, and the contrast between her and men is instructive. Alicia was a grandmother in her fifties. She was the sole support of her household, which included her two high-school-aged granddaughters and her husband, Danilo. She arrived in Costa Rica in 1981 with her granddaughters, whose father, Alicia's son, had been killed in El Salvador. Her husband went to Costa Rica subsequently when it seemed best for the whole family because he had difficulties in El Salvador, the business where he worked burned down, and she found she could not work in Costa Rica without someone to care for the granddaughters. In Costa Rica he had worked in a printer's shop until he had problems with Migración, which was enforcing the law against refugees working.

Alicia was unfailingly and admirably cheerful and helpful; a person could always count on her. It was sometimes difficult for me to distinguish between those things she did for pay and those she did because she was so *colaboradora* (helpful/cooperative). She did a variety of things to earn a living, including various odd jobs and errands, house-sitting, and selling produce. However, much of her work seemed to involve waiting on behalf of other people. If you had an errand in the Migración offices, she would go for you. If it required your presence, she would hold your place in line during the interminable hours of waiting. These varied ways of earning a living required and facilitated the development of a wide network of acquaintances and took her to many different places. They were largely "in the street" in the sense that she was neither at home nor in any other fixed, bounded locale. However, her manner of being in the street was different from that of most men who spent significant portions of their time there. Men could develop further social ties drinking and hanging out; Alicia did not. Even when she had to wait for a bus, if possible she found a place to wait rather than appear to be loitering. When she was out in the street it was because she had something to do, a place to go, or a line to wait in. It could be said that she was "in the street," but it could not be said that she was callejera. She neither acted in socially disapproved ways nor spent time out unnecessarily. Alicia was sometimes criticized for not finding a way to be at home more, although neither often nor excessively, because people sympathized with her poverty and efforts.

Ironically she was similar to her ex-son-in-law, Ramón, in this way of earning a living despite the fact that he had the truck, and she only had her time and alacrity to sell. The similarity between them occurs to me only as I write, but it is ironic because she and he complained about each other incessantly. Neither liked the other, but both told me they could co-operate if it served their mutual interest in assisting Alicia's daughter and granddaughter, Ramón's daughter. They both used their abilities and time networking to earn a living. They maintained their networks through a combination of paid services, friendship, and favors, and used these abilities and resources to connect other people who might be of mutual assistance. It was a difficult and precarious way of earning a living, particularly for a woman.

Alone, Friends, Family

Alicia did not have other people to rely upon since, for whatever reasons, her husband did not work. Nor did she have the resources (monetary or educational) to develop an occupation or more reliable way of earning a living. It is therefore interesting that she did not complain about her situation or talk about being sola, alone. More women than men spoke to me of being sola, and the ways in which they did so indicate the extent to which it was not a purely physical condition. I cannot say that women were more likely than men to feel sola. But if we remember that being alone was a feeling of vulnerability and social isolation from relationships of aid, and if we consider the extra difficulties poor women had in earning a living or gaining access to spaces where they could develop more extensive networks of relationships, then it is plausible that they were more often sola than either men or women in more secure socioeconomic conditions. I first consider how being alone was different for women than men, and then contrast that with the situation of a unified family.

Sofía was from rural El Salvador, where she had taken care of the house and done the varied and unending chores of poor rural women. One day she told me about her life while we were working together in the literacy class; the students' assignment was to write a short essay about their childhoods. She wrote a page, but talked to me at much greater length. She had a difficult childhood because her mother died when she was very young, her stepmother was strict, and her father listened to her step-mother. When she told me this, she told me that her mother had left her sola: There was no one to protect her. She, like many Salvadorans, started working very young; she told me a grinding stone had been her toy. She began by grinding corn for the family's pigs and as she gained exper-tise she graduated to making the *masa* for tortillas. As she recounted her life, she showed me scars she had from her childhood home. Each scar carried the story of what she had done to incur the wrath of her father or stepmother. As an adult, when she was already a grandmother, her family had been among those most brutalized by the state violence. She arrived in Costa Rica as the head of a household composed of her school-age son, a daughter, and two of her grandchildren. She had the address of another daughter who had received her passage out of El Salvador from the UNHCR first. At the airport Sofía asked a woman how to find the ad-dress. The stranger, by chance a Salvadoran also, asked Sofía about herself and told her of the shelter for Salvadorans in Heredia. Sofía lived there with her grandchildren until they managed to move elsewhere.

It is hard to think what else she could have done. Her daughter could not have been in a situation any better than Sofía's. She had no other rela-tives, friends, or acquaintances in Costa Rica. She had few, if any, other resources to draw on. She had only a few months of life in San Salva-dor, spent waiting for her refugee application to be processed, as urban experience, no formal education, and only rural work experience. She had dependents to care for, which, combined with her lack of experience and relative age, would have made working difficult even if it had been legal. The daughter who lived with her was mentally and physically un-able to help.

When I knew her, so many years later, Sofía had an ambiente that still seemed to revolve largely around the organization that grew out of the shelter to which she had originally turned. One daughter had emigrated to Canada, as had her son. She lived with the daughter who was mentally ill and two grandsons in a house that she had recently bought with the assistance of nongovernmental organizations serving refugees. This im-proved her economic situation greatly since she did not have to pay rent, but she was still in a difficult position. Hers was a particularly troubling case since there was no one in the household capable of earning a living; they were among the last families on emergency aid, soon to end com-pletely. Even before the aid ended it could not have been enough, and she did not have many other resources unless her children in Canada could and did help.

Sofía was a thoughtful and generous older woman who, like Alicia, had an amazingly positive attitude despite a life of great hardship. The only time she ever described herself as sola to me was when she remembered the death of her mother. Although she did not complain, in some ways she was sola, based on the way in which other people used the word.

Doña Pilar was also a grandmother from rural El Salvador before moving to Costa Rica and, like Sofía, had not been formally educated. Pilar had been a single mother who raised her children with the help of her brother, who was also single. In El Salvador, she had operated a small store in her home and delivered lunches to agricultural workers. This was probably in addition to other work available in a rural area. In Costa Rica, in addition to receiving emergency refugee assistance, she made and sold tamales for extra money. She had gone to Costa Rica with family: her brother, a daughter, her daughter-in-law (whose husband, Pilar's son, had been killed), and grandchildren by both her daughter and the daughter-in-law, Fernanda. They all lived in a house together, the same one they had found to rent shortly after arriving in the country. Fernanda had one bedroom with her young children who were born in Costa Rica. Pilar shared a bedroom with her daughter, María, and María's two daughters, now in college. Pilar had another son who lived in a nearby house with his family. María and her sister-in-law worked as maids. María was a live-in domestic servant who only spent weekends at home. The sister-in-law went home each evening to care for her own children.

Despite the fact that they all lived together, each of the three women told me how sola she was, how she had no one to help her, and how she hoped for help from one quarter or another. They lived in a single house, but they did not share expenses or domestic tasks. The sister-in-laws not only cooked separately but had separate kitchen areas, each with a stove, sink, and refrigerator. When they spoke with me, they did not mention each other but looked elsewhere for potential aid. María spoke of her brother in the United States as the one person who would help her, but he was getting married so that would surely end, she conjectured, because his new wife would object to his draining resources from the home he was forming in the United States. Fernanda, her sister-in-law, complained of having no one and thought about returning to her family in El Salvador if her grown sons, the ones born in El Salvador, did not find work in Costa Rica. They were not unaccompanied, but each felt sola.

Despite their complaints, the household did appear to benefit from the larger number of people who could contribute and they were in a less precarious position than either Sofía's or Alicia's families. I don't doubt the women felt forsaken and pressured in their attempts to support their families and themselves, but I felt that references to being sola were also a rhetorical device to gain sympathy for the difficulty of their situation. As such it also inadvertently highlighted the many tensions and resentments among the women. The way they used the word "sola" demonstrates that being "alone" could be more a social than a physical state: If they were sola it was because they lacked people on whom they felt they could depend. In this case these women did have family in Costa Rica. When they said they were "alone" they indirectly alluded to the fact that there were problems between the members of this family. They did not entirely rely on each other despite a kind of mutual dependence. Although they were better positioned than Sofía or Alicia, they were still quite poor. They were poor enough that these relationships had to have been crucial to their survival even if they were loath to admit it. None of these women earned enough, or had enough access to income from other people, to live on her own with her dependents. Maids earned approximately eighteen thousand colones a month, and rent for a modest place might have been twelve thousand colones; this would not have left enough to eat, much less pay other expenses.

Sofía and Pilar were older women from very rural areas. Their parents had not thought it necessary to give them formal education and probably could not have afforded it even if the education of girls had been more highly valued. These factors limited the types of employment they could have found, and when I knew them neither was physically capable of paid employment. This limited their ability to expand their social networks. However, Pilar had lived in the same house since she had arrived in Costa Rica. She consequently knew her neighbors better than Sofía, who had recently moved. Pilar was in a similar situation in terms of how she was brought up and her own social sphere, but she was at the center of a larger household with numerous adults who had their own circles of friends and acquaintances. The knowledge or favors that her relatives could obtain from people could also benefit Pilar.

Teresa also was of rural extraction, but she had moved to San Salvador at a young age. Her mother, like Sofía's, died and left her feeling alone and unprotected, sola, despite the fact that she had father and siblings. A neighbor woman took her to work as a maid in San Salvador when she was eleven, not long after her mother died. She was proud of the ability she had shown there. She described to me how she had been able to learn from each new situation in order to progress to better jobs; eventually she had a stand in the market. When she first arrived in Costa Rica she tried to find the address of a friend. She did not find the friend, but she met a family that gave her a place to spend the night. After that initial connection her social network came through her employers in her work as a maid and, once she found God, through the church. She married a Costa Rican whom she met through religious activities. She acquired property with the help of loans obtained through a refugee aid office. Church and religion, more than anything else, gave her an ambiente when I knew her.

Teresa told me she went to Costa Rica sola. She remembered feeling alone and depressed without "parents, uncles, family," no one to help her. She went with her son, but he was about seven, not old enough to help. If Sergio and Antonio told parables of work and making it, Teresa's story had a different moral. She told me that when one comes from a different country, a country of dictatorship and war, one is a "different person." In such a situation a person is *amarga y dura* (bitter and hard), she maintained. Amarga y dura herself, it was no surprise to her, as she looked back on that time, that she had had difficulties with other people. Upon arrival, she was also afraid and lost; she recalled standing on a street corner bemused, without knowing what to do next. When she found God she changed, and consequently her situation changed. After she found God, she lost her bitterness; she understood—she told me that God had taught her psychology.

Her story was markedly different from others in the pivotal role of God and conversion. However, it was like those of many who went to Costa Rica by themselves, or with only dependents, in the disorientation, poverty, and isolation she first felt. It was also similar because the disorientation and isolation were overcome through the help of others as she became part of networks of social relationships. Her story clearly shows how she went from being totally lost to finding her ambiente in Costa Rica. In the absence of family, Teresa made good use of new friends. However, unlike so many of the friends men relied upon, Teresa's relationships were almost all situated in one of two locales: work or church. The one exception was the family that helped her on her first night when she was unsuccessful at finding the friend. Women, unlike men, who obtained help from strangers in this way did so under conditions of great difficulty, not as a standard procedure. They told me about using such connections only in remembering their arrival when they had no one in the country. In both Sofía's and Teresa's stories the strangers appear on their first night in the country when they had barely arrived and ran the risk of spending it outside.

Teresa combined several significant attributes in making her life in

Costa Rica. She was still young enough to work; she capitalized on an innate intelligence; she knew how to take advantage of opportunities available in the city; and she was either lucky or assisted by God. She told me of a Salvadoran family that lived near her that was less knowledgeable. She thought that they could have used loans available to refugees to expand their business making purses and bags. They had not realized this until she had told them, but by then it was too late because the money for refugees was gone. She did not talk of being *sola*, except in remembering both her mother's death and her arrival in Costa Rica, despite the fact that she had fewer relatives in Costa Rica than did the women in Pilar's family. I believe this was because she was not as helpless and overwhelmed in the face of unfulfillable responsibilities as were some women. She had the advantages I have enumerated, which permitted her to expand her network of acquaintances. It was also easier for her to earn a living and meet family responsibilities than it was for women with more dependents. When she arrived she had only one child. Currently she had a husband who worked and no dependents. Her position was very different from that of the women in Pilar's family, who had more children, received less help from men, and were fighting among themselves. Women in families with other cooperating adults were in an easier position than those who had to fulfill family obligations without assistance. Women could share domestic responsibilities and make it easier for mothers to work outside the home. Men could help support the family economically and help women indirectly through their greater ability to negotiate the street. Victoria's is an example of such a family, where the members complemented each other's efforts and, in a sense, pooled the social connections they made.

She went to Costa Rica with her two sisters, brother-in-law, and the four children of one of the sisters and brother-in-law. With so many people it was hard for them to find an affordable place to live, but the women had a relative who wanted to exchange her apartment for a larger one. They found the larger house, and the family moved into the vacated apartment. The apartment had only one bedroom and the landlord would not rent it to a family with four children, so the two daughters, not yet teenagers, went to live with, and work for, nearby families. They hated it; one told me that she cried inconsolably every night. Eventually they quietly moved in with the rest of the family.

The children went to school; they made friends. The two aunts found employment as maids with nearby families. This permitted them to earn money, be with the family, and help with domestic work and family endeavors. The family made and sold tamales during one period of unemployment. The father, Diego, found work in construction when a friend from El Salvador saw a sign at a nearby site. The family that hired one of the aunts became good friends with the whole family. The father of that family worked in a government office and on occasion helped with official business. They met another family through a classmate of one of the daughters.

Eventually Diego applied for a dairy project with one of the organizations working with refugees, and after much time it was approved. He found the land for the farm by talking to a man "in the street." Something unidentifiable about how the man plowed seemed Salvadoran, so Diego spoke to him and the man, who was in fact Salvadoran, knew of some land for rent. When the family moved they maintained contact with the people from their old neighborhood. Some of these families visited the farm on weekends. When the family wished to sell agricultural products those neighbors were among their clients. Some of those neighbors helped by linking the family to other friends and coworkers. The neighborhood in which they first lived was largely middle-class and this benefited them. Other people settled in poor neighborhoods where social connections among neighbors were potentially less useful. Similarly, those in Costa Rica with political connections from El Salvador could benefit in ways that others could not.

This family did help each other, as Javier had observed in other cases, and they were never alone. The family was much more united than Pilar's. It was also younger and did not have the problems caused by the jealousies and torn loyalties often created by tensions between parents, children, and children-in-law when children marry. In this example and the stories of family ties among some men we see that families helped each other by expanding the range of relationships and knowledge available to each individual, sometimes working together, and sometimes finding employment for relatives. For women the help of family could be particularly important. Although the contributions of men and women might be equal in a family, the need was unequal. Women with children but without the assistance of other adults were in a more disadvantaged position than men. This was because they had greater family responsibilities, did not have the same earning potential, and had more limited access to other relationships as a result of the gendered organization of space. In the next chapter we will see this same pattern reflected in the reasons some people did not repatriate. In what remains of this chapter I will consider the concept of ambiente more directly now that we have a sense of how it was used to conceptualize the way in which people adapted to a new space. Further consideration of the term also facilitates consideration of how the two countries were experienced as different kinds of places.

Ambiente

> ambiente. adj. Applied to any fluid that surrounds a body.// Soft air that surrounds bodies.// Painting. Effect of aerial perspective that gives corporeality to what is painted and simulates distances.// Set of circumstances that accompany or surround the situation or state of a person or thing. (Real Academia Española 1981)

Ambiente. I love this word. I like the way it swirls when I say it. I like the concatenation of meanings, meanings to which my growing collection of dictionaries does not do justice. The English/Spanish dictionary on my desk says "environment." The smaller pocket dictionary says "atmosphere, environment." They might have included "ambient" or "ambience," but after looking the word up I feel I know less than I did before. My small Spanish thesaurus disappoints me when I find it has no entry at all. It is true that ambiente is both environment and atmosphere. The word, as in English, can refer to the natural environment and air. People's actions can also create an ambiente, an atmosphere or climate, conducive to particular goals or types of interaction. For example, the Costa Rican newspaper *La Nación* ran an article about the "cold" ambiente of an electoral campaign, which got off to a slow start. This created an ambiente in which many people were undecided; the political parties hoped to "warm" the ambiente in favor of their presidential candidates with public rallies (Feigenblatt 1997). The word is also like ambiance in English: A place, for example a restaurant, can have its own ambiente. Ambiance is an environment, but one peculiar to a place and time and conducive to a particular style of social interaction.

Costa Rica had a different ambiente because the set of circumstances that made it distinct from El Salvador gave it a different social climate. It was more *"tranquilo"*—tranquil, peaceful. People, I was told many times, could do as they wished in Costa Rica as long as they did not do anything bad or illegal. Guillermo, a tailor and shoemaker from San Salvador who went to Costa Rica when he was twenty-three with a group of men with whom he had grown up, recalled the difference between the ambiente of the two countries at the time he arrived in Costa Rica. He spoke of how he and his friends became afraid to spend time out in the evening as the situation in El Salvador worsened. This was despite the fact that they all worked and none was involved in politics—two facts that normally should have kept them out of trouble and safe from suspicion. They had always been afraid of the police, who were abusive, but in the time before they decided to leave, the fear grew worse. Prior to that they had felt safe if they were not doing anything wrong; after that they began to be afraid regardless of what they were doing. In contrast, he said of Costa Rica, "In reality, it was when I arrived here that I felt an air of liberty; I felt a change in the ambiente, in the people." Salvadorans felt that the politico-economic systems of the two countries, which I described in chapter 1, were conducive to different ways of being. A dictatorship, many noted, made people "hard" and encouraged mistrust.[5] It created a climate of generalized fear that included the fear Guillermo described of the police in El Salvador. Other people remembered that at that time in El Salvador they had feared for the safety of family members every time they left the house. Some mentioned ways in which economic problems compounded the climate of fear and insecurity for people who could not adequately provide for children.

In explaining the ambiente of Costa Rica in this way, Salvadorans echoed Massey's (1994) explanation of place as resulting from a coming together of social relations and understandings that create a distinctive style of meaningful space. Furthermore, if we treat space and place as configurations of social relationships, then they are not static because social relations are inherently dynamic. This is true of ambiente also. The ambiente of El Salvador that forced Salvadorans to leave was an effect of a long history of politico-economic relationships. However, it was the increased insecurity and violence of the late 1970s and early 1980s that created the ambiente they left. Similarly, they noticed change in the ambiente of Costa Rica during the years they had lived there. It no longer seemed to them in the mid-1990s as tranquil as it had when they arrived.

People also had an ambiente, although this was so self-evident that I rarely heard it discussed; like many things, ambiente seemed most conspicuous in its lack or potential lack. Salvadorans used this word when talking about how they had adapted to new surroundings, or in the case of people who had repatriated, how others had readapted to old surroundings. The final part of the definition opening this section comes closest to this usage: the "set of circumstances that accompany or surround the situation or state of a person or thing." A person always is in an ambiente, but it is significant that Salvadorans used the phrase "su ambiente" (your/her/his/their ambiente). I have, or am in, my ambiente when that "set of circumstances," that environment, is one that suits me. It is one in which I am, as we say in English, "at home." Sometimes, especially if you leave a known place for an unknown one, you must find your ambiente within that place. If ambiente is translated as "environment," this last possessive sense in which Salvadorans used the word is like "niche" because it refers to the way in which the individual fits into, or has adapted to, a larger social space.

Ambiente in this last sense is a personal relationship with social space. I like the concept of ambiente because it combines spatial connotations with recognition of the importance of social relations and context in human space. Just as in a physical sense we cannot live without the ambiente—the atmosphere and environment—a person cannot be without a social ambiente. Although personal, a person's ambiente is thoroughly social since it involves the way in which a person is in a place through the way in which he or she is embedded in a network of social relations, organizations and institutions. Massey's understanding of place implies that individuals have different experiences of space because they occupy different positions in those social structures and processes that compose it. It is also so because people in different social positions have different resources, including time, money, and knowledge, available to them and they are affected by cultural constructions of what people can do in different ways.

As we have seen, people drew on a range of types of social relations within a context of social structures and institutions that shaped the opportunities available to them. There is consequently an important overlap between what composes an ambiente and what scholars study under the rubrics of networks and social capital. The term "social capital" has become popular in some disciplines to talk about what anthropologists and sociologists have always known, the importance of social networks and ties in accessing resources and knowledge and in the overall well-being of individuals.[6] The term, especially as used by Bourdieu (1986), highlights the fact that social ties can be translated into economic capital or resources. It can be analyzed as having two parts: the social relations themselves and the resources accessed. It is most often used to refer to the ability to capture resources through social connections. It is important then that social position affects one's networks and consequently access to knowledge, resources, and connections necessary for social and economic goals or needs.

Of the two, ambiente is in some ways a broader concept. First it is not primarily utilitarian. Being "solo" is not a problem simply because one might have a harder time surviving economically. It is also lonely. Family and friends do not just potentially help one access resources, they make one feel one belongs both to space and social group. Second, ambiente not only reminds us of how crucial access to places is for creating and maintaining social ties important in developing social capital. In its multifaceted meaning it also focuses our attention toward the dialectic between people and place. It refers not so much to the networks or resources that compose social capital, but to the social climate of a place and the way in which an individual has his or her own social space within that place. It implies recognition of the way in which we create spaces that are propitious for some actions and not others as well as the way in which space in turn shapes our capacity to do things, even things that may not have any potential material benefit, like dancing.

Why, to return to the question that opened this chapter, could some things only be done in one's own country? Another way to think about this is to ask how people make space their own and what factors influence what they feel they can do. The concept "ambiente" highlights the role of social relations and structures in shaping a space that is individualized while remaining socially and culturally conditioned. If we think about space in terms of spatiality or socially produced space, then it is not surprising that being foreign meant different things to different people. Gender, age, family responsibilities, rural/urban experience, class, and personal values all influenced the ways in which people were able to use space, relate to other people, and find ambientes. People who had family with them were in a different position from those who did not because family could broaden a person's access to resources, knowledge, and relationships. This made life easier; it also gave them a social space that was their own from the start. Ideally it gave them people to rely upon, at least initially, when assistance was most necessary, even if later the cooperation eroded. However, the importance of not being alone was also psychological. The people who told me stories of complete disorientation upon arrival were never those who had been with adult family or friends. Those with family or friends had faced difficult times, but had not felt as lost.

Given the ways in which the practice of space in Central America was gendered, it is not surprising that Victoria experienced the change in countries as a change in what she could do, while Antonio experienced it as a temporary shift that less dramatically affected his sense of who he was and what he could do. The effects of gender were intensified by the fact that Antonio could earn a living in more public venues than Victoria, who worked in a private house as a maid and later at home. Women were at a disadvantage relative to men in their ability to meet people not only because of the cultural norms that restricted their use of many public spaces and made them more responsible for family, but also because so often their work kept them at a home—their own or someone else's. These conditions meant Victoria had less opportunity to create an ambiente that could have included opportunities for dancing. A person does not go dancing alone, and she left the lifelong network of relationships within which she had had a space for dancing in El Salvador. She had had very little opportunity to develop a new social group with which she might have been comfortable dancing. People with greater freedom, because of gender or age, to develop a broader range of relationships were less likely to have Victoria's experience of things they could no longer do in the new country.

When they arrived, Salvadorans had little relationship to the space of Costa Rica. They knew few, if any, people, had few resources, and lacked much of the practical knowledge that makes a place one's own. Creating a network of social relations and knowledge of how to do things in Costa Rica was a necessity for survival. In the next chapter I discuss how finding an ambiente led to settlement for some Salvadorans. The process of settling was the same as that of survival and living as they gradually became more enmeshed in social relationships in Costa Rica. This did not happen at the same rate or manner for everyone; but it is difficult to imagine that it did not happen at all, especially as ever more time passed with no foreseeable end to the war. It is also difficult to imagine that people could have easily replicated the same types of networks of social relations, and therefore the same social space, after moving. The fact that they made lives in that country clearly does not imply that they were the same lives as those they had left. The ambiente they came to have in Costa Rica was not the one they had lost in El Salvador.

5

A Second Patria

Patria, País, Pueblo

We were outside the *taller* (workshop) after English class waiting for the rest of the group to catch up with us on the quiet San José evening when José asked me if I often heard from my family. He asked because he did not have much contact with his, only a phone call every six months or once a year. He told me that he was only seventeen when he began separating himself (*cuando se fue apartando*) from them. On another day he recounted that his father had obliged him to leave El Salvador at that age in the early 1980s. Like José's father, other parents also made teenage sons leave so they would not be drafted into the army or arrested on suspicion of subversion. First he had gone to Mexico, then Guatemala; it turned ugly there, and he went to Costa Rica. In Mexico and Guatemala he had felt he needed to disguise the fact that he was Salvadoran by changing the way he spoke. In Costa Rica, finally, he had felt safe without such precautionary measures. Despite the fact that he had made a life there, he told me that he had not yet reconciled himself to the course his life had taken. He was not positive his father had been right to make him leave home.

Of the six children in his family, he was his mother's favorite and he knew that it had been difficult for her to have him gone. At first he wrote, but later he did not as often. Once, after a long silence, he wrote to his mother and a sibling called him to request that he not write because if he was going to write so rarely it was too hard on his mother. Consequently he had little contact with his family. He had no family in Costa Rica, he told me on that evening when he asked about mine. On other days he spoke of his cousin in Costa Rica. His cousin's Russian-born wife taught children dance and sent José business by recommending him to her students' parents when they needed dance shoes. His parents and siblings were all in El Salvador, but he did have some other family, including his Costa Rican partner (compañera) and children, in Costa Rica. In that country he not only felt safe, but also had created a new life.

When he took me, with his compañera and children, to visit a friend's house, he told me that Costa Rica was his "segunda patria," his second country. He would not go back to El Salvador anymore, although sometimes he still thought about it. Upon hearing the latter confession, his compañera looked over and glared darkly at him. That glare made it obvious that his relationship with her was an important element in why Costa Rica was a patria he would not leave. None of the Salvadorans I knew in Costa Rica was likely to repatriate despite the fact that nearly all discussed the possibility, and some at times insisted they would eventually return to El Salvador. Often those who were most adamant that they would go back—even, as Sergio often added, if it was to be buried near his mother after he died—also acknowledged its unlikelihood. Many were like José, for whom Costa Rica had become a second patria. Although it was the patria he would not leave, he still thought of El Salvador as his patria.

He had two patrias or homelands—a state of affairs that has been precluded by most dominant versions of national belonging, although this has begun to change as states grant increased importance to nationals abroad and their descendents. By legal criteria it was impossible in this case. If Salvadorans naturalized as Costa Ricans, they were required to renounce Salvadoran citizenship. While they recognized this legal situation, which complicated the decisions of some people regarding naturalization, they also recognized a broader range of things that made them part of a country. Unlike citizenship, the kinds of criteria they felt tied them to countries were not all of an either-or type and consequently they mobilized a more complex understanding of nation and the connections between people and place. I explore this first by examining the concept of patria directly, and subsequently exploring how people belong to countries through the ways in which Salvadorans continued to feel tied to El Salvador and their discussions of repatriation, which indicated ways they were also tied to Costa Rica.

"Patria" is treated as a synonym for "nation" in both Latin America and scholarly analyses. Scholars working on nations, national identity, and nationalism have emphasized the "socially constructed" nature of national sentiments to counter the primordializing tendencies of both nationalist ideologies and past social science practices. Making selective reference to Anderson (1990 [1983]), they generally analyze how national communities are "imagined" and naturalized through narrative.

> For it is through epic discourses, broadly conceived, that the nation is particularized and centered, imagined as eternal and primordial, and that nationalist love becomes a sacralized and sublime sentiment, indeed a form of piety (Bakhtin 1981:16). And the sacralization of the nation is simultaneously the sacralization of the state. (Alonso 1994:388)

Consequently there has been a privileging of the ways in which the nation is presented to citizens through novels, schools, political rituals, architecture, museums, censuses, and maps. Much of the analytical focus has been on the ways in which the past is selectively remembered in these elite and state projects in order to create a sense of national community that overrides the particularities of different subgroups and areas within the territory of the nation-state (e.g., Alonso 1988; Franco 1989; Pratt 1990; Skurski 1994; Skurski and Coronil 1993; Sommer 1991, 1994 [1990]).

Such "correlative imaginaries" (Radcliffe and Westwood 1996) place people in horizontal integration and a shared space by correlating subjectivities through what Radcliffe and Westwood call "externalities": official symbols, histories, and forms of governance. However, although scholars of nationalism recognize that the horizontal community they study is socially constructed, or "imagined" in Anderson's (1990 [1983]) now immortal term, they have paid relatively little attention to the ways in which the nation is lived and constituted through social interaction. Although it is important that novels and museums are integral parts of national curriculums in public education, for example, we cannot assume that people absorb the lessons in any simple and direct way and need to study when and how dominant ideologies are received, interpreted, and used or transformed by the populace.

In their study of Ecuador, Radcliffe and Westwood show how the nation is in fact de-centered, despite state efforts, except in rare and fragile instances because of the way in which it articulates with other sites of identification. Underlying their work is a theoretical approach to identity as inherently multiple or de-centered in which we can identify multiple sites of subjectivity including geographic (local, regional, national, pan-national) and social (gender, sexuality, class, race, and ethnicity). These interact with each other in dynamic and context-specific ways. Since the nation is not the only source of social identification, the ways in which people experience it, unlike its ideological representation, are necessarily de-centered. This means that an exclusive focus on official and elite representations of the nation is misleading because those discourses attempt to center what rarely is unitary in everyday life. Those instances when people do invest emotionally in a correlative imaginary of the nation offer moments when the nation is centered. War and international sports competitions are two such moments, which "offer a sense of home and belonging" (Radcliffe and Westwood 1996:163).

Bowman (1993), in a comparative study of Palestinian national identity, also notes that national identity is situational, rather than fixed, but he does so to distinguish among types of centering national narratives. Palestinians living under different conditions—in the West Bank, in camps in Lebanon, and in elite exile in Europe and North America—gave Palestinian national identity different meanings as a result of their varied experiences of exile and perceptions of who the external enemy was. The contrast in the meanings of Palestinian identity leads him to note that most scholars have conflated national identity in general with nationalism. He distinguishes between the broad category of national identity and nationalism as a type of national identity. National identity need not be more than a "fairly diffuse recognition of various forms of cultural continuity" (Bowman:77). Nationalism is a form of national identity mobilized toward a political program; I will also call this a nationalist identity. People can experience that sense of belonging described by Radcliffe and Westwood through forms of national identity that are not incorporated into nationalist projects or discourses.

The very term "patria" itself is taken for granted in studies of nations, nationalism, and national identity in Latin America. It is always translated as some variant of "nation" (nation, fatherland, motherland, homeland), implying nationalist projects, but this does not really tell us what it means for most people in their daily life. What did patria mean for Salvadorans I knew in Costa Rica? I began asking myself this question when I realized that my understanding of the word was subtly different from the understandings Salvadorans seemed to express with it. When I knew the term mainly from official contexts and newspapers, I understood it to be a synonym for "country." To me a country implied little more than citizenship and the fact that we live in territorially defined juridical units that claim a right to our loyalty. Country, for me, was primarily an issue of state-based rights and responsibilities. However, when Salvadorans used the word it seemed to presuppose something more complex than simply a country and a much wider range of attachments than a citizen's relationship to a state. Indeed, for them patria often did not seem to depend on states or governments at all. The lesson, once I learned it, was obvious but important. The disjunction between narrow legal criteria and their use of "patria" has been central to my understanding of the way in which some came to have two patrias and others described themselves as more Costa Rican than Salvadoran, even as they retained citizenship in El Salvador.

I owe my first insight into this issue to the ethnographic abilities of a group of Salvadoran friends, the same artisans who were such a prominent part of chapter 3. The first time I went out after English class with Antonio, Daniel, Enrique, and Miguel, Antonio asked me if I was proud of my patria. I answered, "Not particularly." We talked about this, among other topics, over our beer and food in the relatively inexpensive Chinese restaurant they had chosen. Eventually we established that I was not proud of my patria because of how my government had acted, while they were proud of theirs because they were "a people that has fought" ("un pueblo que ha luchado"). "That is the difference," they concluded, satisfied at having figured it out. What they did not add was they were a people that had fought its own government. This, for me, was key because it dramatically illustrated the difference between our understandings of patria. Salvadorans could feel patriotic by opposing their government, although not all Salvadorans nor the Salvadoran state would have accepted this. In contrast, I, like many other United States academics I know, renounced patriotism to denounce activities of my government.

Antonio seemed to find it difficult to remember or accept this difference; he came back to the issue several times over the next year, periodically criticizing me for supposedly not loving my patria. The possibility clearly bothered him despite the fact that he had hated my country, the United States. He perceived a lack of patriotism as a general problem with the United States citizens he met. One day he raised the topic again, and then, pensive with eyes half-focused as if hearing some other conversation, said, "They/you don't even love their/your patria and they/you go around talking nonsense" ("Ni aman a su patria y andan hablando paja"). He refused to specify what *paja*, only saying: "not you, others." That at least clarified the tacit pronoun, although it did not leave me any wiser about either patria or the nonsense that gringos talk. Antonio said that I had to be proud of "mi país" (my country) regardless of the government or anything else. When I asked why, he told me he did not know. He added that maybe he was wrong, but it seemed to him that one had to feel that way. Everyone has to have a patria, and that is where he or she is from. If not, I was told by him and others, nothing would make sense. It is almost like family, Antonio explained. He asked me if when I see another United-statesian it is like family. I replied no, and he said, "That is the difference." For him all Salvadorans were "almost like family." Patria and family were similar because they were the fundamental units of social organization. Family was the basic unit of society that organized individuals into sub-groups and then a patria. Patria, equated with country and the people of a country, was a basic geosocial unit that organized the world into disparate and contiguous spaces. The world was impossible to imagine without either of these units of social organization.[1]

I was still curious about patria, so I asked some other people. I asked Ramiro, an editor from El Salvador, who was among those who went to Costa Rica in the 1970s. He had been trained as an economist and teacher, although he grew up in a large rural family of modest resources, and was among the most formally educated people I met. The first part of his answer captured the way in which people took patria for granted as a fundamental organizing principle: "Well now you have put me in an awkward situation because this is a concept . . . that seems to us so clear." He continued, "Yes, it is as if you put me to explain the light of day." He then generously and carefully explained patria and related concepts. I will return to his explanation momentarily.

I asked Sergio about patria. He told me that he understood it to be "the country, the territory," but he would look it up for me in his dictionary at home. I explained that the dictionary definition was fine, but I wanted to know what he meant when he used the word. He nodded that he grasped the distinction and told me he used it for the territory and the people. This meaning was reiterated in his answer when, on another day, still on guard for how people used the term, I asked him what *mal de patria* was. Sergio explained it as missing one's "patria, its lands, its people" ("patria, sus terruños, su gente"). In English it is homesickness. The next time I saw him, after the day I first asked, as promised he gave me the following hand-written definition:

Patria: Set of persons who are associated among themselves through sentiment; will of a nation. City or district where a great number of men, animals or plants of a specific type are found. Mother Patria: country of origin. Example: Florence is the patria of artists; Arabia is the patria of coffee; celestial patria, heaven.

Synonym, nation: Natural society of men which the unity of territory, origin, history, name and culture inclines to community life and
creates the consciousness of a common destiny. Juridical entity formed
by the set of inhabitants of a country ruled by one government. The
territory of that same country.

The definition Sergio gave me emphasizes the apparently natural nature of patria and the connection between living beings and the place
where they originate. The examples in his dictionary suggest that a person belongs to a patria in the same way that coffee originated in Arabia
or specific varieties of plants and animals (and "men") are found in one
place distinct from another. People and things are necessarily from someplace; that place is a patria. Patria is also people united by sentiment—
presumably, although the first definition does not specify this, people of a
particular place. Interestingly, Florence is the patria of artists, which suggests the possibility of a spiritual or intellectual link between people and
territory that is not based in physical origins or residence. None of the
examples given by Sergio's dictionary is a country, although the synonym
listed is "nation." This provides us with another perspective on patria.
Nation is, according to the entry, a "natural" community fostered by the
unity of land, origin, history, and culture. This is the standard version of
how the world is organized, which underlies both refugee policies and
nationalist discourses. The dictionary continues, with no explicit connection to the earlier definitions, to say a nation is a legal entity composed of
people and territory ruled by a single government. Here, stuck at the end
of the dictionary entry for a synonym, is the definition of patria I had initially assumed. It clearly is not the most important meaning of the word
in this source: While it is not opposed to the primary definitions and examples, they do not imply it.

Ramiro, the editor, explained patria to me, and at first his definition
did not seem to be related to countries although it did echo the definition of "nation" given by Sergio's dictionary. Regarding patria he said:
"Well, I would say, as a first intent to define it, that a patria is a historical, geographical and cultural environment *(entorno)* that a specific population shares and which unites them. And in this sense I would say that
for Central Americans our patria is Central America." He contrasted it to
Venezuela, a different patria that had "another history, other geographical, cultural, environmental characteristics." He continued: "and a patria
has symbols, not just referring to the flag, the shield, the national anthem,
but also to its culture, its beliefs, its arts, its technology. That is to say, it

has paradigmatic manners in each of these areas that go about conforming the things that a person cares about, those he/she abhors, for which one fights, those for which one does not."

Although Ramiro did not speak about national borders directly, his definition presupposes them even when he is not in agreement with the ones in place. This is clear because some of the symbols of patria he lists are official ones. The way in which other people spoke of patria, while still accepting national boundaries, was slightly less dependent on legal jurisdictions.

Salvadorans commonly equated patria, *país* (country),[2] and *pueblo* (people). Julia told me that she liked the television series *Little House on the Prairie* because "it identifies with the country" ("se identifica con el país"); it shows that there are "farmers and everything." In other words, it shows that there is a pueblo and therefore a country. The day she took me to visit doña Marcela, a Salvadoran woman who had lost four of her sons in the war and had another who was arrested (and probably tortured), my status had to be verified in these terms. She studiously avoided talking to me, but periodically darted glances in my direction. Later her son came home and we introduced ourselves. He noted approvingly that I gave my name in Spanish instead of the unpronounceable version and asked if I was "americana." I answered: "Sí, estadounidense" ("Yes, Unitedstatesian"). His mother again glanced at me and asked, "But of the people?" Yes, of the people, Julia vouched. Not everyone made a distinction between the people and government of the gringa patria. Many did not have experiences to permit that, while they often knew too well that system and pueblo had not been the same in El Salvador.

El pueblo (the people), in this usage, gained moral stature from not being part of the system other than to be exploited and repressed. Yet this distinction, which granted the people legitimacy over patria and país, was incomplete since the Salvadoran government also attempted to equate itself with the patria, even at the expense of the pueblo. The Salvadoran government was only partially successful in its efforts to enforce this equation of itself with the patria, although state borders do delimit the patrias of Central America. Antonio, who became a refugee when he deserted from the army, recounted that the army had tried to make new soldiers believe that the pueblo was the enemy of the patria. Despite his hatred of the military and system of the time in El Salvador, they might have convinced him that the war was for the patria, and therefore worthwhile, if it had not been against his own people.

As we continued the interview, I asked Ramiro to define "el pueblo." He said that, when it is not a village, it is all the people of a nationality or patria. I pressed him on this point and told him that sometimes it seemed to me that people used the word to exclude the government or the system. He responded:

> Yes, yes it includes it. What happens is that it would appear not because we are passing through a historical period in which the form of government in El Salvador has presented itself as contradictory and opposed to the interests of the majority. For this reason the majority when it speaks of its popular interests and of its national interests does not include the government because it feels itself in opposition. And of course, how is it not going to resent those persecutions and those massacres!

He explained that he and others who had been politically active in El Salvador had been attempting to create a system that would have benefited everyone in the society and therefore would have been appropriate to the patria. They, in other words, had a nationalist project as defined by Bowman (1993).

However, people did not typically use the term in this sense. When I asked Antonio why I should be proud of my country after all that it had done in El Salvador, he answered that had nothing to do with it. After all, he stated, if what the government did were the indication of how people should feel about their patria, no one would have more reason to hate his than he.[3] This was initially a puzzle for me early in my research, before I began questioning my lack of understanding of patria. I had wondered why they were so proud of being Salvadoran after being betrayed by their country. Similarly, at that time it seemed an impossible contradiction for me that I should love my patria, but denounce the vast resources my government had poured into the war against the Salvadoran people and its continued role in neo-colonialism and imperialism. This was a contradiction Salvadorans answered by saying that there must be good things and people in the United States, although Salvadorans could not know it. Logically there must be good and bad in all countries. Their response did not resolve the contradiction but dissolved it by assuming that patria and government were not necessarily identical. I, as Ramiro insisted was appropriate, had presumed that the government and system were part of the patria; in fact, I had considered them the most essential part. Antonio emphatically did not include those things as an integral and necessary part of patria and used the term to refer to people and territory. From their perspective it was the "system" or "dictatorship" that had been at fault, not the country, and it made no sense to blame the latter. And yet, the state was clearly important in defining the boundaries of what they considered a patria and thus is not entirely excluded from the definition at some level.

When Ramiro told me that a patria has symbols, he included historical and cultural environments, with consequent manners of doing things and beliefs, which shape the things a person most values. These are ambiguous markers because there is no standard to dictate where to find cultural differences and similarities, which are in fact socially constructed and neither inherent nor absolute. It would be possible to draw the geographical borders of a patria, if this is indeed necessary, in different ways. This is clear in the definition from Sergio's dictionary, which said patria is a country but also a place *(lugar)* or even a city.[4] Strong forces in their lives had reinforced the reality of those borders. In Ramiro's own life this ambiguity in the appropriate boundaries of patria was clear in an apparent contradiction during our interview. He felt that he was not at home in Costa Rica, even after twenty-two years, because the surroundings in which he had been raised were in El Salvador. Early in the interview, he had described those surroundings in far more specific terms referring to the region and, especially, to his family home where he had been raised. Of Costa Rica, he told me, "Look, I intend to return to El Salvador. I really only feel entirely at home when I am in El Salvador. When I am here in Costa Rica with all the hospitality, cordiality, and generosity of the ticos, I feel as if I am in another's house. I thank them but my place is there; and so I cherish the dream of returning at some time to El Salvador." He also strongly believed that Central America should be unified and he said that the proper patria of Central Americans was Central America. Thus, in our talk, he quickly shifted between familial, subnational, national, and supranational sites of belonging and home.

Despite the fact that people assumed state boundaries in their use of the term, patria could take on dimensions other than the nation-state even within official discourse. For example, Dr. Arnoldo Mora, then Minister of Culture, Youth, and Sports of Costa Rica, stated in a 1994 conference that the patria of Costa Rica is made up of many smaller patrias. He identified various small patrias within Costa Rica as distinctive cultural spaces (Monturiol F. 1994). On a larger scale, Central America as a whole was called *la gran patria* (the big patria) by media and politicians, and there have been many efforts to unify it economically, militarily, or politically. Radcliffe and Westwood (1996:113) report that rural-urban migrants in South American countries refer to their place of origin as their *patria chica* ("small patria"). Radcliffe and Westwood use this to highlight the fact that there are "scales of affiliation" that de-center the nation by providing spaces of identification that are both smaller and larger than the nation. I agree with their observation and its theoretical implications. However, I maintain that this variable usage of the term "patria" requires that we reconsider our impulses to equate patria with nation in any absolute or simple way. If a locale can be a small patria or a region a large one, the main referent of patria does not seem to be anything so formal as a nation-state.

The primary referent of patria, then, was the sense that people are sentimentally attached to each other and a place through common history, experience, and culture. The essence of the term is the sense of belonging appropriated by nationalism, not the nation-state itself. Given this fact, it is no wonder that Antonio and others were shocked at the idea that I might not love my patria. Patria defines one's being through the practices, experiences, and people of a place within which a person is embedded. Not to love it would make a person unnaturally atomistic and disconnected from his or her society and culture.[5] I was consequently more struck by the resonance it had with the English word "home" than by any connection to the affairs of countries. "Home" does not correspond in any easy way to Spanish terms. It can be translated as *hogar*, but hogar is only the house that is a home. Home in the larger sense, which has uncertain dimensions, no absolute boundaries, and implies sentimental attachment to peoples and places where a person has lived, is very like patria except that patria usually is more closely tied to connotations of legally bounded countries.

The ways in which Salvadorans spoke of El Salvador reflect considerations emphasized by scholars who have used the idea of home to talk about identity. Home indicates a place where one is from or "belongs." Kondo (1996) uses home as a trope for "racial and ethnic identities" and writes that "It stands for a safe place, where there is no need to explain oneself to outsiders; it stands for community; more problematically, it can elicit a nostalgia for a past golden age that never was, a nostalgia that elides exclusion, power relations, and difference" (95). She examines ways in which Asian-Americans have dealt with the problems created by a Eurocentric "American" home to which they do not entirely belong and argues that they need to "write [themselves] into existence" by telling their stories (110). She examines a particular instance of story-telling, a play, which succeeded in making her feel at home through its evocation of distinctive linguistic practices, sensory memory, place, and people. These gave her a sense of belonging. The production of the play reinforced these literary devices because it created a sense of community among those people involved.

Feminist scholars have questioned the way in which "home" as a trope for identity intimates a sense of safety: perhaps that sense of safety and shelter that children ideally feel since home, like patria, is often said to be the place where we grew up. Kondo highlights the ways in which "people on the margins," including "peoples in diaspora," may not have a home or have a home that is not safe. Bell hooks (1990:41–49) writes of the work women did when she was a child to create homes where African-Americans felt safe and even had a space of resistance. She and other feminists also have pointed out that for those who are relatively powerless safety can be difficult to attain. The experiences of Salvadorans are illustrative of the fact that home is not always safe. One thing they appreciated about Costa Rica was that it had given them safety. They also show that home does not need to be safe to be a home and a site of belonging. Above I quoted Kondo as saying home "stands for a safe place, where there is no need to explain oneself." Clearly these two characteristics are not necessarily linked. I here set aside the issue of safety to consider the relationship between common understanding and belonging or "home."

Heller (1995) defines home as ways in which we "reduce contingency." This does not require safety, only a measure of predictability. In this sense, home and being at home share a great deal with the concept of "trust" theorized with reference to refugees by Daniel and Knudsen (1995). They argue that "the capacity to trust needs to be underwritten by the capacity to tame chance, especially the chance of being hurt. This capacity is not an individual matter but a gift that a cultured society gives a person" (2). They argue that refugees are produced when their society no longer provides that level of trust. They use trust not in the quotidian sense of belief, but in a way that is closely related to culture and the human capacity to make and find meaning. Like Heller's use of "home," "trust" in this case references the predictability of our sociocultural world. Daniel and Knudsen explain: "By 'trust,' we do not intend a largely conscious state of awareness, something akin to belief, but rather its opposite: something more akin to what the French anthropologist Pierre Bourdieu called 'habitus' or what Martin Heidegger called 'being-in-the-world' " (ibid., 1). Heller does not elaborate on the philosophical underpinnings of her way of thinking about home, but the parallel with the theoretical discussion of trust by Daniel leads to phenomenology and the importance of place.

Phenomenological approaches to place, inspired by Heidegger, start from the proposition that the perception of being in place is primary. This means that the body is primary because perceptions are embodied. Perception is neither presocial or precultural nor passive. The philosopher Edward Casey writes that

> I am not proposing a merely mute level of experience that passively receives simple and senseless data of place. Perception at the primary level is synesthetic—an affair of the whole body sensing and moving. Thanks to its inherent complexity, bodily perceiving is directed at (and is adequate to) things and places that come configured, often in highly complicated ways. Moreover, the configuration and complication are already meaningful and not something internally registered as sensory givens that lack any sense of their own: the sensory is senseful. . . . To perceive synesthetically is to be actively passive; it is to be absorptive yet constitutive, both at once. (Casey 1996:18)

Casey adds: "It is also to be *constituted*: constituted by cultural and social structures that sediment themselves into the deepest level of perception" (ibid.). Casey echoes Bourdieu's (1977) concept of habitus, which focuses our attention on the ways in which the structures of culture and society, the ways in which the place in which we live is structured, inculcate sets of dispositions for how we interpret and act. Ramiro noted that patria was not only people and place but also a historical and cultural context in which people live. This in turn, he told me, induces values and ways of living. He was making a point that is congruous with the arguments of Casey and Bourdieu except he put a name, the name of patria, to that place and set of structures. Keeping in mind this understanding of patria, the rest of this chapter will consider the connections people felt to the two countries in which they had made homes. An examination of, first, the connections they felt to El Salvador in exile and, second, ties to Costa Rica that were important in decisions about repatriation, will help us to understand how they came to be and to feel a part of the latter country, as well as the ambiguities of that belonging.

Memories of El Salvador

A country would seem to be something one must leave behind when one migrates, whether as a refugee, tourist, or labor migrant. Yet, if patria is not just a bounded territory, but the land and its people bound together through culture, history, and values, then perhaps it becomes partially portable. Patria as land and people, or community, are the least transportable, but even these proved not to be completely rooted. Although the communities they had known in El Salvador were not in Costa Rica, other Salvadorans were there including, in many cases, family and childhood friends. This permitted a displaced connection to the people of their patria. During the 1980s, the Salvadoran organizations I mentioned in the introduction facilitated social interaction among Salvadorans in the country. Even in the 1990s, although all Salvadorans in the country had ties, often family relations, with Costa Ricans, they continued to value opportunities to spend time with other Salvadorans. People commented that they felt Salvadorans, and sometimes other Central Americans, could understand them in ways that Costa Ricans could not.

Patria as land proved portable in the form of plants. The day Alicia took me to visit her house she sent me away with a piece of sugar cane. When I gave it to the women where I lived, they were puzzled, but prepared to eat it, until I intervened and told them she had sent it because it was from El Salvador. Then they understood, put down the machete, planned where to plant it, and began debating exactly what variety of cane it was. Specific varieties of plants they believed could not be found in Costa Rica were, for many Salvadorans, prized gifts and possessions smuggled from El Salvador.

Ramiro also included history, practices, and values as defining characteristics of patrias. Salvadorans carried these within themselves as a part of who they were. Some social practices, especially food and language, were important and evoked the feel of home. Many Salvadorans mentioned they attempted to retain a sense of being Salvadoran, although they recognized that they had changed, through these practices. For example, Guillermo and Lucrecia commented that all societies have different customs and continued:

> GUILLERMO: Yes, and from all this one learns, bit by bit I would say. It is gradual, right? Identifying oneself with the society in which one lives, but never losing that of oneself. Because in reality we still have

customs from there, our customs with which we were raised by our parents. We have mixed the two societies, we could say.

LUCRECIA: Yes, they have mixed a bit. Always one tries to preserve one's roots.

HAYDEN: How do you do this . . . preserve your roots? What is it that you preserve?

GUILLERMO: Say, for example, in the case of food they are almost the same thing, what happens is that sometimes one cooks in the Salvadoran style: the kinds of seasonings. The rest, I don't know. Sometimes even in the way of speaking.

Lucrecia added that a person could feel he or she had changed, but other people would say no, that one spoke the same as always. Some Salvadorans commented on the reverse phenomenon: They felt they had not changed, but were told that they had.

Salvadorans felt that the process of change was natural. Even so, it remained a potential point of disagreement among them because people changed to different degrees and at different rates and because these changes indicated attitudes toward the patria. Some, like José whom you met at the beginning of this chapter, felt it had not been necessary to change dramatically in Costa Rica because there was no real source of danger. He disapproved of symbolically or implicitly renouncing Salvadoraness through unnecessary change, but he also felt that it was wrong stubbornly to resist all change. Others disagreed with his position and changed more thoroughly and rapidly to be more like Costa Ricans, although in some cases it might not have been clear if this was done consciously. For some it was a tactic to avoid prejudice. Sometimes Salvadorans wondered at, even mildly criticized, compatriots who seemed to have changed very little; sometimes they wondered at and criticized those who seemed too eager to change and reject the fact that they were Salvadoran. Regardless of their position on this issue or how much they felt they had changed, they recognized a sense in which national identity was mutable. Some considered remaining Salvadoran a virtue, but it was one that was difficult. It could not be accomplished simply by retaining citizenship and it was almost impossible to live in another country without adopting its ways of being and acting.

Food was one practice everyone commented on as a mark of national difference. Lucrecia was more specific than her husband in this regard during our interview. She mentioned wild plants they had eaten in El

Salvador that were not eaten in Costa Rica. To be more precise, I would say that these plants were not eaten in urban Costa Rica where they had settled, but they had been eaten in San Salvador where both had grown up. From this fact they extrapolated national characteristics, despite the fact that I don't think any of us knew if these plants were eaten in rural Costa Rica. Sometimes Lucrecia would find these plants and make a meal to remember El Salvador. Other foods, particularly *pupusas* and *quesadilla*, took on increased meaning and symbolic value to represent a distinctly Salvadoran cuisine.[6]

Aspects of language also served as markers of nationality. All Salvadorans commented on differences in vocabulary and pronunciation between the two countries. One woman told me that she was not really very Salvadoran because she did not use language typical of El Salvador. This, she explained, was because she was raised in San Salvador by two elderly aunts who were very particular about language. As a consequence she felt different, less Salvadoran, particularly in contrast with rural El Salvador. She also felt she had a distinctive style of cooking that made her less Salvadoran. Other people commented on how they had to learn Costa Rican Spanish when they arrived in that country. Some found this change in language disorienting or embarrassing. Others, at least in retrospect, considered it a minor inconvenience quickly overcome. Two women independently commented to me on the predicament of trying to buy *chayotes* in Costa Rica with the Salvadoran word *güisquil*, which to Costa Rican ears sounded like "whisky." It made an uncomfortable impression on them when they were directed to the neighborhood bar, not a respectable place for women, when they tried to buy vegetables to make lunch. Some Salvadorans told me they initially had avoided asking for anything by name; in the market they pointed, in sodas they listened before requesting the same foods they overheard Costa Ricans request.

In the 1990s most Salvadorans who remained in Costa Rica rarely used Salvadoran words. They had, consciously or unconsciously and to varying degrees, modified both their vocabulary and pronunciation to be closer to, even identical with, Costa Rican usage. Thus speech served as a major marker of how much people had changed. Although I knew a few people, older rural women, who retained strong forms of Salvadoran pronunciation and vocabulary, most only spoke in those ways occasionally and among themselves for fun. In addition to accent and vocabulary, the pragmatics of language were different. Salvadoran distrust of strangers, reticence, and avoidance of direct questions were contrasted with Costa Rican openness. Even younger Salvadorans who had spent most of their lives in Costa Rica and did not exhibit these traits themselves noted this difference. People who commented on this to me normally explained these differences as consequences of the political system in El Salvador, although in one discussion one man claimed that Salvadorans had been this way even before the war. People who had grown up in El Salvador seemed less likely to have changed these aspects of speech than pronunciation or vocabulary. Pragmatics is more closely tied to other more essential ways of being than the other aspects of speech.

Food and language were two more easily identifiable differences. Other differences, like the pragmatics of speech, were so much a part of the way people were, the ways in which they lived their lives and performed daily tasks, that Guillermo's "I don't know" was appropriate. People who had grown up in El Salvador often said that "something," something not wholly identifiable but distinctive, about other people had made them believe they were Salvadoran. In this way patria was embodied and was the name given to aspects of a person's habitus (Bourdieu 1977). It also supports Ramiro's observation that the environment of a patria influences the ways in which a person does things and what one values. The degree to which nationality was embodied, or expected to be embodied, is illustrated by many of the differences Salvadorans noted between Salvadorans and Costa Ricans. These often included bodily practices such as ways of dressing or performing mundane tasks. Some of these differences were arbitrary, either because I have counterevidence or because they were referenced inconsistently and idiosyncratically, but the fact that they made such comparisons is indicative of the hegemony of patria as a way of organizing experience. It was expected that compatriots should have similar beliefs, habits, and customs. For example, one Salvadoran woman told me that I peeled potatoes like a Costa Rican. When I asked her how she knew, she contrasted the way in which people peeled in her family to the way in which they did it at the home of a Costa Rican friend she had once visited. I had little faith in this particular example of difference because a Costa Rican woman also once told me I peel potatoes backward.

Salvadorans noted other differences more consistently, and these were often more plausibly linked to the kinds of structuring effects that Bourdieu theorizes. Salvadorans considered their compatriots to be good workers, at least while they lived in El Salvador.[7] Adela, who had worked as a clerk in a luggage store in San Salvador, explained this to me. She noted that there she had made every effort to sell as much as possible.

To do this she had carefully attended to customers' needs. She had even anticipated what customers might have plausibly needed in the future to sell more and make her job more secure. In Costa Rica clerks, justly or unjustly, were notorious for their unavailability and unhelpful attitude: One woman described them as acting as if they were doing you a favor by letting you buy. Adela felt this was because it was easier to earn a living in Costa Rica, so workers were less concerned about their jobs. In El Salvador she had known she was fortunate to be employed and therefore did all she could to avoid losing the position. In other words, in her interpretation and that of others, the socioeconomic conditions of the country contributed to structuring basic personality characteristics as part of a national character.

A final, and particularly poignant, example of how patria was embodied is that many Salvadorans told me that you could recognize Salvadorans by the sadness in their eyes. Antonia reported to me that other Salvadorans had told her she did not look Salvadoran because she did not have sad eyes. She considered this a criticism of how she lived her life, but believed that a time came when a person had to let go of the past. Salvadorans had, or were expected by many compatriots to have, sad eyes because of their history; in this way they carried within themselves a piece of their patria that marked them to each other. It also symbolized the reasons they had had for leaving El Salvador and the reasons some parents had wanted to remove their children from that country. When one man told me about how it was possible to recognize Salvadorans by their eyes, he told me he had left El Salvador with his family to spare his children from lives of constant fear. He did not want his children to have eyes that reflected back the sadness of their country.

In El Salvador it probably would have been meaningless to say that all Salvadorans were "like family." In another country there was an expectation that people would be worth talking to, until they proved otherwise, simply for sharing a patria. The reason they gave for preferring the company of other Salvadorans was that they understood each other better than Costa Ricans understood them because of the common history of living under a dictatorship, in war, and in a violent society. These were things the Costa Ricans did not share: Alberto said his Costa Rican wife would never totally understand him because she was not, as he was, "a child of war." Compatriots, by more fully understanding each other in these regards, made them feel at ease—at home. Sad eyes were important to some, then, because they reflected the experiences Salvadorans shared and therefore the reason they could understand each other.

In fact, eyes represented the reason compatriots could understand only one very important part of who they were since, despite the expectations of national solidarity, in practice of course people did not automatically like, respect, or wish to spend time with all compatriots. Even the reasons they would want to speak with compatriots excluded some Salvadorans, including those wealthy Salvadorans whom they were unlikely to meet in any case. Being from the same country was just one of many possible connections that could be made between people. When Sergio told me he liked working in an office with other Salvadorans, I asked why. He answered because it was "part of his identity." It was part of who he was, but not everything. Ramiro clarified that he "identified with" the good Salvadorans, not all of them. As Radcliffe and Westwood (1996) note, there were also other sites of affiliation including education, class, gender, and politics. Among the forms of affiliation that were important were those that tied them to Costa Rica.

Thoughts on Repatriation

Sometimes there is no best solution to the problems we face. In a conversation about reasons for remaining in any particular country, Antonio asked me, "What is patria, is it only the place where a person was born?" I reminded him that he was supposed to tell me. In response, he commented that nationalism only causes problems. He was not satisfied with it, but the dominant understanding of national belonging underlay both his question and policies toward refugees. We are supposed to belong to only one country; ideally it should be that patria where we were born. When conditions permit, refugees are expected to repatriate. Permanent settlement in the host society is accepted as a second solution, but in either case the refugee must choose one country. Authorities, at least officially, do not recognize that there is any problem in that choice. The only problem is people who are not in the country where they belong on a permanent basis, not the difficulty of deciding where that is. However, that policy ignores the importance of both family and other social relationships and the passage of time in favor of a belief in timeless and primordial attachments of individuals to nations. In practice the decision to remain in Costa Rica was rarely so simple as deciding where one belonged;

in some sense people belonged in both countries. The decision was even more complex because it rarely concerned only one individual's preferences. Doña Elena clearly expressed her quandary regarding repatriation during our conversation. The contradictory forces affecting her exemplify problems with the assumption that repatriation is the most desirable outcome for refugees.

Elena grew up poor, working in the market in San Salvador. Her mother did not send Elena or her siblings to school because, according to Elena, she believed they would not need an education, although it is possible that cost was another factor. Elena learned to read by playing school with a neighbor who was enrolled. At age eleven, she enrolled herself in school for three years. Subsequently she worked with nuns, first finishing three more years of schooling with them and then training to become a nurse's aide. This training proved useful in Costa Rica, where the UNHCR hired her to care for ill refugees in a hospice setting. Her husband, Arturo, grew up in a rural area and then moved to the city where he worked as a taxi driver. They met and married. She began working at home as a seamstress because her husband did not want her to work outside of the house; there one did as the man said, she explained. Together they saved enough to buy property. They progressed to be what she described as middle class. They were visiting Costa Rica when someone telephoned to warn them the family should not return to El Salvador. In Costa Rica, she had returned to a life of poverty that, she explained, had shocked her out of the complacency and self-satisfaction her remarkable progress in El Salvador had given her.

She loved Costa Rica because she believed it had saved the lives of her children, who were thirteen and fourteen when they left their native country. If they had stayed longer in El Salvador, she feared her son would have been drafted into the army and her daughter dangerously involved in politics. Her daughter was now a nurse in a Costa Rican hospital. Her son was married to a Costa Rican and had a young daughter. However, despite fourteen years in the country, doña Elena did not feel completely comfortable. The family retained the land and house they owned in El Salvador in case they returned and for the eventuality that a new president were elected in Costa Rica who would decide to deport all foreigners, as Monge had threatened during his presidential campaign in the 1980s. The possibility always remained, in the minds of many Salvadorans, even after so many years and despite the fact that at the moment they faced no such problems, that Costa Rica or Costa Ricans could reject, even eject, them.

Even so, until she spoke of her children's lives, I thought she was well settled in Costa Rica. They had recently bought the house where we met. It was the kind of comfortable old Costa Rican house I love: wood (although concrete is now considered preferable) with extraordinarily high ceilings. Although it was in a part of San José that was considered dangerous, it was a lovely home. She, like so many others, had mentioned that for a long time they had lived day-to-day, not acquiring excess belongings, always expecting to return soon. The house surely indicated they had settled and made peace with the fact that they were staying in Costa Rica permanently. Then, unexpectedly, she proved me wrong in a moving description of the contrast between the lives of her two children and her reaction to their contrasting experiences.

She described the situation of the two:

I have the two children: woman and man. In the case of the man, he does feel good here. He feels fine because he has his spouse, he has his daughter, a good job and everything; in contrast Isabel, since she is single, she is twenty-seven years old, single. . . . I don't know. She feels hurt. And she gets these depressions . . . these depressions! [They are so bad that] she has to go to the psychologist.

Yes, she feels very bad and she told me: "*Mami*, I don't even know where I am from. Half of my life I have here, half of it I have there," she says, "but I feel bad here. I cannot adapt to the life here."

I asked why she could not adapt. Isabel's mother answered: "¡Idiay, es que no!" She just couldn't.

Elena resumed her narrative. Her daughter was dissatisfied despite the fact that she was a nurse with a decent job and salary. However, she was not entirely happy in that job. She felt that she was criticized unfairly by supervisors and that this was a consequence of being foreign. Her mother thought she was in part right; she knew from personal experience that Costa Ricans did things that made her feel unwelcome.[8] The slights they experienced bothered them a great deal, "don't believe [they don't]."

She continued, commenting on how the contrast between her son and daughter made her feel: "And there it is that I would like to divide myself: leave one part here with my son and granddaughter and the other part go with her [Isabel] to El Salvador. And we are both the same, as much Arturo as I, the same. Because he loves the girl [i.e., the granddaughter]." It was even more difficult for Arturo, Elena's husband, at the time of this conversation because family had recently called from El Salvador to tell him his father was ill and he feared his father might die. He wanted to be with his father. He also wanted to be with his granddaughter, wife, and children. "It's as if . . . if he would like us all to go together," Elena told me. The only resolution would have been if the wife of Geraldo, Elena's son, had gone. The daughter-in-law would have liked to go to El Salvador, but only to visit. She would not stay there because her family was in Costa Rica. Her father was old and she feared he would die while she was in El Salvador if she moved. Although Elena told me that for years the family had longed to repatriate, the option was now tearing her apart.

Elena's son was content to remain in Costa Rica; her daughter was miserable yet ambivalent about returning to El Salvador. The daughter Isabel's unhappiness with Costa Rica seemed ineluctably connected to her unhappiness with her life. Her mother recognized this by focusing on the fact that her daughter, despite her relatively advanced age, had not created a home or family of her own and was unhappy at work, while Elena's son was happy with family, love, and job. The connection between creating a home and feeling at home is clear. This link was an experiential one more than an ideological one. Some people had histories similar to those of José, from the beginning of the chapter, and Geraldo, Elena's son. They meant to go back, then they found someone, had children, and now their home was in Costa Rica. Others, like Elena and Arturo, went to Costa Rica with family who became comfortable in the new country and no longer wanted to leave. Ramiro, the editor from earlier in this chapter, intended to go back, but he told me that after twenty-two years in Costa Rica he was not in such a hurry as he had once been. He, like some other men, said he would wait until his children were grown, in his case until they graduated from college.

For all these people, if repatriation remained an alternative it was one that had become much less imaginable because it would take them away from people they loved. Rather than an immediate option, it was a dream for some indefinite future; something they occasionally considered, perhaps on those occasions when work or family were less satisfying; or no longer a viable alternative. Sergio often said he intended to repatriate, but one day he added that he had been saying this for fourteen years so . . . . He left the sentence hanging in recognition that he was unlikely to leave Costa Rica. The frequent repetition of his desire to repatriate had become a formulaic reiteration of past intentions rather than a concrete plan for future action, although this could change again in the future. For others repatriation was not even something they currently desired as they recognized that their future was in Costa Rica, regardless of the fact that they had never intended that to happen. Family not only made a country a home, but also could create multiple homes that came into conflict because of the practical difficulties of distance and state borders.

Family, especially children, was a primary reason for staying in Costa Rica for Salvadorans who were either parents or grandparents. Families with children did repatriate, so this was only one consideration. Among the people I knew with children in Costa Rica, what mattered was not where the children had been born, but how old they were and practical concerns, including the desires of other members in the family and where economic prospects were better. Guillermo and Lucrecia told me that they would not repatriate because of the age of their oldest son. He was entering adolescence and they felt that this was a difficult period even without taking him from the life he knew to another country. Guillermo explained that personally he would have liked to return to El Salvador. He thought that if he sold everything the family had acquired in Costa Rica, it would be enough to resettle in El Salvador. But then the money would have been gone, and they would have had to start over finding a new way to earn a living for the family. They would have been in the position they had been in during their early years in Costa Rica, when they had owned nothing and constantly searched for ways to earn a living. This was no longer how they felt they should expend their energies ("no estamos por eso"), which they now felt should be directed to the needs of their children's upbringing and education. This is why it was easier for Sergio and Ramiro to imagine returning after their children were grown and no longer needed their fathers. Ramiro was explicit in telling me he did not feel that he had the right to uproot his children, two of whom were in college. Fate had forced him to leave his country, and he would not do that to his children without necessity. These men clearly did not envision a day when they would have to depend economically on their children. Nor had they thought through the implications of their sentimental attachments to family, which eventually could put them in the position of Elena and Carlos who could not leave for love of their son and granddaughter.

Economic prospects were another important consideration; for some they were more important than family. Elías, a shoemaker from San Salvador, spoke of the possibilities of returning. In 1992 and 1993, he had visited El Salvador and decided that he would not repatriate because it would be too hard to earn a living. Now he was beginning to think it was becoming more difficult in Costa Rica and maybe it would be easier in El

Salvador. His compañera was Honduran; he joked to me that their infant son did not know what he was: Salvadoran, Honduran, or Costa Rican. I asked him what she would do if he decided to repatriate. She would return to her family in Honduras with the child. The only consideration he spoke of in making the decision was how difficult it would be to earn a living, so his attachment to his compañera and children seemed relatively weak. He also made clear how far removed his deliberations were from issues of national belonging, identity, or citizenship. He had been uninterested in politics in El Salvador and was equally uninterested in Costa Rica. It did not bother him and others that they could not vote in the latter country. No matter who won, in either country, they would still have to work. When they discussed repatriation, citizenship was not an issue people discussed except in terms of practical implications such as the inconvenience of obtaining permission to be in either country, the amount of bureaucracy involved in naturalization, or how it might facilitate access to employment. Other aspects of citizenship seemed of little interest, although a few said they would not renounce their Salvadoran citizenship.

For some, especially poorer women, for whom it is more difficult to earn an independent living, the sentiment and economics of family were more obviously mixed. Fernanda, whom you met in the last chapter, spoke to me, on the same day that she told me about being sola, about possibly repatriating. She complained that life was too difficult in Costa Rica; she had no one to help her. If she went to El Salvador, she had family; they might help her. Or maybe her grown sons would find jobs in Costa Rica; if so, things would be easier for her since they would help, and she would remain in the country. If she did repatriate, she would not leave until December, when the school year ended, because she wanted to let her younger children finish classes without unnecessary disruption. In Fernanda's deliberations and uncertainties, we find each of the factors I have been discussing. She hoped that she would be better positioned economically if she repatriated, but if her grown sons could help she could stay in Costa Rica with fewer economic worries. If she did repatriate, she could not do it at a time that would disrupt the schooling of her young children. Family and economics were intertwined concerns. The twin possibilities of residency in Costa Rica and repatriation to El Salvador were two sources of dreams for how things might work out. These dreams, although they recognized the importance of sentiment, were as much, and usually more, about managing the problems of survival. Fernanda, a single mother with little earning power and many dependents, was caught between equally difficult and unlikely options. It was not at all certain either that her sons would be able to help or that if she repatriated the family she had not seen in fourteen years could (or would) significantly better her situation. In fact, December came and went while she remained in Costa Rica working as a maid, living with her young children, unemployed sons, and in-laws.

There were rumors regarding the intentions of Pilar, her mother-in-law, among people who knew her. People claimed that Pilar had told them she was going to repatriate soon. She was fighting with the daughter with whom she lived, by refusing to speak to her, at the time. Perhaps spreading a rumor that she was leaving was intended to make her daughter worry and treat her as she wished; at the time, she told me privately that she never would repatriate. I asked her, during a conversation about other people who were visiting El Salvador or thinking about doing so, if she did not wish to go. She said yes, she would have gone already if her back did not hurt. Because I had heard the rumors, I inquired whether she would have visited or repatriated. She told me she would not repatriate because she had nothing in El Salvador.

Pilar reiterated to me on another occasion that she would never go back, except to visit her daughter who had remained in El Salvador. This time she explained this was because her family was now in Costa Rica: Although she had a daughter in El Salvador and a son in California, the family she had depended upon and lived with for so long was all in Costa Rica. She pointed to the college-aged granddaughter who was working in the kitchen while we sat at the table having coffee and said "that one" and her sister would not go back to El Salvador, so she would not leave, either. The granddaughter, who had remained silent during our conversation, inserted "not even dead." She and her sister were taken from El Salvador too young to remember very much, if anything. They had spent nearly all their lives in Costa Rica. Like other children raised in Costa Rica, they were Costa Rican in their ways of being. They had their friends and studies in that country. Their ambiente was in Costa Rica.

While people who were older were more tied by economic concerns and family to Costa Rica, younger people would have been uncomfortable in El Salvador culturally as well as socially. The younger people were when they went to Costa Rica, the more likely they were to feel it was their only patria rather than a second one. One young woman was five when she left El Salvador; she told me that she did not remember anything and considered herself Costa Rican. She felt no curiosity to go to El Salvador, although she would have liked to visit Miami, a very different cultural center and reference point. Guillermo and Lucrecia said that the oldest of their children accepted that he was Salvadoran, but only because he knew he had been born there. Until the war ended, he had been embarrassed to be Salvadoran. His father thought perhaps it was because he was at a rebellious age or had a contrary temperament. His mother said that it was because he talked with other children in the neighborhood and he had been embarrassed by the violence in El Salvador. They heard about it in the news and that was all he or his friends knew about El Salvador. Guillermo and Lucrecia's other children insisted they were Costa Rican despite their parents' efforts to make them feel Salvadoran. Their parents told them that they had been born in Costa Rica, but had Salvadoran blood. The children did not accept this argument. They had only recently become interested in El Salvador as the birthplace of their parents and older brother.

Some parents were bothered when their children felt Costa Rican instead of Salvadoran. Because people considered values and ways of behaving primary markers of nationality, this was at least in part about who was most influential in the lives of children. If children learned more of their values, character, and sense of self from parents, then children born in Costa Rica should have felt Salvadoran. If friends were more influential, then children would feel Costa Rican. Legally children born there were considered Costa Ricans by the government. A visa is required, even of citizens, to leave Costa Rica. One of the requirements, for people with children born in Costa Rica, is proof that children will be provided for in the parent's absence. One woman could not repatriate because she could not guarantee that her disabled Costa Rica-born child would get adequate medical care in El Salvador. Children could choose their citizenship, that of their birth or that of their parent's country of origin, when they turned eighteen. Costa Rica did not permit them to choose both, however, and no one really believed a child raised in Costa Rica would choose El Salvador.

After so many years away, even older people could find that they no longer had their ambiente in El Salvador. Teresa told me she would not repatriate. She loved her country, but her future was in Costa Rica. In Costa Rica she had acquired property; in El Salvador she had nothing. In addition, she no longer liked the heat or other aspects of life in El Salvador. For example, when she had visited El Salvador once she found it difficult to avoid conversing freely with strangers. When Victoria visited El Salvador, she was unhappy despite the fact that she stayed with a sister. Some people speculated that she would remain in El Salvador, but others disagreed because, they said, her family—the family she had been living with for so long—was now in Costa Rica. She did miss her family in Costa Rica. She was lonely, by herself most of the day while her sister worked, and she no longer knew many people. Sergio sympathized and commented that when he visited family in El Salvador he knew almost no one, but he was able to meet people. As a man, he observed, he would go out to see who was visiting in the street and join the conversation. A woman would not be able to do that, he added. In contrast, one man commented that it seemed to be the case that those who had repatriated did fine because it was there that they had their *ambiente*.

To repatriate was a big step, and one that people could not afford—economically or emotionally—to take lightly. Repatriating in many regards would have been like the original leaving, but without the same level of necessity. Leaving Costa Rica would have reproduced difficulties people had first faced in the country, but at stages in their lives when they no longer felt able to deal with them. Leaving would have meant losing relationships that people depended on emotionally, socially, and economically. For most, probably all, it would have involved going where they no longer knew many people, either because no one they had known was still where they had lived in El Salvador, or because they had been gone for so long that social ties had been strained or broken. They would have had to rediscover ways of earning a living and rebuild networks of relationships at a point in their life when this was potentially even more difficult than the first time because they were older.

With all of the practical considerations, there was the fact that they had grown unaccustomed to life in El Salvador. One young man, who had been a child in an isolated rural area of El Salvador, told me that those who were from rural El Salvador had grown accustomed to the "amenities" of life in Costa Rica—amenities like running water and electricity. They were no longer tolerant of the heat in El Salvador after living so many years in the much cooler Central Valley of Costa Rica. El Salvador was more violent and dangerous even after the war was over; people worried a great deal about crime when they planned trips to El Salvador. They had also changed in ways that seemed appropriate to the differing environments (*ambientes*) of the two countries. For example, some men told me that they did not get in fights in Costa Rica as they had in El Salvador.

This, they explained, was because social relations were more peaceful in the former country, so if someone did something to them it probably was not intended as a provocation. In making this kind of adjustment, they invested in the Costa Rican historical narrative I presented in chapter 1 because they adjusted in ways appropriate to that understanding of the national character.

Given all these facts, why repatriate if it were not necessary? Why, as doña Pilar asked me rhetorically, go to nothing? Javier, the shoemaker who explained the ambiente of Costa Rica in chapter 4, told me why he would not go back to El Salvador, despite his discontent with options in Costa Rica and his undiminished love for El Salvador. He told me that he no longer had his ambiente there. His ambiente in Costa Rica, as a foreigner and without family, was difficult but better than the prospect of starting over with nothing and no one. Other people had more satisfying home lives than he, but similar reasons not to repatriate. The decision to repatriate or not was also a decision regarding which set of memories to pursue, but this decision involved highly practical concerns about where it would be possible to live and with whom one wished to be.

I began this chapter by asking how people thought about patria and their connections to it. It was a hard question to answer; patria was many things. One short definition people gave was that it was the place where one was born. Through an analysis of the term, I suggested that patria shares core aspects of its meaning with the English concept of home. The Costa Rican poet Virginia Grutter provides another answer that supports this argument in a poem titled "La Patria." The poem begins:

> Donde está la escuela de mis hijos
> Donde está el techo que cubre mi cabeza
> Donde da fruto el árbol que sembré
> Donde esperan que pase mi pena
> Antes de pedirme que sonría.

> Where my children's school is
> Where the roof that covers my head is
> Where the tree I planted gives fruit
> Where they wait until my pain is past
> before they ask me to smile.

She continues with more examples that emphasize freedom ("Where I do not have to serve anyone"), a sense of being at home ("Where the air and the street belong to me"), where things make sense ("Where two and two are four"). The poem ends:

> Donde sucede todo esto
> Donde sucederá todo esto
> Allí queda mi patria
>
> Where all this happens
> Where all this will happen
> That is where my patria is.
>   Grutter (1985:386)

It was in this sense that Costa Rica became a patria for many Salvadorans. It was the country where they had found peace, where their children were in school, where grandchildren had been born, where despite the prejudice and discrimination they had sometimes felt from Costa Ricans they had made lives with relative freedom. It was, most importantly, the place where they had their ambiente and where, in varied ways and to varying degrees, they were now at home. Yet El Salvador remained their patria as well. It was the place that gave them birth, where they were raised, where they had acquired core values. It was the country where trees they had planted were bearing fruit, where they had gone to school, where some relatives remained. Grutter ends her poem with a shift of verb tense from present to future, which suggests that the place where all the things she lists now happen is the same place in which they will happen in the future. For Salvadorans, however, those places had proven to be different. Not only was there a split between past and present, but that split continued into the future. There was no choice that would have brought those activities into alignment for most people. There would always be people they cared about and important life experiences in both countries.

If patria is not primarily a legal category, but the place where a person is or was at home, then it is perfectly reasonable for people to have more than one. There are many possible kinds of attachments to a place or country. Citizenship, residence, memories of childhood, a feeling of being culturally at ease, all those connections that Grutter lists in her poem, political commitments and values, one's mother, the home of one's children and grandchildren . . . these were all attachments that had different meanings for different people and even different meanings on different days for a single person. There is no reason these ties all should or could have been transferred to only one country. It was possible for there to be many different configurations of attachments to countries because such ties are not always spun together into a single strand. People could have cultural affinities not only with multiple countries but also with a country in which they no longer had their ambiente. Citizenship was in one country, residency in another. The country where people were born was different from that where their children were born. Where they were born was not always the country where they now felt most socially, economically, or culturally at ease.

The multiple possible attachments of a person to a country generally form a fairly unified whole for people who have not migrated and consequently have all their life-forming experiences in one place. The experiences of Salvadorans in Costa Rica were very different from this unified whole. Over the course of their lives they, particularly those who left El Salvador as adults, came to have pieces of their lives in two, and sometimes more, different countries. It is no wonder that Elena's daughter Isabel said that she did not even know where she was from with half of her life in one country and half in another. It is significant, however, that she phrased this dilemma as she did. She was from, or not from, both countries. The ways in which most people talked about patria highlighted sociocultural ties and personal, but socially situated, experiences. This made it possible for Salvadorans eventually to feel they were from Costa Rica. If patria had been understood in other ways they could not have adopted the second country as their own. At the same time, there was a certain ambivalence in this for many people. Throughout this book, I have looked at the situated and historically specific nature of how ideologies were mobilized. In the concluding chapter I will consider the importance of this way of understanding the conditions in which refugees, and other migrants, are received through an examination of how the varied interpretations of national identity in Costa Rica met to create that sense of ambivalence many Salvadorans expressed about their place in that country.

6

To Be from Here

Conditions of Reception

Miguel, a shoemaker who knew a great deal about trends in social science although he had attended school only through sixth grade, suggested that Salvadorans formed a diaspora like the Jewish one. I never heard anyone else propose this description, but almost everyone I knew had friends and family in multiple countries. This is not surprising given the high levels of migration from El Salvador, both during and after the civil war of the 1980s. I have heard of Salvadorans in Italy, Sweden, and Saipan (Flood 1992) in addition to Australia, Mexico, Canada, the United States, Belize, Honduras, Guatemala, Nicaragua, Costa Rica, and Panama. In the mid-1980s there were, by an extremely conservative count, a half million Salvadorans internally displaced, a quarter million in the rest of Central America and Mexico, and a half million in the United States (Montes Mozo 1985:35).[1] There are now an estimated two million Salvadorans in the United States alone, and El Salvador is often described as a country of migration. In a real sense, the country's main export is its people: The largest source of foreign currency is remittances from the United States.

Relatively little information is available on Salvadoran migration, and until recently most of what had been published examined the causes and structures of migration, established demographic profiles of Salvadorans in different countries, or documented Post Traumatic Stress Disorder among Salvadorans in the United States. The overwhelming majority of the research has been on Salvadorans in the United States, and this emphasis seems to have only increased since the war ended. This may be warranted in terms of the relative impact of the migration, but it threatens to distort our theoretical understandings. In the preceding chapters of this book, I examined the process of settlement for Salvadorans in Costa Rica. Although they had been affected by the same historical circumstances and articulated their experiences through shared discourses, their experiences and ultimate relationship to Costa Rica and El Salvador were varied. I explored vectors of this variation within the common themes and cultural categories expressed in stories people told me. My intention has not been to provide sociological profiles of "typical" experiences, but to consider factors that affected how people were positioned differently in larger structures and processes so that their experiences were at once shared and varied. In this chapter, I draw together the strands of my argument and consider how the case of Salvadorans who migrated to countries other than the United States may enrich our understanding of migration more generally.

Enough has been published on Salvadoran migration for a schematic comparison of social, although not cultural and interpretive, aspects of their experiences in several countries. I begin this chapter with a presentation of those politico-economic conditions that seem to explain the varied ways in which Salvadorans related to different countries in which they lived and to El Salvador. This by no means comprehensive comparison reconfirms arguments by other scholars about the importance of politico-economic context in the reception of Salvadorans in the United States (e.g., Landolt et al. 1999, Menjívar 2000). It also throws new light on the arguments in chapter 5 and denaturalizes the outcome of Salvadoran migration to Costa Rica, which otherwise so closely conforms to the traditional models of migration in the social sciences.

The comparison is not my main objective in either this book or this chapter, however, and it remains superficial in part due to the relative paucity of information on Salvadorans in countries other than the United States. Nor do I do justice to the work on Salvadorans in the United States, since this would require comparing migration to the different cities within that country and a much more detailed description of structural conditions. Menjívar (2000:77) notes, and a comparative reading of her, Repak (1995), and Mahler (1995a, 1995c) confirms, the importance of three broad forces important in thinking about the conditions of reception of migrants: government (i.e., national) policy, local economy, and the organization of the receiving community. I focus here on the level of national government policy within a global context as this affected Salvadoran relations to the countries in which they lived. However, my discussion in prior chapters suggests that this should not be separated either from the constitution of the national economy or understandings of national identity.

An important factor in how Salvadorans were received everywhere was the way in which the war in their country was enmeshed in the Cold War. Salvadorans I knew often insisted that the revolution in their country was not implicated in the Cold War because it was about national injustices, not global politics. This was a strategic argument against United-statesian military support of the Salvadoran government. It was also to argue that the exploitation and injustice within El Salvador had their own long history to justify rebellion, and that Salvadoran opposition had an equally long history that did not require outside instigation. Interpreting the war in El Salvador in terms of global politics seemed to delegitimize the revolutionary effort by drawing attention away from the injustices of the Salvadoran system. Despite the fact that their own interpretations of the war tended to focus on endogenous conditions and historical antecedents, elsewhere it was interpreted in Cold War terms and therefore it was part of that politics.

Salvadorans were well treated in Nicaragua under the Sandinistas, where they received the same access to resources as nationals in addition to special assistance for refugees. This reflected the political sympathies of the Sandinista government, which also facilitated ties with the FMLN in El Salvador. This permitted Salvadorans to remain connected to events in their home country (Montes Mozo 1985:111). That country was fighting the Contra war, faced a blockade by the United States, and had severe economic problems; so the political support and climate were probably important attractions for those who chose to stay there. The situation of Salvadorans in Nicaragua changed dramatically after the Sandinistas lost the elections of 1990. Subsequently the Nicaraguan government, it is said under the instigation of its Salvadoran counterpart, persecuted Salvadorans in that country as it searched for caches of FMLN weapons (Morel 1991). At least in part as a result of the change in political climate some Salvadorans repatriated from Nicaragua in four groups in 1991; at least one of these groups formed a new community together in El Salvador (ibid.). The contrast between the treatment of Salvadorans under the two Nicaraguan governments is as striking as is the contrast with other countries.

Despite animosity between Honduras and El Salvador, which fought a brief war in 1969 and had an outstanding border dispute, the armies of those two countries formed an alliance under the influence of the United States and the Honduran government's fear of insurrection. Salvadorans who fled military sweeps in border areas of El Salvador were sometimes met by a hostile Honduran army when they attempted to cross the river into Honduras. Salvadoran refugees in that country were isolated in camps controlled by the UNHCR, which they could not leave. These camps kept them under the surveillance of the military and prevented them from competing with Hondurans for work during the economic crisis. At times the Honduran government permitted the Salvadoran military to enter camps and search for people it suspected of being involved in the FMLN (Fagen and Eldridge 1991:122–23). Salvadoran refugees were consequently separated from Honduran society despite long-standing social ties between Salvadoran and Honduran communities near the border (Phillips 1996). In contrast, the camp organization encouraged the creation of communities within the refugee camps. These had structures of governance, education, and production that were transferred to El Salvador when the occupants of these camps chose to repatriate even before the war had ended.[2]

In the United States, official support for the Salvadoran government meant Salvadorans had little chance of receiving refuge: Only 2.6 percent of Salvadoran applicants received asylum between 1983 and 1990 (Mahler 1995a:174).[3] Under these political conditions, most Salvadorans in the United States did not apply for asylum and instead remained as undocumented migrants. Nearly half of the Salvadorans in the United States are undocumented; this makes them the most undocumented national group in the United States (Lopez et al. 1996). This contributes to their vulnerable and disadvantageous position in the labor market and consequent economic insecurity. Both Menjívar (2000) and Coutin (2000) also comment on the sense of not existing or being fully part of the society caused by being undocumented.

The relationship between Salvadorans in the United States and El Salvador is very different from the relationship between Salvadorans in other countries and El Salvador. Those in camps in Honduras repatriated as communities formed in exile rather than as individuals to the places from which they had originated. Those in Costa Rica, who had lived dispersed among Costa Ricans, repatriated as individuals, families, or small groups, or settled in Costa Rica. Those in the United States, in contrast, have created extensive transnational links between the two countries through circular migration, remittances, businesses and institutions related to those remittances, family ties, political action and civic activism, and other social forms (DeCesare 1998; Landolt 1997, 2000; Mahler 1995a; Hamilton and Chinchilla 2001). In contrast, very few Salvadorans in Costa Rica maintained the kind of sustained social involvement in and orientation toward multiple countries that social scientists call transnational. The actual degree of transnational connections Salvadorans in the United States maintain varies, but the contrast in density and diversity of ties between the countries as a result of migration is striking.

This can be explained in part by the economic position of the different countries in the world system and the expectations that people in El Salvador had of opportunities in different places. The United States is a rich country, and although Central Americans had access to stories about migrants who did not succeed, there was a prevalent belief that it is a place of economic opportunity in addition to difficulty and racism. People earn more in the United States than they do in Central America. They consequently almost always expect to help family through remittances or to save for their own future home or business upon return to Central America. Some analysts suggest that Salvadorans in the United States maintain transnational ties under difficult economic conditions at the cost of community ties with other Salvadorans within the United States (Mahler 1995a, 1995b; Menjívar 1994, 1997a, 1997b, 2000). The insecurity of their position in the United States increases the importance of the transnational ties because it makes permanent settlement less likely and they will need a social network to rely on in El Salvador when (and if) they return or are deported (cf. Landolt 2000).

Salvadorans in Costa Rica were not generally faced with the difficult expectations that they help people in El Salvador. Although some people expected more economic opportunities in Costa Rica than in El Salvador, it was another poor country. Nicaraguans do send remittances from Costa Rica (Agencia AFP 1998; Leitin 1998; Muñoz N. 1997), so the position of Costa Rica in the world economic system does not entirely explain this lack of expectations for Salvadorans. However, it is highly implausible that remittances earned anywhere in Central America are ever expected to equal those from the United States.[4] Remittances are an important method of maintaining family and community ties across national borders, so a logical consequence of this difference would be that the break between families at home and abroad seems to have been greater between El Salvador and Costa Rica than El Salvador and the United States. Salvadorans in Costa Rica were less oriented toward maintaining social ties to El Salvador and more dependent on relationships within Costa Rica than is described in studies of the migration to the United States. This does not mean that the family Salvadorans retained in El Salvador was not important to many (but not all; this, too, varied), but they had fewer resources to remain actively involved in their natal country. In many cases communication between family members in Costa Rica and El Salvador increased after the war, but it was not tied into systematic economic arrangements or plans for return with investment money or a nest egg earned abroad, as is the case with those in the United States. Other sources of participation, particularly political, were important for some Salvadorans in Costa Rica but were by their nature relatively exclusive.

Despite the greater geographical proximity, ties between Costa Rica and El Salvador were more difficult during the war for people I knew than they generally were between El Salvador and the United States. Poverty in both El Salvador and Costa Rica made communication more difficult. For example, in Costa Rica telephones were not as common as they are in the United States.[5] Formal and informal courier services between El Salvador and the United States are well developed, but not between El Salvador and Costa Rica. Finally, Salvadorans in the United States appear to have been less likely to have been direct victims of the political violence than those in Costa Rica.[6] Some Salvadorans in Costa Rica told me they had been afraid to have contact with people in El Salvador, for either their own safety or that of others. Others recounted the fear they had felt the first time they finally returned to visit.

Salvadorans did not intend to integrate into Costa Rica. They initially hoped to repatriate within three months to a year. Despite that fact, the conditions in which they lived made some degree of integration necessary. They arrived in San José on their own and were neither put in camps nor automatically guided by any bureaucracy or social agency. Salvadorans in Costa Rica were not made into a socially distinguished group through the isolating mechanisms of refugee policies in the way that refugees placed in camps often are and Salvadorans in Honduras were. Nor were they markedly different from the rest of the society in terms of language or culture. In Costa Rica, they first had to orient themselves to available resources and institutions, find a place to live, and find a social space that would permit them to survive until they could return to El Salvador. This process depended upon access to relationships with other people. The gendering of space that I analyzed as "house" and "street" affected how all people used space, but ensured that the experience of the new country was different for women than for men or children. The experience of migration was also very different for people who went by themselves than for those who were with family and who carried a bit of their social world with them. Finally, it varied with class.

In the process of living in Costa Rica, to some degree all had to develop networks of social relationships upon which they came to depend. They either made families or watched the maturation of the families with which they arrived. Even as life in Costa Rica required developing a social network, the conditions of poverty and the violence they had left dictated that it was difficult to maintain relationships with people in El Salvador. Many Salvadorans found themselves completely cut off from relatives and friends in that country, while others could only maintain sporadic contact. Consequently their current social world came to be almost entirely in Costa Rica. When the war ended some no longer had family in El Salvador for a variety of reasons. Many people had been killed, a great number migrated to other countries, some had lost contact, and others no longer felt they had anything in common with people from whom they had been separated for so long. When the war ended many of those who chose not to repatriate, but not all, began visiting between the two countries. For almost everyone, however, these were visits only and did not represent a sustained involvement across borders as described in the literature on transnational migration.

Consequently, for a complex mixture of reasons Salvadorans in Costa Rica had more restricted use of transnational space than those in the United States, but far freer access to their host society than those in Honduras. Both contrasts are paradoxical for geographic reasons. Costa Rica is closer to El Salvador than the United States, and therefore we might reasonably have expected contact to be easier from Costa Rica. On the other hand, there were preexisting community ties between El Salvador and Honduras that did not exist in Costa Rica. As we have seen, these paradoxes are easily understood in the political and economic contexts of the 1980s. A consequence of these very different configurations of relations (local, national, and international) that coalesced for Salvadorans in different places was that people had different orientations to national spaces. This part of my argument largely supplements Malkki's observations regarding the ways in which the social conditions in which refugees live shape their attitudes toward, and use of, national and migratory categories. They do so by creating conditions in which particular types of social relations are possible and in which different categories of social identification are useful and meaningful. My analysis thus complements Menjívar's discussion of how politico-economic context affects social networks for Salvadoran migrants in the United States. My discussion also illustrates some ways in which we can extend Malkki's insights through ethnographic attention to the varied ways in which national categories and ideologies inform the actions of different people and sectors of society.

The factors that Menjívar and other sociological studies of migration emphasize in analyzing the conditions of reception are structural. My analysis has primarily focused instead on an aspect of context that is little considered in other studies: the cultural and ideological context, especially understandings of nation, space, and forms of belonging. The case of Salvadorans in Costa Rica illustrates the importance of not only objective sociological, economic, and political structures but also of structures of feeling (R. Williams 1977) and meaning. In this regard, for example, a factor that I believe significant and yet is little mentioned in studies of migration to the United States is that there exists in that country the possibility of hyphenated identities. It is possible to be Salvadoran-American; it was not, in contrast, possible to talk of Salvadoran-Costa Ricans. The term simply did not exist; there were only Costa Ricans and Salvadorans and consequently no language readily available for thinking about the changes Salvadorans felt over time. At the same time, I have shown that these structures of feeling are not completely independent from the economic, sociological, and political conditions of possibility.

The structural conditions summarized above alone do not explain why many Salvadorans came to feel part of a Costa Rican patria. Nor do they explain how they could feel that it was possible to have two patrias when most interpretations of the dominant ideology of nations say that a person has only one. One important aspect of the reception of Salvadorans in Costa Rica was how different people understood national identities. Malkki emphasizes the ways in which refugees relate to categories of social identity, but does not explore the nationalist ideologies of the host society as these influence the treatment of refugees. Other scholars have written on how ideologies of the nation influence the ways in which migrants are represented in receiving countries (e.g., Berlant 1996; Borneman 1986; Gutiérrez 1996), although more rarely considering the interaction between nationalist discourses and perceptions of the national character of people from specific other countries. The ways in which migrants are interpellated through nationalist and ethnic or racial discourses of the society they enter may in turn influence their own self-understandings (Glick Schiller et al. 1995). It is necessary to consider all of these perspectives in addition to the relationship between national discourses and politico-economic context to understand the experiences of migration and settlement. In the next section I elaborate on the theoretical implications of my analysis for integrating the study of nationalist discourses and migration. I conclude the chapter with a consideration of how all these forces came together to create contradictions in Salvadoran understandings of their place in Costa Rica.

National Identities and Discourses

Malkki directs our attention to the importance of nations in the contemporary world and observes "that the modern system of nation-states requires study, not just as a political system narrowly understood, but as a powerful regime of order and knowledge that is at once politico-economic, historical, cultural, aesthetic, and cosmological" (1995a:5). She rightly points out that the way in which this hegemonic cultural order organizes the world has political consequences for those people, including refugees, who are excluded from it. Interpreting the national order as a system of classification, she applies Douglas's (1984 [1966]) insights on purity and contagion in systems of classification to illuminate why refugees are treated as sources of danger because they are anomalous in that order.

Malkki's study of the national order as a system of classification provides us with important insights into the ideologically charged representations of refugees and the assumptions behind refugee policies. However, people are motivated by their images of specific nations more than the abstract ideology of a system of equal nations. Therefore a politicized study of the national order must take into consideration the different positions that countries have and the historically specific relationships between the nations involved. Outside of the ideology of a "family of nations," nations are not interchangeable units. They are not equal and they are not autonomous; they are instead organized in hierarchies of power and value. This has been recognized by scholars through the many spatial models that have been used to explore those politico-economic relations: center/semi-periphery/periphery; first, second, and third worlds; East/West, North/South. This inequality is encoded in the structure of even the United Nations, perhaps the ultimate institution representing the idea of a family of nations, in the permanent seats on the Security Council. These global relations are important in structuring the political and economic climate in which refugees and other migrants are created and received, the actions of states, and even the expectations migrants have of themselves. This was clearly seen in my comparison of Salvadorans in different countries.

In addition to this global unevenness, specific nations are formed in contrast to other nations. This does not mean that the external contrast is the most salient aspect of the nation at all times, but it is an element of nationalist discourses that can be very important. For example, Radcliffe and Westwood (1996) note that it was in opposition to Peru that Ecuadorians most shared an understanding of their nation. The fact that refugees remain nationals and are not received as nationless means that their reception is inflected by the nationalist discourses where they settle. Most often that is in a neighboring country, so it is probable that most refugees are received by people with very definite ideas of the national character of the refugees in their country. As with migrants more generally, they are incorporated into national projects as well as racial, ethnic, and class ideologies and transformations (Basch et al. 1994). Thus, while it is true that there are ways in which refugees are excluded from the national order, they are at the same time a part of that order. First they are created and maintained by it. The United Nations definition of refugees refers to nations, and nation-states subsidize many of the programs to assist them. I consider the second way in which refugees are part of the national order to be at least as important: Refugees are received by host countries not just as refugees, but as nationals.

"Refugee" is one category in another system of classification based on criteria of residence and citizenship, which we can call a migratory system of classification. This system defines the relationship between people and the state in which they live, delimiting the legal rights people can claim. However, people often do not use these categories as parts of abstract systems, but with specific nations in mind. The national and migratory systems of classification consequently may inform each other. This means that refugees are pulled back into the national order even as they are categorized as refugees and consequently excluded from it. The connotations El Salvador and Nicaragua had for Costa Ricans as a consequence of the way in which Costa Rica was defined in opposition to the rest of Central America informed the meaning of the term "refugee." It did this within a historically specific politico-economic moment that made some issues more important than others as the crisis threatened the fundamental bases of Costa Rican distinctiveness. This process, I argued, was so powerful that it ultimately influenced the legal structure of migration in Costa Rica.

The insights gained from Malkki's approach to refugees in "the national order of things" are thus made more compelling when read in conjunction with an understanding of the more localized versions of that order. This point is evident in Malkki's (1995a) ethnography, but she does not integrate it into her theoretical framework and it is consequently elided in her analysis. To understand more fully refugees' experiences, including their own use of national categories, we must locate the specificities of different nations more centrally in our analyses. This specificity needs to take place in three dimensions. As Malkki notes, we need to analyze the ways in which refugees themselves think of their national affiliation(s). We also need to consider the ways in which nations, nationalisms, and national identities shape their reception. Finally, we must not ignore the refugee's interpretation of that reception.

I am especially arguing against reading context from a decontextualized nationalist ideology. Meaning is always socially situated so that it partially emerges from context. There is no fixed meaning to be extracted from a nationalist discourse as represented in novels, newspapers, museums, and rituals. The hegemonic discourse of Costa Rican national history and identity did not dictate how people would use that discourse to justify their own preferred responses to the refugees. The same discourse could be used to justify both a degree of xenophobia and acceptance of Central American refugees. It did not even dictate which dimensions of that ideology would be most important for distinguishing Salvadorans from Costa Ricans. For example, few Salvadorans told me they had been called "Indian" by Costa Ricans drawing on the "racial" dimension of Costa Rican nationalism. Other themes in the nationalist ideology were more important in the reception of Salvadorans, despite a common perception that Salvadorans tend to be darker than Costa Ricans. Nor was race an important part of official or mass media representations of refugees in the 1980s. Those representations tended instead to focus on class and social welfare. Government officials also sometimes commented on the cultural correlates of the Costa Rican system and argued that Central American refugees needed to learn to live in a democratic and peaceful country.

This illustrates a final complication in the way that nationalist discourses influence the reception of all migrants, including refugees: Costa Rican nationalism contained varied themes that could be used selectively. Yuval-Davis (1997) argues that there are three dimensions to constructions of nationalism: common origins (i.e., historical), culture, and citizenship in a state. Identifying these as dimensions is useful because all three may be present in any version of nationalism to different degrees. I would add that this also means that a dimension may be more salient at some times or in some contexts. It is significant that although all three were present in Costa Rican nationalism, it was the cultural dimension that predominated in discussions of Salvadoran refugees. Yuval-Davis notes that the cultural dimension facilitates assimilation of immigrants because it is more changeable. If Costa Ricans and Salvadorans had emphasized race or "blood," as Germans do (Peck 1995), in defining national identity, then Salvadorans could not have come to feel Costa Rican no matter how long they lived in the country.

The focus on culture as the defining characteristic of Salvadoran identity in chapter 5 and in most discussions I had regarding Salvadoran and Costa Rican distinctiveness contrasted with the politicized and nationalist reading of history as a form of Salvadoran national identity in chapter 1. There was, then, no single way to be Salvadoran. Although these two forms, and there may be more, of national identity were not mutually exclusive, they did not depend upon each other. The nationalist version of Salvadoran national identity used to promote support for the revolution focused on the dimension of historical origins identified by Yuval-Davis. In contrast, the modality of national identity I presented in chapter 5, to which most Salvadorans I knew referred when they spoke of what made El Salvador and Salvadorans distinctive, did not support a nationalist project. This cultural dimension did, however, facilitate Salvadorans' sense that they could have two patrias, could feel Costa Rican regardless of citizenship, or could mix nationalities. Yuval-Davis's third dimension of nationalism, citizenship in a state, was the one that least concerned Salvadorans I knew. This reflects the widely shared sense that the government was not an integral part of the patria. It probably also reflects their position in society. When they raised the topic, people commented that they would always have to work, so they did not think the government really mattered.

The meaning of patria more closely associated with juridical units had an important effect on people, even if it was not the core meaning of the term. It affected them legally and in the ways in which it shaped the hegemonic framework available for interpreting their experiences even when it contradicted aspects of their own experiences. Discussions about what makes a person be a particular nationality, including discussions of children born in El Salvador but raised in Costa Rica, evinced the fact that experiences called into question formerly unquestioned assumptions about patria. When birth, blood, and culture did not agree, which dictated national identity? Most often the answer was values and culture. However, the fact that patria was not primarily a legal category meant that there was a multiplicity of possible ties that composed it. This in turn meant that over time people came to have different configurations of ties (familial, economic, sentimental, cultural, historical) with different countries. Different people experienced and interpreted this mixture in distinct ways.

The range of dimensions to national belonging combined with the wide variety of experiences people had of both countries to produce many different kinds of outcome. Each person's sense of how he or she did or did not belong in the two countries was unique, and I would be reluctant to attempt a grand generalization. These issues were resolved by different people in different ways, apart from the decision to repatriate or not. Some interpreted their experiences as a straightforward, if sometimes problematic, shift from one nationality to the other. Others, like Guillermo and Lucrecia in chapter 5, felt they mixed national characteristics. A few suggested that they had become a Central American synthesis. In choosing this interpretation, consciously or unconsciously, they drew, in a novel way, on the political tradition of Central American unity that meant so much to Ramiro. They were Central American because they were neither Salvadoran nor Costa Rican in their ways of acting and speaking; they were both and consequently neither. Even in this case, however, they continued to recognize that El Salvador was a patria because it was where they had been born.

The difficulty of describing what they came to be, however, reflects more than the diversity of experience and more than the complexity of what it means to be from a place. It also evinces the lack of a clear language in which to express this experience of multiple belonging. Finally, it is indicative of the conflicts in Salvadoran experiences of Costa Rica and national belonging, a conflict that some told me they felt when they visited El Salvador also. They were no longer Salvadoran in the same way as Salvadorans who had remained in El Salvador; a few reported that Salvadorans in El Salvador had even questioned their continued Salvadoraness. However, their sense of being part of Costa Rica was at least as conflicted. In the final section of this chapter I consider these contradictions.

Contradictions of Reception

"You're not from here, right?" ("¿No es de aquí, verdad?") This is a question I often heard from Salvadorans in Costa Rica. Many Salvadorans told me of being asked this question by Costa Ricans. When they told me this story, they made it clear they had been hurt. They felt it to be a sign of rejection *(rechazo)* despite the fact that they quoted the same question when telling me how they had met people, suspected they too were Salvadoran, and asked to confirm their suspicions. Hector, the first time I met him, told me about being asked this question by a Costa Rican. He not only recounted the question as so many others did; he enacted a response for me. He said, "What do you mean, 'I'm not from here?' I've lived here twelve years." Then he added, "Soy centroamericano" ("I am Central American"). The question is deceptively simple, and Hector's answer elegantly complex.

On the surface, the question appears to be only a statement of fact. Costa Ricans who asked it could have been innocent of any intentions other than curiosity or a desire to make conversation. However, the full meaning of this question could only be understood within its social context. Regardless of unknowable Costa Rican intentions, when Salvadorans told me how Costa Ricans had asked this, it was always to illustrate a social climate in which they had felt unwelcome. The prejudice they had felt in Costa Rica, especially in the 1980s, was, they believed, latent, and this question reminded Salvadorans of it. Yet, when Salvadorans asked others this question it was a sign of inclusion and potential solidarity. Then the question stood in for another one: You too are from there, El Salvador?

One half of Hector's answer—"I've lived here twelve years"—forces us to consider the meaning of "from" in the question "You're not from here, right?" Salvadoran hurt at being excluded from Costa Rica through this question reflected at least a partial rejection of the idea that a person belongs only to the country where he or she was born. Their use of the same question with compatriots seems to accept it. Hector's answer reflects an alternative to dominant ideologies about how one comes to be from a country. He suggested that time, as much as birth, could make a person be from a place even without the legality of naturalization. As I discussed in chapter 5, many Salvadorans who chose not to repatriate felt this way as they came to have more of their lives in Costa Rica and adopted Costa Rican manners of speaking, acting, and interpreting events.

Although the question was given as an example of a more generalized climate, it was the fact that it called into dispute the way in which they had come to feel that Costa Rica was a patria for them that seemed to make this particular instance of rejection so important to those who raised the topic. The question reminded people that they were in fact foreign, even if they usually forgot that in their daily lives. Those who felt both Salvadoran and Costa Rican were obliged to recognize that Costa Ricans might understand things differently. Costa Ricans, some told me, would consider them foreign regardless of how long they stayed in the country, even if they naturalized as Costa Rican citizens, because they had been born elsewhere. For example, in chapter 4, Javier told me his life in Costa Rica might be easier if he naturalized because that would give him access to some resources he did not have as a foreigner. However, he doubted that it would help very much because he believed that Costa Ricans would still consider him foreign. A difficulty with Salvadorans' sense of dual belonging was that most people without the experience of displacement and reemplacement only recognized that people belonged to one patria, the one where they were born. It hurt them to realize that no matter how long they lived in the country or how well settled they felt, perhaps they still did not belong.

Hector's second answer—"I am Central American"—directs our attention to the meaning of "here" in the hated question. In the context of this question, we all understood that the deictic "here" meant Costa Rica and not a city or the supranational region of Central America. However, this answer indicates that even if Hector had to be from someplace, that place did not have to be a country. There are multiple levels of spatial belonging that articulate with the national level (Radcliffe and Westwood 1996). This is true not just with subnational space, but also beyond the level of the nation state. Different situations focus attention on different levels of geographical or social contrast; this changes the meaning of the nation for people in that moment. For example, Costa Rica was not exactly the same country when defined in contrast to Central America as it was when contrasted to the United States or Europe. In the one case it was "advanced"; in the other it was "underdeveloped." At the subnational level, in Costa Rica some Salvadorans identified not only with El Salvador and the region in which they had lived in that country, but also with both Costa Rica and the town or city in which they lived or had first settled.[7] They could be integrated into Costa Rican national space through the ties they developed with more localized spaces. I believe that the experiences of displacement, including the experience of refugee policies and the rhetorics inspired by a Costa Rican nationalist discourse, made nationality a more important category for explaining experience than it would have been for most people most of the time within El Salvador. At the same time, there also was a supranational spatial unit with a long tradition that was available as a category of social identification. Central America potentially could have linked Salvadorans and Costa Ricans in a single historical and geographical unit of identification. The ideal of Central American unity has been stronger in El Salvador than Costa Rica, so it may be that it was easier for Salvadorans like Hector to resort to it as a source of identification than Costa Ricans.[8]

However, Hector could not rely on the fact that he was Central American to grant him rights to be from "here" if Costa Ricans did not recognize the referent of "here" as Central America. Aspects of how he told this story to me are important in this context. The way in which he performed the first answer ("I've been here twelve years") made it clear that this is what he had said to the Costa Rican: an interpretation confirmed on another occasion when he mentioned how long he had lived in Costa Rica. When he gave the second answer ("I am a Central American"), he shifted footing (Goffman 1981) non-verbally so that it seemed directed to me rather than reported speech. I don't believe that he gave both responses to the Costa Rican. The shift between the two answers requires a shift in the referent of "here" and the pertinent level of space. It is improbable that he could have accomplished this with the Costa Rican, who had already defined him as not from "here" and in doing so had excluded Central America as a possible interpretation.

All of these observations regarding the question and Hector's answers complicate the observations I made in chapter 5. Salvadorans could not have claimed Costa Rica as a second patria without the cooperation of Costa Ricans. The reactions of both Salvadorans and Costa Ricans to the arrival of Central American refugees in Costa Rica were important to the manner in which Salvadorans integrated into Costa Rica. In addition, it was not just how Costa Ricans received Salvadorans, but also Salvadorans' understandings of their reception that mattered. In that regard those who arrived in the 1980s had received mixed signals. The Costa Rican government feared enclaves of poor, revolution-trained foreigners who could turn into disadvantaged minorities and possibly foment revolution. It therefore encouraged social integration of refugees into Costa Rican society. They settled with relative freedom, restricted only in their ability to work legally, and had good relations with their Costa Rican neighbors and coworkers. In the context of a severe economic crisis, however, this integration was limited. Refugees were Central Americans against whom many Costa Ricans felt prejudice. Some government officials and the mass media created a climate prejudicial to refugees, and Salvadorans' access to employment was initially limited. They met with "persecution" (as some called it) from migration authorities, read the negative representations of refugees in the press, and put up with rude treatment from bureaucratic employees. The tension between acceptance and rejection by Costa Ricans was reflected in Salvadorans' uncertainty about their integration into the society many years later. The two sides of their reception were both justified by the same nationalist discourse. The tension between the two readings of Costa Rican history had a real impact on refugee policies and Salvadoran sensibilities even many years later.

If Salvadorans have formed a diaspora, as Miguel suggested, then the case of Salvadorans who remained in Costa Rica demonstrates one problem with current migration theory. Migration theory is primarily developed in work on migration to the United States and Europe from poorer regions of the world. The study of Salvadoran migration is similarly dominated by the consideration of migration to the United States. Consequently, transnationalism has come to dominate the study of migration to such a degree that the terms are sometimes treated as synonyms, or any connection that extends beyond a national border is called transnational. Furthermore, work on transnationalism is often over-romanticized. Anything that seems to work against the hegemony of nation-states is often valorized, obscuring both the continued, if changed, significance of states and the pain and ambiguity caused by the continued importance of distance and borders.

Yet Salvadoran migration is not always transnational in any interesting sense of the term and it is nearly always rooted in melancholy, pain, disillusion, and separation. Those who migrated in the 1980s left a country torn apart by violence, war, and poverty. Salvadorans continue to leave their country at an astounding rate, despite the fact that those who left during the war thought that peace would permit them to return. Nor is it only the poor who leave; middle-class Salvadorans with good jobs are also so disillusioned with current prospects that many are willing to sell everything and attempt to make a life elsewhere, not always in the United States although that remains the primary destination. In December of 2001 and January of the following year, for example, the newspapers in El Salvador were filled with the drama of over six hundred Salvadorans who had gone to Sweden erroneously believing that country would give them political asylum due to the difficult economic and social conditions in El Salvador.

Work on transnationalism in migration often does not include a national perspective and at times this leads to romanticization of transnational strategies by migrants. This is particularly true when variables such as gender, class, and race are not examined in relation to nationalist discourses and the construction, and transformation, of identity through the lived experience of those discourses. Too often obscured in studies of migration is the pain of poverty, displacement, and prejudice. The experiences of Salvadorans in Costa Rica direct our attention to the conditions that make transnationalism possible or desirable, the ways in which national identities are forged and experienced, and the relationship among levels of spatial belonging. They also suggest that we take seriously the ambiguities and contradictions of lived experience, the pain of exclusion, and the difficulties of lives that have been split in half.

Notes

Introduction: Displaced Lives

1. Ramírez says 3 percent, but simple math shows this can only be a typographical error and it should be about 33 percent (Ramírez Boza 1987:76). Basok reports that two-thirds of Salvadorans in Costa Rica were receiving UNHCR assistance in 1983 (Basok 1993b:26); to receive this aid they had to have been registered as refugees. Sources vary on the number of refugees in the country even when they mean only documented refugees.

2. Wiley (1995) argues that the Costa Rican government enforced the strict labor laws with documented refugees in order to create a public perception that it was not permitting foreign competition with Costa Rican labor in the context of depressed wages and rising unemployment in the 1980s. The ironic consequence, he finds, was that undocumented Central Americans occupied a better position in the labor market than documented refugees.

3. Larson (1992) makes the same argument with regard to Nicaraguans.

4. For an analysis of the development and strategies of the war from both the military and guerrilla perspectives see Lungo Uclés (1990).

5. State violence against civilians was worst in 1981 when approximately 14,000 people were killed; this decreased to almost 6,000 in 1982 (Americas Watch Committee [U.S.] 1991:10–11). A different source estimates 4,419 people were killed and 1,045 disappeared in 1982. In the first half of the next year, those numbers were reduced to 1,787 and 840; in the second half of 1983, 588 died and 476 were detained (Montgomery 1995:172–73). Yet another source, the Comisión de Derechos Humanos de El Salvador, in 1984 estimated deaths in 1980 at just over 12,000, in 1981 over 16,000, in 1982 over 12,000, in 1983 nearly 6,000, and in 1984, 2,000 (cited in Booth and Walker 1989:156). In each case the general pattern remains constant despite the difficulty of fully documenting the violence.

6. Blanco S. et al. (1985:109) report that most Central American refugees re-

ceiving aid in Costa Rica were women and single, while those in projects were more likely to be married men. Rural people would have been at a disadvantage in negotiating the urban labor market and setting and it was difficult for single mothers to earn a living with the combined effect of their family responsibilities and the lower earning potential of women.

7. A survey of refugees in the Central Valley had 53 percent female Salvadoran respondents; in contrast 66.6 percent of Nicaraguans were male (Zúñiga S. 1989:30). The same survey had nearly 55 percent of the Salvadorans in some form of marital union (formal or free-union). The government agency responsible for refugee affairs said that 51.8 percent of Salvadorans were women (DIGEPARE 1989c). In contrast, an NGO found that 51 percent of Salvadoran refugees were men (CASP/Re 1986).

8. They had no record of either how many of these repatriations were children who had been born in Costa Rica or how many people eventually returned to Costa Rica. At least some did, although people I met had a sense that this was more common among Nicaraguans. These numbers include only those who had refugee status and took advantage of the UNHCR's assistance in returning. That organization paid the expenses of the move, including transportation of refugees' belongings. Salvadorans were apparently more organized than Nicaraguans about first researching conditions in El Salvador before returning. DIGEPARE (the government agency for refugee affairs) reported far fewer repatriations, only 57 Salvadorans by October of 1987. According to these statistics, 2.2 percent of repatriations (of all nationalities, not necessarily Salvadorans) were Costa Rican-born children (Secretaría Técnica de Población—MIDEPLAN 1988:21).

9. As of 1987, sixty-one Salvadorans had been resettled in third countries from Costa Rica through official programs (DIGEPARE 1987).

10. See Warner (1994) for a discussion of the relationship between voluntary repatriation as the preferred solution for refugees and the conception of the world that equates people and geopolitical units.

11. Malkki gives more detailed discussions of this. See Barré (1985) for an example of representations of Central American refugees as without a patria (country).

12. See Vargas Cullel and Carvajal (1988) for a discussion of the issues involved in the definition of the metropolitan region around San José. They also provide a history of the development of this urbanized area.

13. Meseta Central and Valle Central are the names for the intermountain valley where the Aglomeración is located, although in geographic terms it is not a single valley, but interconnected sub-valleys. Seventy percent of the country's population lives in the Valle Central (PREALC 1987 cited in Kutsche 1994:28).

14. The main exceptions to this are Limón, Guanacaste, and some less accessible indigenous reservations. In Hayden (1999) I discuss the way in which these exceptions are frequently excluded from normative Costa Ricanness.

15. Two rural areas of settlement were Los Angeles in Guanacaste and Guápiles

in Limón. The former was a refugee camp/agricultural project with 350 people in 1982. I concentrate on the urban population, although I knew some people who had either lived in one of these rural areas or still had family there.

16. See Basok (1993b:48–52) for more details on community organization in the 1980s. See Anónimo (1991) for a comprehensive list and description of organizations serving refugees.

17. Costa Rica and El Salvador are the smallest countries in Central America. Costa Rica is 19,238 square miles in size and El Salvador 8,236 square miles. The population of El Salvador was 4.75 million and that of Costa Rica was 2.5 million (LaFeber 1984:10–11).

18. People did sometimes talk of "family" as primarily those relatives with whom they had been living and upon whom they relied.

19. See the works by Rodríguez, Francisco (1993) and Quizar (1998) for testimonials from Salvadorans in Costa Rica. The former was a Salvadoran refugee in Costa Rica. Quizar's book contains the stories of a group of women who ran a cooperative day-care center in Costa Rica. She found that the first study she hoped to do among Salvadorans was difficult because people were tired of being studied for no good reason. The women she instead studied used the occasion of the interviews in 1988 to send their politicized stories to the United States.

Chapter 1. Two Histories

1. Some historians suggest that the Natives of what became Costa Rica resisted a great deal and that this is what led it to be settled by the Spanish later than the rest of the region (Woodward 1987). This is not the version of history I have heard from Costa Ricans. See Hayden (1999) for a discussion of Columbus Day in Costa Rica and the politics of racial identification in Costa Rican history.

2. See Láscaris (1980), a Costa Rica philosopher who emigrated from Spain, for an exposition on Costa Rica as a mountainous country and how that has dominated the national character.

3. Among other things, capital for growing indigo had come from Guatemalan merchants, and this was withdrawn; movement to the Atlantic ports was disrupted; and the Pacific shipping was blockaded by the British in an effort to collect debt payments in 1842, 1844, and in a period between 1850 and 1851. Synthetic dyes from Europe began replacing natural dyes from Central America (indigo and the red cochineal that was produced in Guatemala), and this further reduced the market for indigo from El Salvador.

4. Circa 1820, at the end of the colonial period, the population density of El Salvador was 11.9 people per square kilometer. In Costa Rica, it was only 1.2 per square kilometer. Guatemala had the second highest population density, with 5.5 per square kilometer, while that of the other three countries was comparable to Costa Rica's (Gudmundson and Lindo Fuentes 1995:2).

5. It is hard to know how much land was in use by indigenous communities in

the Central Valley, but the native population was relatively small and concentrated in towns at the periphery of the Meseta (Hall 1978:27). Hall also reports that at the end of the century only 10 percent of the Costa Rican territory had been colonized. She documents variation in the size of landholdings in different parts of the country, but overall the tradition of relatively small growers predominated despite the simultaneous existence of important large plantations.

6. San José, in 1821, distributed coffee plants, obtained through voluntary monetary donations by citizens, to indigents and the municipality gave land for cultivation of these plants. Soon other municipalities followed the example set by San José. In 1831, it was decreed that those who cultivated coffee in formerly unused lands for five years would receive title to them (Hall 1978:35).

7. For this chapter, Browning (1971) is my main source of information on the early development of coffee and its effect on the population in El Salvador.

8. The revolt of 1832 is the best known. Anastacio Aquino led three thousand indigenous peasants in a year-long fight against the government in Los Nonualcos. Other than that of 1832, these uprisings are not well documented. Browning (1971: 272) reports that they do not even show up in the contemporary press.

9. An important exception to this has been on the banana enclaves, which were owned and managed by people from the United States, where the history of labor relations is more conflict-ridden. This is an important part of the country's history I cannot adequately present here. Unlike Honduras, where the banana companies effectively ran the country, Costa Rica usually maintained greater national sovereignty. I focus most on the history of the central part of the country. This is the region where most Salvadorans lived, and it has been considered most typically Costa Rican. The interpretation of Costa Rican history that results from the political and economic dominance of the Central Valley was the one that was influential in the reception of refugees from the rest of Central America.

10. Estimates vary widely. Anderson, who is the main authority on the events of 1932, accepts a conservative estimate of between eight and ten thousand, although thirty thousand is widely quoted and accepted as realistic. He considers that the maximum number of people killed by the rebels was one hundred (Anderson 1971).

11. The population of the country was five hundred thousand (Edelman and Kenen 1989:76).

12. The Communist Party rose in Costa Rica in 1931 and was strongest in the banana plantations and among some urban intellectuals and artisans. It did not have strong support in the coffee-growing countryside, where many wage-workers were also independent growers who therefore shared interests with larger growers. Stone argues that class relations were more paternalistic and personalized in Costa Rica, where growers lived on and managed their estates (Stone 1990:78). In El Salvador many large growers lived in the city and hired managers.

13. Supporters and dominant history say he did so to avoid the abuse of power by the military, which was evident in the rest of the region. Detractors claim it was

to prevent a coup against himself. These are not, as Edelman and Kenen (1989:88) also point out, mutually exclusive explanations.

14. It is also said either that they were given citizenship at this time, or that the acquisition of citizenship was facilitated. Harpelle (1993) takes a much less benign view of the period. He argues that the West Indians (mainly from Jamaica) in the country essentially were forced to either choose Costa Rican citizenship or leave the country. My concern in this chapter, however, is for dominant and popular historical narratives, especially as found in the Central Valley.

15. During the decade 1961–70, multinationals repatriated $799.9 million, while Central America received $322.9 million in new foreign investment (Castillo Rivas 1980 cited in Russell 1984:53).

16. This was of a total of approximately three hundred thousand Salvadorans in Honduras at the time. They also worked in the banana plantations of that country.

17. The United States provided close to $6 million of military aid to El Salvador in 1980. In 1981, that rose to $35.5 million, and in 1982 it rose again to $82 million (LaFeber 1984:286). Military aid reached $136.5 million for 1984 (Dunkerley 1988: 401). Direct and indirect military aid together were $412.59 million in 1984 (Montgomery 1995:285).

18. Barry (1991:164) also reports this (adding other venues I did not hear about, like theaters) and says that boys as young as fourteen were conscripted in this way.

19. See Sewastynowicz (1986) for a discussion of how the frontier in Costa Rica created possibilities for the poor to improve their economic position. They could compensate for their lack of capital through " 'two-step' migration": because land increases in value after initial settlement, people could increase their capital by being among the earliest settlers on consecutive frontiers and selling fertile land when land values rose with increased development and population. This was possible in Costa Rica because of the short distances between frontiers and negligible interference from the state or corporations.

20. In 1963 only 43.2 percent of landholdings was in micro-units in Costa Rica versus 91.4 percent in El Salvador. Micro-units cannot produce enough for a family to survive. In that same year, 35.1 percent and 20.1 percent were in small and medium farms in the former country and 6.7 percent and 1.5 percent respectively in El Salvador (Dunkerley 1988:180).

21. In 1980, the poorest 20 percent of Costa Ricans received 4 percent of the national income and the richest 20 percent, 49 percent. In El Salvador it was 2 percent and 66 percent, respectively (Torres Rivas and Jiménez 1985:41).

22. There are seven provinces in Costa Rica. Four of these have their capitals in the Central Valley: San José, Heredia, Alajuela, and Cartago. The remaining three provinces are poorer and more rural, although all seven provinces have relatively distant rural areas.

23. Combined spending on social services went from $55 million in 1973 to $114 million in 1975 (R. Williams 1986:185).

24. Costa Rica was second only to Israel in per capita assistance from the United States. It went from $15.3 million to $51.7 and $214.1 million in 1982 and 1983 respectively (Dunkerley 1988:631).

25. See Hayden (1999) for a more detailed discussion of public representations of this history of distinctiveness, especially as presented in the media at the time that Salvadorans were arriving in Costa Rica.

Chapter 2. Meanings of Refuge

1. Costa Ricans did not always assume or suspect Salvadorans were from elsewhere. Key features marking difference were accent and skin color, but neither was definitive or reliable. Salvadorans living in Costa Rica were probably better and more sophisticated at spotting other Salvadorans, although still without 100 percent accuracy. Although I did not believe them initially, especially when they said one person "looked" Salvadoran because she was tall and another because she was short, over time I also learned to do so. It is more like recognizing the similarities among members of families.

2. There are a number of reviews of Costa Rican refugee policies. Most works give an overview, but for more in-depth discussions see Barthel (1987), Larson (1992), and Wiley (1991).

3. The UNHCR relied on NGOs and the government to administer refugee aid programs.

4. See Yundt (1989) for an analysis of Latin American legal instruments regarding refuge, the search for a consensus on how to interpret these, and the failure of the Organization of American States to respond to the Central American refugee movement.

5. In the international legal instruments, both *refugio* and *asilado* are sometimes used interchangeably to refer to those with territorial refuge (cf. ACNUR—División de Protección Internacional 1984:100, 110). In Costa Rica, I have encountered the term *asilado* for people admitted under either form of asylum.

6. This provides an interesting contrast to the observation often made in work on refugees published in English, which emphasizes the political nature of the category of "refugee." Following the United Nations definition of refugee, a state implicitly or explicitly criticizes the country of origin when this status is granted. In Costa Rica, in contrast, that category became the more neutral term and *asilado* was more likely to indicate a critique of the government of origin.

One reason people might want to obtain the status of refuge in many countries is to deligitimize the current government in their country of origin and draw attention to problems in that country. In contrast, Salvadorans in Costa Rica did organize to draw attention to the political injustice and violence in their country, but they did so as Salvadorans and not as refugees per se.

7. My own perusal of newspaper clippings found relatively few of these.

8. These were lawyers so they focused on issues of law, among other things the propriety of strengthening the police force and the wisdom of reforming the constitution to make naturalization more difficult. Previously Central Americans could naturalize after one year of residency and other Ibero-Americans after two years. This was changed to five years for Latin Americans and six for others.

9. In 1986 a poll published by *La Nación* found that 50 percent of the Costa Rican population thought refugees should be accepted while 32 percent thought they should be expelled or not permitted to enter (Ramírez Boza 1989:12). Few Salvadorans volunteered direct instances of Costa Ricans saying things to them; mostly they spoke of official actions or the general climate in the country—as represented in newspaper articles, for example—in addition to a few chance comments. Whether this was because of greater tolerance among working-class Costa Ricans who lived among refugees or politeness, I am not sure. It seems to be in part politeness. Some Salvadorans described Costa Ricans as people who would only talk behind their backs. Costa Ricans, using more positive terms, describe the national character as one that avoids direct confrontation. Larson found that Nicaraguans had not felt widespread discrimination from Costa Ricans but were aware of the negative stereotypes because they read the newspapers (Larson 1995:31). However, Costa Ricans do disparage Nicaraguans a great deal, so Larson's finding almost certainly must be explained by politeness. Some Salvadorans told me that they were present when Costa Ricans spoke about Nicaraguans and suddenly, chagrined, stopped to ask if the Salvadoran were Nicaraguan.

10. This is only one example of this argument. It is, for me, the most striking because of the linkage made between refugees and retirees. See Chacón for similar concerns: refugees not only competed with working class and impoverished Costa Ricans for resources, they also made social inequality more visible by increasing the size of the "marginal" population (Chacón Araya 1989:49–50).

11. My observation here is congruent with that of Ramírez Boza (1989:3–4), who argues that Costa Rican ideology framed refugee policies in the abstract while the enactment of policies responded to economic concerns.

12. For example, malaria was controlled in the 1970s and reappeared as a problem in the 1980s with half of all cases among refugees (Morgan 1987).

13. There is evidence that the United States and the Contras operated from Costa Rica, but the Salvadoran opposition did not use the country for military training.

14. One man who had been subjected to such a search reported it to me during my research. It is also reported in published accounts of Salvadorans in Costa Rica (e.g., Basok 1993b:32; Rodríguez, F. 1993:116).

15. Fallas (1980 [1941]:202) mentions the press blaming the 1934 banana plantation strike on Nicaraguans.

16. This observation was often made to me while I was in the country doing my fieldwork, and I too was impressed by how often foreigners were blamed for all evil. However, it seemed to me that this began changing during the early 1990s when

Costa Ricans in the newspapers began criticizing their society more and stopped attributing all problems to outside influences.

17. This did not lead to significant changes in gender relations or roles in the cases I observed. Men can take care of children, when necessary, but need not do it or other housework with the same attitude or care that women do. Although men watched the children, they left the other housework for when women came home.

Chapter 3. In the Street

1. The term machismo was widely used although it did not necessarily carry the full range of connotations that it is often said to have elsewhere, especially Mexico. Most often it was used to mean something like "male chauvinism." It indicated unwarranted exhibitions of, or belief in, male superiority. The word implied criticism; people who felt a male prerogative was warranted would probably not have used the term. I do not deal with this term or the attitudes it implies here. For a discussion of machismo in El Salvador from the perspective of a social psychologist see Martín Baró (1986). Lancaster (1992) gives a discussion of machismo in urban Nicaragua, and Gutmann (1996) provides a sensitive antidote to the predominant stereotypes of machismo as an extreme or exaggerated form of masculinity among working-class Mexicans.

2. In El Salvador in 1979, 27.8 percent of people over fifteen were formally married and 26.4 percent were in a free-union partnership, for a total of 54.2 percent in a marital relationship (García and Gomáriz 1989–90:143). In Costa Rica in 1980, 45.6 percent of men and 46 percent of women were married while 8.3 percent of men and 8.5 percent of women were in free-union arrangements, for a total of 53.9 percent of men and 54.5 percent of women (ibid., 69). As one moves up the economic hierarchy, a greater proportion of people in both countries opt for formal marriage. Throughout this chapter, I choose statistics from the early 1980s (when possible) because that was the basis of the comparisons Salvadorans made upon arrival.

3. It is important to note that this contrast is simplified since it does not take into consideration age, regional differences within countries, or changes over time. See Biesanz et al. (1988 [1982]:100–105) on changes in dating in Costa Rica from the early twentieth century to the early 1980s. Nonetheless, these considerations do not ultimately invalidate the basic contrast and can be set aside for the purposes of this chapter.

4. It is not the same to be born outside of a legal marriage as to be unrecognized by one's father because fathers can recognize children by women to whom they are not married. Given the lack of data, this was the best comparison the editors of the two-volume *Mujeres centroamericanas* felt could be made (García and Gomáriz 1989–90:408). This fact, however, can only increase the contrast between the countries by increasing the percentage of recognized children in Costa Rica.

5. This was an increase from 5.8 percent in 1973. This probably reflected the economic crisis and increased poverty of those years.

6. Menjívar (2000:41–42) argues that this originates with internal labor migration in the late nineteenth and early twentieth centuries that separated families for part of the year, leading some men to form second households. This is an important historical fact; however both Menjívar and my arguments imply that this pattern would not have continued so strongly if economic conditions had not encouraged it in the present.

7. Twenty-three percent of men and 29 percent of women in El Salvador over age ten had not finished primary education versus just 7 percent in Costa Rica for both sexes. Costa Rica had higher rates for each level of education, including twice the rate of university studies: 8 percent of Costa Rican men and 7 percent of women, versus 4 percent and 3 percent for El Salvador (García and Gomáriz 1989–90:448).

8. Extended families predominate among peasants where fathers can retain control over the labor of grown children through control over the family patrimony (Deere 1978).

9. Biesanz et al. (1988 [1982]:86) observe that in Costa Rica "since heavy drinking is identified with machismo, abstinence is sometimes considered a sign of effeminacy." I have not found this attitude (which does not mean that some men do not hold it or did not at the time that the Biesanzes were writing), but their observation supports my point that behaviors marking gender were linked conceptually in such a way that would permit such inferences. Note that they also seem to be using the word "machismo" to mean manliness, which differs from my experience of the term.

10. All of the observations in this chapter were unelicited. It is possible that if I had questioned them, people would have agreed with the observations made by members of the opposite sex. However, it seems significant that in eighteen months this did not happen spontaneously.

11. It is not clear to me that this was because Salvadorans had ever seen a Costa Rican man do housework other than help with marketing. My own experience of Costa Rica was that it was considered undesirable for men to have to do housework, although they would if necessary.

12. See, for example, the neighborly teasing that Tula (1994) reports her husband suffered in El Salvador because he helped her with housework while she was pregnant. Chant's article does not discuss the meanings people gave to actions, so it is impossible to do more than conjecture on the interpretations Costa Ricans might have had of the behaviors she documented. I provide the observations that follow as examples of what we need to consider in order to avoid simplistic readings of women's "liberation" or gender relations from observed behaviors.

13. Callejero describes someone who is habitually in the street *(calle)* without adequate reason.

14. "Tu" seemed to have gained popularity among urban university students and

was felt by some to be a form of foreign copying. Instead of "tu," Costa Ricans generally used either "usted," even with children and animals, or "vos." "Vos" is a third form of singular "you" with an intermediate level of formality and its own verb conjugations. See Vargas D. (1974) for a history of "vos" and an analysis of its grammatical and pragmatic usage in Costa Rica in the mid-1970s.

15. *Callejear* is a verb for spending excessive amounts of time in the street (calle) without adequate reason. *Callejeando* is the gerund form of this verb, "streeting."

16. This did not seem, in the urban setting I knew, where people from many places and class backgrounds mixed, to be strictly correlated to class or class trajectory. The complicated life histories of most people I knew and the rapid socioeconomic change since the 1950s made this situation far more complex than I can adequately deal with here.

17. This desire appeared contradictory, at least to an English speaker. He did say that he wanted to be alone *(solo)* and he did complain that he could not because none of his family and friends would or could accompany him. The usage seemed idiosyncratic even in context, but it is consistent with my discussion of being alone in chapter 5. There I discuss being alone as a state of lacking people upon whom one could depend. Antonio was not "alone" enough because he had too many people depending upon him. He did not want to be physically alone, but to have a temporary break from so much responsibility.

18. This was one of the many "productive projects" that were started as a form of aid to Salvadoran refugees. Productive projects were a form of development program combined with refugee aid that provided access to the materials needed to set up small businesses in an effort to promote self-sufficiency without creating job competition with Costa Ricans. It also incorporated them into the country's overall development plan and, it was hoped, would contribute to the growth of Costa Rica's productive capacity (Basok 1993b:62-63, Campos V. et al. 1985:125, CONAPARE 1983). The government wanted the projects to incorporate both refugees and nationals, although this was not successful at least in part because of lack of funding (Blanco S. et al. 1985:55, Rodríguez S. 1984). Initially, projects were primarily for groups and donated. Subsequently, individuals and families were given projects.

19. See Simonson (1994) for this argument for subproletariat men in the Dominican Republic.

20. See Bencastro's (1997 [1990]) novel *Disparo en la catedral* for an account of life in San Salvador during the early years of the war. Among other things, he recounts the great difficulty the young male narrator had finding work.

21. In 1980 approximately 19 to 24 percent of Costa Rican, versus 23 to 34 percent of Salvadoran, women were employed (García and Gomáriz 1989–90:75, 153). For Costa Rica this was an increase from 15 to 17 percent in 1960, and the percentage of women working has continued to increase between 23 and 32 percent in 1990 (ibid., 75). Salvadoran women show a similar trend but always with higher employment rates than Costa Ricans.

22. Only 15 percent of all Salvadoran women workers were salaried; the rest had temporary positions. This was an important additional source of economic insecurity.

23. For an indication of consumption differences between the two countries, see Dunkerley (1988:174). In the 1970s, Costa Rica used 791 kilowatts of electricity per capita versus 291 in El Salvador. There were twice as many telephones in Costa Rica than in El Salvador although Costa Rica had only half as many people. Costa Rica had 42 televisions per 1,000 people versus 14 in El Salvador. In contrast, far more radios were used in El Salvador—a much less expensive technology that is easier to run off of batteries where necessary.

24. Costa Ricans also often commented to me on the importance of conspicuous consumption (particularly of imported goods) in their society (e.g., Denton L. 1971:9). This does not necessarily mean that Costa Ricans, as a whole or by class, were more "consumeristic" than Salvadorans, an assertion I cannot judge, but that the capacity to consume was greater among much of the population.

25. Responsibility for home, on average, should have been easier because families in Costa Rica were smaller than in El Salvador. The average number of children in Costa Rica was 3.5 and in El Salvador 5.2 (García and Gomáriz 1989–90:440).

26. A survey of women workers in Costa Rica found that 23 percent of university women who worked did not contribute to household expenses and only 15 percent gave all of their earnings to the household. In contrast, 90 percent of female working-class (and non-student) workers (*obreras*) gave all of their salary to their households (Carlos et al. 1985 cited in Vega R. 1992:37).

27. See Guy (1994) for a brief discussion of this issue for Latin America more generally.

Chapter 4. Only in One's Own Country

1. She was not his biological grandmother, but the woman who had raised him in El Salvador. Now that she was old, he was caring for her.

2. Other Salvadorans also spoke of the difficulty of finding a place to rent during their early years in Costa Rica. This, they said, was because they were foreign and because they could not afford homes Costa Rican landlords considered adequate for the number of people in many families.

3. Bazars in Costa Rica are small stores of miscellaneous goods. Some people installed them in a front room of their houses. They sold to neighbors whatever the owner had stocked: clothes, towels, pencils, cards, wrapping paper, shampoo, toys. . . . Some filled the front room of houses; Doña Elena had only a few shelves of items.

4. At the time, the early 1980s, the organizations serving refugees on behalf of the UNHCR had Salvadoran "collaborators" or volunteers, in part to mediate between the Costa Ricans and the refugees. They were given a monetary donation or

stipend, rather than wages, in return for their work. This was a way to circumvent the laws that did not permit refugees to work.

5. See the work by Martín Baró (1984, 1989) for psychosocial analyses of the effects of the war on interpersonal relations in El Salvador.

6. There is a large body of work on social capital; see Portes (1998) for a critical review of it. See Menjívar (2000) for a discussion of social capital and migration, particularly as applicable to Salvadorans in the United States. My primary interest in this chapter and this book is in the sense of belonging and possibility that we can come to feel with relation to particular spaces and not the material or political resources we access or social structure per se. Consequently my discussion of social capital is limited in comparison to other studies of migration.

Chapter 5. A Second Patria

1. These social units contrast with other social groupings, such as gender or class, because the latter transverse and divide the basic units. Consequently they need not follow the same sociocultural logic and cannot serve as metaphors for the nation. Not only have I been told that family is the basic unit, but some constitutions, including the Salvadoran, specify this fact. My analysis of the logic of house and street reflects one way in which this centrality is practiced.

2. Although the root of "país" in Spanish is like the French and English words in referring both to "country" in the juridical sense and to rural areas, I have not encountered the latter connotation in use in Spanish. I do not believe that many people were aware of the etymology any more than they were cognizant that "patria" is from the same root as "father" (*padre*). I know they did not make the latter connection because they did not find the term "madre patria" (mother fatherland), used by some people to refer to Spain, as oxymoronic or humorous as I did.

3. Rodríguez (1993:114), a Salvadoran who lived in Costa Rica, also writes of this disassociation between patria and government. He writes that Salvadoran refugees in Costa Rica hated the military and government, and that some hated any official symbol. He did not hate the symbols, just the system, but felt shame that symbols such as the national flag could be used to justify assassinations in the name of the patria.

4. My Spanish dictionary defines patria as "our own nation, with the sum of material and nonmaterial things, past, present and future that capture the loving loyalty of patriots" and "place, city or country in which one has been born" (Real Academia Española 1981).

5. Antonio manifested this same concern in a different way on another occasion. He was preoccupied by his perception, which was widely shared, that North Americans (Unitedstatsians and Canadians) do not care about family. This made them very solitary. He told me that he did not see how a person who did not care about family could care about anything or feel solidarity with anyone because family is

the first social grouping. Both patria and family were fundamental units of social organization, and not loving them indicated similar problems of social atomism.

6. Salvadoran quesadilla is a slightly sweet quick bread, or cake, made with rice flour, cheese *(queso)*, and cream. Pupusas are like a tortilla stuffed (before it is cooked) with ground pork, beans, cheese, or some combination of these. Pupusas serve the same symbolic function as a marker of national identity for Salvadorans in other countries. Restaurants specializing in them are found in the United States where there are Salvadoran migrants, and they show up on World Wide Web sites devoted to Salvadorans abroad.

7. Many felt that Salvadorans had lost this disposition in Costa Rica and that they were consequently less Salvadoran and less meritorious. In El Salvador, also, it is said that being hard workers is an important aspect of the national character.

8. Some Salvadorans reported Costa Rican rejections that were clearly intentional and malicious. Other cases of rejection I was told of might conceivably be explained by cultural misunderstandings between the two groups and Costa Rican obliviousness about how they were being understood.

Chapter 6. To Be from Here

1. These numbers are extremely conservative. Montes used the UNHCR's statistic of ten thousand Salvadorans in Costa Rica, but this only included those who were receiving assistance from the agency. The actual number was greater than fifteen thousand and probably was close to twenty thousand. Estimates of Salvadorans in the United States run as high as one million. Montes listed one hundred twenty thousand Salvadorans in Mexico, but other scholars estimated that there were as many as five hundred thousand in that country (Alvarado Umanzor 1992:7). Similar discrepancies could be cited for each country.

2. See Macdonald and Gatehouse (1995) for a description of one of these repatriated communities.

3. This fact led to a class action suit (American Baptist Churches vs. Thornburgh, also known as ABC) against the U.S. government on behalf of Guatemalan and Salvadoran asylum applicants in the United States. The plaintiffs argued that the Immigration and Naturalization Service (INS) had not adjudicated their cases legally, but based their judgments on Cold War political ideology. The government agreed to an out-of-court settlement to give those people a rehearing of their cases.

4. Mahler (1995a:16) reports that the median monthly remittance to El Salvador from Salvadorans in Long Island, New York was $200. In contrast, yearly remittances from Nicaraguans in Costa Rica are estimated to be between $400 and $666 per worker (Agencia AFP 1998). The estimate for Nicaraguans is based on dividing the total remittances the bank in Costa Rica reported sending by the estimated number of Nicaraguans in the country. It is therefore not necessarily reliable because it probably does not include all methods of sending money, estimates of

how many Nicaraguans are in Costa Rica vary widely, and it assumes that all Nicaraguans are sending remittances.

5. Telephones were more common in Costa Rica than El Salvador. High demand created another problem in accessibility, however, because people in Costa Rica waited as long as a year for a phone line after making their deposit.

6. A number of sources attempt to weigh the relative importance of economic and political motivations in Salvadoran migration to the United States during the 1980s (Alvarado Umanzor 1992; Stanley 1987; Jones 1989). There is general agreement that the migration was partially motivated by economic concerns. This interpretation is supported by the fact that much of it was from the regions of the country least involved in military campaigns (Jones 1989). At the same time, the migration was correlated with levels of violence, so the war was an influential cause (Stanley 1987). What the case really demonstrates is the impossibility of completely disentangling economic and political causes of migration.

7. Some people followed the soccer team of the Costa Rican town in which they had first lived. I knew Salvadorans who identified groups of Salvadorans by the city in which they lived in Costa Rica and associated those groups with social characteristics. Some people, for example, referred to those who lived in Heredia as more dependent or less astute in negotiating life in Costa Rica. I do not know how widespread this perception was, although I heard it several times. Those who made this distinction contrasted themselves with other Salvadorans in terms of capabilities they believed they had developed by living independently and unassociated with aid organizations.

8. One clue that this might have been true is the change in naturalization law Costa Rica enacted in response to the refugee crisis. Previously Central Americans had been able to naturalize after one year of residency, and other Latin Americans could after two years. In the early 1980s, in response to the refugee crisis, Costa Rica changed this to five years for all Ibero-Americans and six years for other people. In making this change the government erased an indication of common Central American identity.

References

ACNUR. División de Protección Internacional
  1984   Recopilación de instrumentos internacionales relativos al asilo y a los refugiados (versión provisional). Ginebra.

Acuña M., Olga M., and Carlos F. Denton L.
  1979   *La familia en Costa Rica.* San José: Ministerio de Cultura, Juventud y Deportes e Instituto de Estudios Sociales en Población.

Agencia AFP
  1998   BICSA abre sucursal en Nicaragua. *La Nación Digital* (San José, Costa Rica), sec. El País. 20 May. http://www.nacion.co.cr/ln__ee/1998/mayo/20/ultima5.html

Alonso, Ana María
  1988   The Effects of Truth: Re-presentations of the Past and the Imagining of Community. *Journal of Historical Sociology* 1(1):33–57.
  1994   The Politics of Space, Time and Substance: State Formation, Nationalism and Ethnicity. *Annual Review of Anthropology* 23:379–405.

Alvarado Umanzor, Raimundo Adalberto
  1992   La investigación en migraciones internacionales en Centroamérica. In *La migración internacional: su impacto en Centroamérica*. San José, Costa Rica: IDESPO, Gobierno de Costa Rica, ICT, FNUAP.

Americas Watch Committee (U.S.)
  1991   *El Salvador's Decade of Terror: Human Rights since the Assassination of Archbishop Romero.* Human Rights Watch Books. New Haven: Yale University Press.

Anderson, Benedict
  1990 [1983]   *Imagined Communities: Reflections on the Origin and Spread of Nationalism.* New York: Verso.

154   *References*

Anderson, Thomas
:::1971   *Matanza: El Salvador's Communist Revolt of 1932.* Lincoln: University of Nebraska Press.
Anónimo
:::1991   *Situación de la familia y los refugiados en Costa Rica.* Biblioteca Nacional, San José, Costa Rica. Ms.
Ardener, Edwin
:::1971   Introductory Essay: Social Anthropology and Language. In *Social Anthropology and Language*, Edwin Ardener, ed., pp. ix–cii. Association of Social Anthropologists Monograph, 10. London: Tavistock.
Arendt, Hannah
:::1973 [1951]   *The Origins of Totalitarianism.* New York: Harcourt Brace Jovanovich.
Arguedas C., Carlos
:::1984   Preocupa a gobierno tener refugiados en zona urbana. *La Nación* (San José, Costa Rica), p. 12A. 8 December.
Armstrong, Robert, and Janet Shenk
:::1982   *El Salvador: The Face of Revolution.* Boston: South End Press.
La Asociación Nacional de ONG's de Costa Rica
:::1991   *Diagnóstico de la población refugiada en Costa Rica.* Asociación Regional de ONG's que trabajan con población refugiada y desplazada en Centroamérica, San José, Costa Rica.
Bailey, Adrian J., and Joshua G. Hane
:::1995   Population in Motion: Salvadoran Refugees and Circulation Migration. *Bulletin of Latin American Research* 14(2):171–200.
Bakhtin, M. M.
:::1981   *The Dialogic Imagination.* Michael Holquist, ed. Austin: University of Texas Press.
Barboza Chavarría, Lorena
:::1988   Los huéspedes forzados. *La República* (San José, Costa Rica), p. 8. 25 July.
Barré, Marie Chantel
:::1985   Los sin patria: destierro y migración en Centroamérica. *Nueva Sociedad* 79:123–31.
Barry, Tom
:::1991   *Central America Inside Out: The Essential Guide to Its Societies, Politics and Economics.* New York: Grove Weidenfeld.
Barthel, Klaus
:::1987   A Right of Refuge—A Right of Flight: Costa Rican Refugee Policy, 1978–1987. Thesis (Masters)—University of Kansas.
Basch, Linda G., Nina Glick Schiller, and Cristina Szanton Blanc
:::1994   *Nations Unbound: Transnational Projects, Postcolonial Predicaments and Deterritorialized Nation-States.* Langhorne, Pa.: Gordon and Breach.

Basok, Tanya

1989   How Useful Is the "Petty Commodity Production" Approach? Explaining the Survival and Success of Small Salvadorean Urban Enterprises in Costa Rica. *Labour, Capital and Society* 22(1):42–64.

1990   Welcome Some and Reject Others: Constraints and Interests Influencing Costa Rican Policies on Refugees. *International Migration Review* 24(4): 722–47.

1993a   Individual, Household and Cooperative Production: The Case of Salvadorean Refugees in Costa Rica. *Canadian Journal of Latin American and Caribbean Studies* 18(35):17–38.

1993b   *Keeping Heads above Water: Salvadorean Refugees in Costa Rica.* Montreal: McGill-Queen's University Press.

1993c   Too Much or Too Little: Urban Employment Projects for Salvadorean Refugees in Costa Rica. In *Refugee Empowerment and Organizational Change: A Systems Perspective*, Peter W. Van Arsdale, ed., pp. 99–118. Arlington, VA: American Anthropological Association.

Beattie, Peter M.

1996   The House, the Street, and the Barracks: Reform and Honorable Masculine Social Space in Brazil, 1864–1945. *Hispanic American Historical Review* 76(3):439–37.

Bencastro, Mario

1997 [1990]   *Disparo en la catedral.* Houston: Arte Publico Press.

Berlant, Lauren

1996   The Face of America and the State of Emergency. In *Disciplinarity and Dissent in Cultural Studies*, Cary Nelson and Dilip Parameshwar Gaonkar, eds., pp. 397–493. New York: Routledge.

Biesanz, Richard, Karen Zubris Biesanz, and Mavis Hiltunen Biesanz

1988 [1982]   *The Costa Ricans.* Prospect Heights, Ill.: Waveland Press.

Blanco S., Carlos R., M. Consuelo Briceño A., Rocío Ramírez L., and Zaida Sánchez R.

1985   La situación de los refugiados centroamericanos en Costa Rica: satisfacción de necesidades básicas de los refugiados Nicaragüenses y Salvadoreños. Seminario de graduación en trabajo social—Universidad de Costa Rica.

Blumberg, Rae Lesser

1978   The Political Economy of the Mother-Child Family Revisited. In *Family and Kinship in Middle America and the Caribbean: Proceedings of the 14th Seminar of the Committee on Family Research of the International Sociological Association*, Arnaud F. Marks and René A. Römer, eds., pp. 526–573. Leiden: Department of Caribbean Studies of the Royal Institute of Linguistics and Anthropology.

Booth, John A.
   1991   Socioeconomic and Political Roots of National Revolts in Central America. *Latin American Research Review* 26(1):33–73.
Booth, John A., and Thomas W. Walker
   1989   *Understanding Central America*. Boulder: Westview Press.
Borneman, John
   1986   Emigres as Bullets/Immigration as Penetration: Perceptions of the Marielitos. *Journal of Popular Culture* 20(3):73–92.
Bourdieu, Pierre
   1977   *Outline of a Theory of Practice*. New York: Cambridge University Press.
   1986   The Forms of Capital. In *Handbook of Theory and Research for the Sociology of Education*, J. G. Richardson, ed., pp. 241–58. New York: Greenwood.
Bowman, Glenn
   1993   Tales of the Lost Land: Palestinian Identity and the Formation of Nationalist Consciousness. In *Space and Place: Theories of Identity and Location*. Erica Carter, James Donald and Judith Squires, eds., pp. 73–99. London: Lawrence & Wishart.
Briggs, Charles L.
   1992 [1986]   *Learning How to Ask: A Sociolinguistic Appraisal of the Role of the Interview in Social Science Research*. Studies in the Social and Cultural Foundations of Language, no. 1. New York: Cambridge University Press.
Brown, Susan E.
   1975   Love Unites Them and Hunger Separates Them: Poor Women in the Dominican Republic. In *Toward an Anthropology of Women*, Rayna R. Reiter, ed., pp. 322–32. New York: Monthly Review Press.
Browning, David
   1971   *El Salvador: Landscape and Society*. Oxford: Clarendon Press.
Burns, E. Bradford
   1984   The Modernization of Underdevelopment: El Salvador, 1858–1931. *The Journal of Developing Areas* 18:293–316.
Campos V., Nidia, Olga Guevara B., Virginia Murillo, and Dunia Pérez
   1985   Desfase entre la formulación y la aplicación de las políticas en materia laboral del refugiado en Costa Rica. Seminario de graduación para licenciatura en trabajo social—Universidad de Costa Rica.
Carlos, M. J., et al.
   1985   Machismo y socialización: un estudio de casos en mujeres universitarias. Seminario de graduación, Escuela de Trabajo Social—Universidad de Costa Rica.
Casey, Edward S.
   1996   How to Get from Space to Place in a Fairly Short Stretch of Time: Phenomenological Prolegomena. In *Senses of Place*, Steven Feld and Keith H. Basso, eds., pp. 13–52. Santa Fe, N.M.: School of American Research.

CASP/Re
1986   *Refugiados urbanos y semi-urbanos en cifras.* San José, Costa Rica.

Castillo Rivas, Donald
1980   *Acumulación de capital y empresas transnacionales en Centroamérica.* Mexico City: Siglo XXI.

Central de Trabajadores Costarricenses
1989   *Seminario nacional: la marginalidad social en Costa Rica.*

Cevo, Juan, Chester Zelaya, Esther Jimeno, Claudio Segura, and Florencio Magallón
1980   *Costa Rica, nuestra comunidad nacional: estudios sociales, sétimo ano.* San José, Costa Rica: Editorial Universidad Estatal a Distancia.

Chacón Araya, Germán Ricardo
1989   Analisis sociológico del Programa de Atención al Refugiado "Urbano" (1983-1988). Tesis para licenciatura en sociologia—Universidad Nacional de Costa Rica.

Chanady, Amaryll Beatrice, ed.
1994   *Latin American Identity and Constructions of Difference.* Minneapolis: University of Minnesota Press.

Chant, Sylvia
1991   Gender, Households and Seasonal Migration in Guanacaste, Costa Rica. *European Review of Latin American and Caribbean Studies* 50:51-85.

Chodorow, Nancy
1974   Family Structure and Feminine Personality. In *Woman, Culture, and Society*, Michelle Zimbalist Rosaldo and Louise Lamphere, eds., pp. 44-66. Stanford: Stanford University Press.

Chomsky, Avi
1994   West Indian Workers in Costa Rican Radical and Nationalist Ideology, 1900-1950. *The Americas* 51(1):11-40.

CONAPARE (Comisión Nacional para los Refugiados)
1983   *Plan global de criterios para proyectos de solución durable de refugiados y costarricenses.* San José, Costa Rica: Gobierno de Costa Rica.

Coutin, Susan Bibler
2000   *Legalizing Moves: Salvadoran Immigrants' Struggle for U.S. Residency.* Ann Arbor: University of Michigan Press.

CSUCA (Programa Centroamericano de Ciencias Sociales)
1978   *Estructural demográfica y migraciones internas en Centroamérica.* Ciudad Universitaria Rodrigo Facio. San José, Costa Rica: EDUCA.

Dalton, Roque
1983   *Poesía escogida.* San José, Costa Rica: Editorial Universitaria Centroamericana.

daMatta, Roberto
1991 [1979]   *Carnivals, Rogues, and Heroes: An Interpretation of the Brazilian Dilemma.* Notre Dame, Ind.: University of Notre Dame Press.

1991 [1985]   Espaço: Casa, rua e outro mundo: o caso do Brasil. In *A casa & a rua: espaço, cidadania, mulher e morte no Brasil*, 4th ed., revised and expanded, pp. 33–70. Rio de Janeiro: Guanabara Koogan.

Daniel, E. Valentine, and John Chr. Knudsen, eds.

1995   *Mistrusting Refugees*. Berkeley: University of California Press.

de Certeau, Michel

1988 [1984]   *The Practice of Everyday Life*. Steven Rendall, trans. Berkeley: University of California Press.

DeCesare, Donna

1998   The Children of War: Street Gangs in El Salvador. *NACLA Report on the Americas* 32(1):21–29.

de Mora, Nini

1995   Listos para el proceso "sostenible." *La Nación* (San José, Costa Rica), sec. Opinión, p. 15A. 2 February

Deere, Carmen Diana

1978   The Differentiation of the Peasantry and Family Structure: A Peruvian Case Study. *Journal of Family History* 3(4):422–38.

Denton L., Carlos F.

1971   *Patterns of Costa Rican Politics*. Boston: Allyn and Bacon.

DIGEPARE (Dirección General Para Refugiados)

1987   Descripción esquemática de la situación de la población refugiada en Costa Rica, Gobierno de Costa Rica, San José, Costa Rica.

1988   Recopilación sobre el flujo migratorio: su magnitud y datos generales sobre las areas de ubicación, Gobierno de Costa Rica, San José, Costa Rica.

1989a   Encuesta de opinión a población refugiada sobre servicios en salúd, educación, trabajo y alimentación, Gobierno de Costa Rica, San José, Costa Rica.

1989b   Opinion de los costarricenses sobre la presencia de refugiados en el país, Gobierno de Costa Rica, San José, Costa Rica.

1989c   Situación de los refugiados y desplazados en Costa Rica, Gobierno de Costa Rica, San José, Costa Rica.

1991   Boletin Informativo. Vol. 3.

DIGEPARE (Dirección General Para Refugiados). División de Ingresos, Emergencias y Seguridad

1987   Plan nacional de emergencia para la atención de los refugiados, Gobierno de Costa Rica, San José, Costa Rica.

Douglas, Mary

1984 [1966]   *Purity and Danger: An Analysis of Concepts of Pollution and Taboo*. Boston: Ark Paperbacks.

Dunkerley, James

1982   *The Long War: Dictatorship and Revolution in El Salvador*. London: Junction Books.

1988   *Power in the Isthmus: A Political History of Modern Central America.* New York: Verso.

Echeverria Esquivel, Carlos
1994   A propósito de los mal llamados "chapulines." *La República* (San José, Costa Rica), sec. Opinión, p. 15A. 23 June.

Edelman, Marc, and Joanne Kenen, eds.
1989   *The Costa Rican Reader.* New York: Grove Weidenfeld.

Fagen, Patricia Weiss, and Joseph T. Eldridge
1991   Salvadoran Repatriation from Honduras. In *Repatriation under Conflict in Central America,* Mary Ann Larkin, Frederick C. Cuny, and Barry N. Stein, eds., pp. 117–86. Washington, D.C.: Center for Immigration Policy and Refugee Assistance (CIPRA) and Intertect Institute.

Fallas, Carlos Luis
1980 [1941]   *Mamita Yunai.* San José, Costa Rica: Libreria Lehmann.

Feigenblatt, Hazel
1997   PUSC y PLN a calentar ambiente. *La Prensa Libre* (San José, Costa Rica). 30 October. http://www.prensalibre.co.cr/nacional2.html

Fernandez, Janina, José Carlos Vasquez, Mario Ramirez, Viria Sanchez, and Antonio McHugh
1986   Situaciones socio-económicas críticas de la población refugiada en Costa Rica. San José, Costa Rica: CASP/Re.

Fernández Pacheco, Janina
1988   *Inestabilidad económica con estabilidad política: el caso singular de Costa Rica, 1950-1982.* San José, Costa Rica: Editorial de la Universidad de Costa Rica.

Flood, Nancy Bohac
1992   Alien Workers. *Focus* 42:28–30.

Flores Gamboa, Guillermo A.
1989   Plan maestro para la atención de la problemática del refugiado y desplazado externo en Costa Rica. San José, Costa Rica: DIGEPARE.

Foster, Robert J.
1991   Making National Cultures in the Global Ecumene. *Annual Review of Anthropology* 20:235–60.

Franco, Jean
1985   Killing Priests, Nuns, Women, Children. In *On Signs,* Marshall Blonsky, ed., pp. 414–20. Baltimore: Johns Hopkins University Press.
1989   The Nation as Imagined Community. In *The New Historian,* H. Aram Veeser, ed., pp. 204–12. New York: Routledge.

Gallardo, Helio
1995   Del latinoamericano otro, o de la estupidez. *Semanario Universidad* (San José, Costa Rica), sec. Opinión, p. 17. 27 January.

Galván Bonilla, José Guillermo, and Julio Alberto Quintanilla Arevalo
1987   Los refugiados salvadoreños en Costa Rica. Trabajo de Graduación (licen-

ciatura). Universidad Centroamericana, José Simeón Cañas. San Salvador, El Salvador.

García, Ana Isabel, and Enrique Gomáriz

1989–1990   *Mujeres centroamericanas: ante la crisis, la guerra y el proceso de paz.* 2 vols. Santiago, Chile: FLACSO.

Glick Schiller, Nina, Linda Basch, and Cristina Szanton Blanc

1995   From Immigrant to Transmigrant: Theorizing Transnational Migration. *Anthropological Quarterly* 68(1):48–63.

Goffman, Erving

1981   *Forms of Talk.* Philadelphia: University of Pennsylvania Press.

Gólcher, Erika

1993   Reflexiones en torno a la identidad nacional costarricense. *Anuario de estudios centroamericanos* 19(2):91–99.

González, Vinicio

1983   Diferencias e igualdad en la situación de la mujer: una aproximación a su estudio en Costa Rica. *Revista de ciencias sociales* 25:91–106.

González de la Rocha, Mercedes

1995   The Urban Family and Poverty in Latin America. *Latin American Perspectives* 85:22(2):12–31.

Green, Linda

1994   Fear as a Way of Life. *Cultural Anthropology* 9(2):227–56.

Gregory, Derek

1995   Imaginative Geographies. *Progress in Human Geography* 19(4):447–85.

Grutter, Virginia

1985   La Patria. In *Las armas de la luz: antología de la poesía contemporánea de la América Central*, Alfonso Chase, ed. San José, Costa Rica: DEI.

Gudmundson, Lowell, and Héctor Lindo Fuentes

1995   *Central America, 1821–1871: Liberalism before Liberal Reform.* Tuscaloosa, Ala.: University of Alabama Press.

Guidos Vejar, Rafael

1980   La crisis política en El Salvador (1976–1979). *Revista mexicana de sociología* 42(1):235–65.

Gupta, Akhil, and James Ferguson

1992   Beyond "Culture": Space, Identity, and the Politics of Difference. *Cultural Anthropology* 7(1):6–23.

Gutiérrez, Ramón

1996   The Erotic Zone: Sexual Transgression on the U.S.—Mexican Border. In *Mapping Multiculturalism*, Avery F. Gordon and Christopher Newfield, eds., pp. 253–62. Minneapolis: University of Minnesota Press.

Gutmann, Matthew C.

1996   *The Meanings of Macho: Being a Man in Mexico City.* Berkeley: University of California Press.

Guy, Donna
    1994   Future Directions in Latin American Gender History. *The Americas* 51(1): 1–9.

Hall, Carolyn
    1978   *El café y el desarrollo histórico-geográfico de Costa Rica*. San José, Costa Rica: Editorial Costa Rica.

Hamilton, Nora, and Norma Stoltz Chinchilla
    1991   Central American Migration: A Framework for Analysis. *Latin American Research Review* 26(1):75–110.

    1996   Global Economic Restructuring and International Migration: Some Observations Based on the Mexican and Central American Experience. *International Migration* 34(2):195–227.

    2001   *Seeking Community in a Global City: Guatemalans and Salvadorans in Los Angeles*. Philadelphia: Temple University Press.

Hareven, Tamara K.
    1978   Postscript: The Latin American Essays in the Context of Family History. *Journal of Family History* 3(4):454–57.

Harpelle, Ronald N.
    1993   The Social and Political Integration of West Indians in Costa Rica: 1930–50. *Journal of Latin American Studies* 25:103–20.

Hartsock, Nancy C. M.
    1987   The Feminist Standpoint: Developing the Ground for a Specifically Feminist Historical Materialism. In *Feminism and Methodology: Social Science Issues*, Sandra Harding, ed., pp. 157–80. Bloomington: Indiana University Press.

Harvey, David
    1990 [1989]   *The Condition of Postmodernity: An Enquiry into the Origins of Cultural Change*. Cambridge, Mass.: Basil Blackwell.

Hayden, Bridget A.
    1999   Half a Life: Social Space and Nation in the Settlement of Salvadoran Refugees in Costa Rica. Thesis (Ph. D.)—University of Michigan.

Heller, Agnes
    1995   Where Are We at Home? *Thesis Eleven* 41:1–18.

hooks, bell
    1990   *Yearning: Race, Gender, and Cultural Politics*. Boston: South End Press.

Jackson, Michael
    1995   *At Home in the World*. Durham, N.C.: Duke University Press.

Jameson, Fredric
    1984   Postmodernism, or the Cultural Logic of Late Capitalism. *New Left Review* 146:53–92.

Jelin, Elizabeth, J. Ann. Zammit, and Marilyn Thomson
    1994 [1990]   *Women and Social Change in Latin America*. Atlantic Highlands, N.J.: Zed Books.

Jones, Richard C.

  1989   Causes of Salvadoran Migration to the United States. *Geographical Review* 79:183–94.

Kearney, Michael

  1986   From the Invisible Hand to Visible Feet: Anthropological Studies of Migration and Development. *Annual Review of Anthropology* 15:331–61.

  1991   Borders and Boundaries of State and Self at the End of Empire. *Journal of Historical Sociology* 4(1):52–74.

  1995   The Local and the Global: The Anthropology of Globalization and Transnationalism. *Annual Review of Anthropology* 24:547–65.

Kincaid, A. Douglas

  1989   Costa Rican Peasants and the Politics of Quiescence. In *The Costa Rica Reader*, Marc Edelman and Joanne Kenen, eds., pp. 178–86. New York: Grove Weidenfeld.

Kondo, Dorinne

  1996   The Narrative Production of "Home," Community, and Political Identity in Asian American Theater. In *Displacement, Diaspora, and Geographies of Identity*, Smadar Lavie and Ted Swedenburg, eds., pp. 97–117. Durham, N.C.: Duke University Press.

Kutsche, Paul

  1994   *Voices of Migrants: Rural-Urban Migration in Costa Rica*. Gainesville: University Press of Florida.

LaFeber, Walter

  1984   *Inevitable Revolutions: The United States in Central America*. Expanded ed. New York: W. W. Norton.

Lamphere, Louise, Helena Ragoné, and Patricia Zavella

  1997   *Situated Lives: Gender and Culture in Everyday Life*. New York: Routledge.

Lancaster, Roger N.

  1992   *Life Is Hard: Machismo, Danger, and the Intimacy of Power in Nicaragua*. Berkeley: University of California Press.

Land, Geoffrey

  1988   *La inserción laboral de los refugiados en Costa Rica*. Escuela postgraduada de relaciones internacionales y estudios del pacifico—Universidad de California, San Diego.

Landolt, Patricia

  1997   Salvadoran Transnationalism: Towards the Redefinition of the National Community. Working Paper 18, Program in Comparative and International Development, Johns Hopkins University.

  2000   Embeddedness and Transnational Settlement Strategies: The Case of Salvadoran Migrants in the US. Working Paper 00-02-H, Center for Migration and Development, Princeton University.

Landolt, Patricia, Lilian Autler, and Sonia Baires
1999   From Hermano Lejano to Hermano Mayor: The Dialectics of Salvadoran Transnationalism. *Ethnic and Racial Studies* 22(2):291–315.

Larson, Elizabeth M.
1992   Costa Rican Government Policy on Refugee Employment and Integration, 1980–1990. *International Journal of Refugee Law* 4(3):326–42.
1993   Nicaraguan Refugees in Costa Rica from 1980 to 1993. *Conference of Latin Americanist Geographers Yearbook* 19:67–79.
1995   Through the Eyes of the Media: Perceptions of Nicaraguan Refugees in Costa Rica in the 1980s. *Yearbook, Conference of Latin American Geographers* 21:25–35.

Láscaris, Constantino
1980   *El costarricense*. 3d ed. San José, Costa Rica: Editorial Universitaria Centro Americana.

Lauderdale Graham, Sandra
1992 [1988]   *House and Street: The Domestic World of Servants and Masters in Nineteenth-Century Rio de Janeiro*. Austin: University of Texas Press.

Lefebvre, Henri
1991   *The Production of Space*. Cambridge, Mass.: Blackwell.

Leitin, Patricia
1998   Pinolero en problemas. *La Nación Digital* (San José, Costa Rica), sec. Noticias de Economa & Negocios. 18 July. http://www.nacion.co.cr/ln__ee/1998/julio/18/economia.html

Lopez, David, Erik Popkin, and Edward Telles
1996   Central Americans: At the Bottom, Struggling to Get Ahead. In *Ethnic Los Angeles*, Roger Waldinger and Mehdi Bozorgmehr, eds., pp. 279–304. Newbury Park: Russell Sage Foundation Press.

López A., Agustín
1994   Inseguridad ciudadana. *La Nación* (San José, Costa Rica), sec. Opinión, p. 12A. 2 December.

Lungo Uclés, Mario
1990   *El Salvador en los 80: contrainsurgencia y revolución*. Colección Debate. San José, Costa Rica: Facultad Latinoamericana de Ciencias Sociales: Editorial Universitaria Centroamericana.
1995   Building an Alternative: The Formation of a Popular Project. In *The New Politics of Survival: Grassroots Movements in Central America*, Minor Sinclair, ed., pp. 153–79. New York: Monthly Review Press.

Lungo Uclés, Mario, ed.
1997   *Migración internacional y desarrollo*. 2 vols. San Salvador: FUNDE.

Macdonald, Mandy, and Mike Gatehouse
1995   *In the Mountains of Morazán: Portrait of a Returned Refugee Community in El Salvador*. New York: Monthly Review Press.

Mahler, Sarah J.

1995a   *American Dreaming: Immigrant Life on the Margins*. Princeton, N.J.: Princeton University Press.

1995b   The Dysfunctions of Transnationalism. Paper presented at the 94th Annual Meeting of the American Anthropological Association, Washington, D.C. Ms.

1995c   *Salvadorans in Suburbia: Symbiosis and Conflict*. Boston: Allyn and Bacon.

1999   Vested in Migration: Salvadorans Challenge Restrictionist Policies. In *Free Markets, Open Societies, Closed Borders? Trends in International Migration and Immigration Policy in the Americas*, Max J. Castro, ed., pp. 157–173. Miami: North South Press.

Malkki, Liisa H.

1990   Context and Consciousness: Local Conditions for the Production of Historical and National Thought among Hutu Refugees in Tanzania. In *Nationalist Ideologies and the Production of National Cultures*, Richard G. Fox, ed., pp. 32–62. American Ethnological Society Monograph, 2.

1992   National Geographic: The Rooting of Peoples and the Territorialization of National Identity among Scholars and Refugees. *Cultural Anthropology* 7(1):24–44.

1994   Citizens of Humanity: Internationalism and the Imagined Community of Nations. *Diaspora* 3(1):41–68.

1995a   *Purity and Exile: Violence, Memory, and National Cosmology among Hutu Refugees in Tanzania*. Chicago: University of Chicago Press.

1995b   Refugees and Exile: From "Refugee Studies" to the National Order of Things. *Annual Review of Anthropology* 24:495–523.

Mandel, Ernest

1987 [1972]   *Late Capitalism*. Joris De Bres trans. New York: Verso.

Martín Baró, Ignacio

1984   Guerra y Salud Mental. *Estudios centroamericanos* 429-30:503–14.

1986   La ideología familiar en El Salvador. *Estudios centroamericanos* 41(450): 291–304.

1989   Political Violence and War as Causes of Psychosocial Trauma in El Salvador. *International Journal of Mental Health* 18(1):3–20.

Massey, Doreen B.

1994   *Space, Place, and Gender*. Minneapolis: University of Minnesota Press.

Meléndez Chaverri, Carlos, and Quince Duncan

1981 [1972]   *El negro en Costa Rica*. 7th ed. San José, Costa Rica: Editorial Costa Rica.

Menjívar, Cecilia

1994   Salvadoran Migration to the United States in the 1980s What can we learn *about* it and *from* it? *International Migration* 32(3):371–99.

1997a   Immigrant Kinship Networks: Vietnamese, Salvadorans, and Mexicans in Comparative Perspective. *Journal of Comparative Family Studies* 28:1–24.

1997b   Immigrant Kinship Networks and the Impact of the Receiving Context: Salvadorans in San Francisco in the Early 1990s. *Social Problems* 44(1): 104–23.

2000   *Fragmented Ties: Salvadoran Immigrant Networks in America.* Berkeley: University of California Press.

Montes Mozo, Segundo
1985   *Investigación: desplazados y refugiados salvadoreños*, Instituto de Investigaciones de la Universidad Centroamericana de El Salvador José Simeón Cañas (UCA), San Salvador, El Salvador.

1986   La familia en la sociedad salvadoreña. *Estudios centroamericanos* 41(450): 305–19.

1987   *El Salvador 1987: Salvadoreños refugiados en los Estados Unidos.* San Salvador: Instituto de Investigaciones e Instituto de Derechos Humanos de la Universidad Centroamericana de El Salvador, José Simeón Cañas.

1989   *Refugiados y repatriados: El Salvador y Honduras.* San Salvador, El Salvador: Dept. de sociología y ciencias políticas e Instituto de Derechos Humanos, UCA José Simeón Cañas.

Montes Mozo, Segundo, and Juan Jose Garcia Vasquez
1988   *Salvadoran Migration to the United States: An Exploratory Study.* Washington, D.C.: Center for Immigration Policy and Refugee Assistance, Georgetown University.

Montgomery, Tommie Sue
1995   *Revolution in El Salvador: From Civil Strife to Civil Peace.* 2d ed. Boulder, Colo.: Westview Press.

Montoya, Rosario
1997   Revolutionary Geographies and the Male Backlash: Nicaragua, 1979–1990. Ms.

Monturiol F., Silvia
1994   "Ticos: generación de apátridas". *UNA Informa* (Heredia, Costa Rica), p. 8. September.

Mora Salas, Minor, and Franklin Solano Castro
1994   *Nuevas tendencias del desarrollo urbano en Costa Rica: el caso del Area Metropolitana de San José.* Ciudad Universitaria Rodrigo Facio, San José, Costa Rica: Editorial Alma Mater.

Morel, Augusto
1991   *Refugiados salvadoreños en Nicaragua.* Managua, Nicaragua: ACRES.

Morgan, Lynn M.
1987   Health without Wealth? Costa Rica's Health System under Economic Crisis. *Journal of Public Health Policy* 8(1):86–105.

Muñoz Jiménez, Krysia

1985   *Los refugiados en Costa Rica en proceso conyuntural-política período 1978-1984.* Tesis para la licenciatura en ciencias políticas—Universidad de Costa Rica.

Muñoz N., Miguel

1997   Nicas obtienen salarios de ¢2.000 millones al año . *La Prensa Libre* (San José, Costa Rica), sec. Nacionales. 30 October. http://www.prensalibre.co.cr/1997/10/30/nacional1.html

La Nación

1988   Refugiados cubrirán déficit laboral. *La Nación* (San José, Costa Rica), p. 5A. 4 April.

Nagengast, Carole, and Michael Kearney

1990   Mixtec Ethnicity: Social Identity, Political Consciousness, and Political Activism. *Latin American Research Review* 25(2):61–91.

Oficina de Orientación y Asistencia Social a Refugiados Salvadoreños

1982   *Actividades: Oficina de Orientación y Asistencia Social a Refugiados Salvadoreños.* Heredia, Costa Rica: Iglesia Fátima.

Paige, Jeffery M.

1997   *Coffee and Power: Revolution and the Rise of Democracy in Central America.* Cambridge: Harvard University Press.

Palmer, Steven

1993   Getting to Know the Unknown Soldier: Official Nationalism in Liberal Costa Rica, 1880–1900. *Journal of Latin American Studies* 25:45–72.

Pastor, Rocio

1993   Urgen reformar ley del Día de la Raza. *La República* (San José, Costa Rica), p. 4A. 12 October.

Peck, Jeffrey M.

1995   Refugees as Foreigners: The Problem of Becoming German and Finding Home. In *Mistrusting Refugees*, E. Valentine Daniel and John Chr. Knudsen, eds., pp. 102–25. Berkeley: University of California Press.

Pellegrino, Adela

1992   La migración internacional de latinoamericanos en los censos de los 80. In *La migración internacional: su impacto en Centroamérica.* San José, Costa Rica: IDESPO, Gobierno de Costa Rica, ICT, FNUAP.

Phillips, James

1996   The Politics of Refugee Identity in Central America. In *Selected Papers on Refugee Issues: IV*, Ann M. Rynearson and James Phillips, eds., pp. 222–40. Arlington, Va.: American Anthropological Association.

Porras Zúniga, Anabelle

1987   *Deterioro de la salud en Costa Rica debido a la migración de nicaragüenses.* San José, Costa Rica: Ministerio de Salud, República de Costa Rica.

Portes, Alejandro
  1998   Social Capital: Its Origins and Applications in Modern Sociology. *Annual Review of Sociology.* 24:1–24.
Prado, Rosane
  1995   Small Town, Brazil: Heaven and Hell of Personalism. In *The Brazilian Puzzle: Culture on the Borderlands of the Western World*, David J. Hess and Roberto daMatta, eds., pp. 59–82. New York: Columbia University Press.
Pratt, Mary Louise
  1990   Women, Literature, and National Brotherhood. In *Women, Culture, and Politics in Latin America*, E. Bergmann et al., eds., pp. 48–73.
PREALC (Programa Regional de Empleo para América Latina y el Caribe)
  1987   *Migraciones internas y mercado de trabajo en San José, Costa Rica.* Santiago, Chile: PREALC, Oficina Internacional de Trabajo.
Quesada, Juan Rafael
  1993   *America Latina: memoria e identidad, 1492–1992.* San José, Costa Rica: Editorial Respuesta.
Quizar, Robin Ormes
  1998   *My Turn to Weep: Salvadoran Refugee Women in Costa Rica.* Westport, Conn.: Bergin & Garvey.
Radcliffe, Sarah A.
  1993   Women's Place/El Lugar de Mujeres: Latin America and the Politics of Gender Identity. In *Place and the Politics of Identity*, Michael Keith and Steve Pile, eds., pp. 102–16. New York: Routledge.
Radcliffe, Sarah A., and Sallie Westwood
  1996   *Remaking the Nation: Place, Identity and Politics in Latin America.* New York: Routledge.
Ramírez Boza, Mario A.
  1987   La problemática del refugiado y las perspectivas de integración socio-económica: el caso de Costa Rica. *Ciencias sociales* 36:71–85.
  1989   *Refugee Policy Challenges: The Case of Nicaraguans in Costa Rica.* Washington, D.C.: Hemispheric Migration Project, Center for Immigration Policy and Refugee Assistance, Georgetown University.
Real Academia Española
  1981 [1950]   *Diccionario manual e ilustrado de la lengua española.* 2d ed. Madrid: Espasa-Calpe, S.A.
Renan, Ernest
  1996 [1882]   What Is a Nation. Reprinted in *Becoming National: A Reader*, Geoff Eley and Ronald Grigor Suny, eds., pp. 42–55. New York: Oxford.
Repak, Terry A.
  1993   Labor Market Experiences of Central American Migrants in Washington, D.C. *Migration World* 21(2–3):17–22.

1994   Labor Recruitment and the Lure of the Capital: Central American Migrants in Washington, D.C. *Gender and Society* 8(4):507-24.

1995   *Waiting on Washington: Central American Workers in the Nation's Capital.* Philadelphia: Temple University Press.

La República

1982a   Mil salvadoreños entran al mes. *La República* (San José, Costa Rica), p. 2. 11 July.

1982b   Desaparecieron 11 mil refugiados salvadoreños. *La República* (San José, Costa Rica), p. 3. 7 October.

1983a   La única solución es poner a trabajar a refugiados. *La República* (San José, Costa Rica), p. 3. 14 November.

1983b   Señalan infiltración roja en campo de los refugiados. *La República* (San José, Costa Rica), p. 2. 22 November.

Rodríguez, Francisco

1993   *Vida para los que vienen después en El Salvador.* San José, Costa Rica: Litografía La Jornada.

Rodríguez, Julio

1994   En vela. *La Nación* (San José, Costa Rica), sec. Opinión, p. 15A. 18 November.

Rodriguez, Nestor P.

1987   Undocumented Central Americans in Houston: Diverse Populations. *International Migration Review* 21(1):4-26.

Rodriguez, Nestor, and Jacqueline Maria Surroca Hagan

1989   Undocumented Central American Migration to Houston in the 1980's. *Journal of La Raza Studies* 2(1):1-4.

Rodríguez E., Miguel Angel

1994   Frente el tercer milenio. *La Nación* (San José, Costa Rica). 19 May.

Rodríguez Soto, Maritza

1984   Características psicosociales de la mujer campesina salvadoreña en su condición de refugiada en Costa Rica. Tésis para la licenciatura en psicología—Universidad de Costa Rica.

Rosaldo, Michelle Zimbalist

1980   The Use and Abuse of Anthropology: Reflections on Feminism and Cross-Cultural Understanding. *Signs* 5(3):389-417.

1989 [1974]   Woman, Culture, and Society: A Theoretical Overview. In *Woman, Culture, and Society*, Michelle Zimbalist Rosaldo and Louise Lamphere, eds., pp. 17-42. Stanford: Stanford University Press.

Rosaldo, Michelle Zimbalist, and Louise Lamphere, eds.

1989 [1974]   *Woman, Culture, and Society.* Stanford: Stanford University Press.

Rouse, Roger

1987   Migration and the Politics of Family Life: Divergent Projects and Rhetorical Strategies in a Mexican Transnational Migrant Community. Ms.

1989 Mexican Migration to the United States: Family Relations in the Development of a Transnational Migrant Circuit. Thesis (Ph.D.)—Stanford University.

1991 Mexican Migration and the Social Space of Postmodernism. *Diaspora* 1: 8–23.

1992 Men in Space: Power and the Appropriation of Urban Form among Mexican Migrants in the United States. Ms. in author's possession.

1995a Questions of Identity: Personhood and Collectivity in Transnational Migration to the United States. *Critique of Anthropology* 15(4):351–80.

1995b Thinking through Transnationalism: Notes on the Cultural Politics of Class Relations in the Contemporary United States. *Public Culture* 7:353–402.

Russell, Philip
1984 *El Salvador in Crisis*. Austin: Colorado River Press.

Sánchez P., Arturo
1982 Urgen medidas para garantizar seguridad. *La República* (San José, Costa Rica), p. 14. 22 September.

Sassen, Saskia
1988 *The Mobility of Labor and Capital: A Study in International Investment and Labor Flow*. New York: Cambridge University Press.

Scott, Joan W.
1991 The Evidence of Experience. *Critical Inquiry* 17:773–97.

Secretaria Técnica de Población—MIDEPLAN
1988 *Informe sobre la situación del refugiado en Costa Rica*. San José, Costa Rica: Comisión Nacional de Políticas de Población.

Seligson, Mitchell A.
1989 Agrarian Reform in Costa Rica. In *The Costa Rica Reader*, Joanne Kenen and Marc Edelman, eds., pp. 169–75. New York: Grove Weidenfeld.

Sewastynowicz, James
1986 Two-Step Migration and Upward Mobility on the Frontier: The Safety Valve Effect in Pejibaye, Costa Rica. *Economic Development and Cultural Change* 34(4):731–54.

Simonson, Peter
1994 Masculinity and Femininity in the Dominican Republic: Historical Change and Contradiction in Notions of Self. Thesis (Ph.D.)—University of Michigan.

Skurski, Julie
1994 The Ambiguities of Authenticity in Latin America: Doña Bárbara and the Construction of National Identity. *Poetics Today* 15(4):604–42.

Skurski, Julie, and Fernando Coronil
1993 Country and City in a Postcolonial Landscape: Double Discourse and the Geo-politics of Truth in Latin America. In *Views beyond the Border*

Country: Raymond Williams and Cultural Politics, Dennis L. Dworkin and Leslie G. Roman, eds., pp. 231–47. New York: Routledge.

Sommer, Doris

1991   *Foundational Fictions: The National Romances of Latin America.* Berkeley: University of California Press.

1994 [1990]   Irresistible Romance: The Foundational Fictions of Latin America. In *Nation and Narration*, Homi K. Bhabha, ed., pp. 71–98. New York: Routledge.

Soto Badilla, Claudio

1982 [1979]   La industria. In *Costa Rica contemporánea*, Chester Zelaya, ed., pp. 189–209. San José, Costa Rica: Editorial Costa Rica.

Stack, Carol B.

1975 [1974]   *All Our Kin: Strategies for Survival in a Black Community.* New York: Harper & Row.

Stanley, William Deane

1987   Economic Migrants or Refugees from Violence? A Time-Series Analysis of Salvadoran Migration to the US. *Latin American Research Review* 22(1): 132–54.

Stein, B. N.

1986   Durable Solutions for Developing Country Refugees. *International Migration Review* 20(2):264–82.

Stone, Samuel

1990   *The Heritage of the Conquistadors: Ruling Classes in Central America from the Conquest to the Sandinistas.* Lincoln: University of Nebraska Press.

Torres Rivas, Edelberto, and Dina Jiménez

1985   Informe sobre el estado de las migraciones en Centroamérica. *Anuario de Estudios Centroamericanos* 11(2):25–66.

Tripp, Robert

1983   Domestic Organization and Access to Property in a Town in Eastern El Salvador. *Anthropological Quarterly* 56(1):24–34.

Tula, María Teresa

1994   *Hear My Testimony: María Teresa Tula, Human Rights Activist of El Salvador.* Lynn Stephen, trans. and ed. Boston: South End Press.

United Nations Development Programme

1997   Human Development Report. Web page. Available at http://www.undp.org/undp/hdro/97.htm.

United Nations, ECLAC (Economic Commission for Latin America and the Caribbean)

1995   Latin America (13 Countries): Changes in Household Income Levels and Distribution. Web page. Available at http://www.eclac.org.

Valverde R., José Manuel, and María Eugenia Trejos Paris

1993   Diez años de luchas urbanas en Costa Rica. *Ciencias Sociales* 61:7–16.

Vargas Cullel, Jorge, and Guillermo Carvajal
1988   El surgimiento de un espacio urbano-metropolitano en el Valle Central de Costa Rica, 1950-1980. In *La estructuración de las capitales centroamericanas*, Rodrigo Fernández V. and Mario Lungo Uclés, eds., pp. 185-228. San José, Costa Rica: Editorial Universitaria Centroamericana.

Vargas D., Carlos Alonso
1974   El uso de pronombres "vos" y "usted" en Costa Rica. *Revista de ciencias sociales* 8:7-30.

Vega C., Jose Luis
1984   Central American Refugees in Costa Rica. San José: Hemispheric Migration Project. Mimeograph.
1986   Migrantes centroamericanos en Costa Rica. *Estudios sociales centroamericanos* 40:87-98.

Vega R., Isabel
1992   Cambios en los patronos organizacionales de la familia. In *El nuevo rostro de Costa Rica*, Juan Manuel Villasuso, ed., pp. 25-44. Heredia, Costa Rica: Centro de Estudios Democráticos de América Latina (CEDAL).

Voloshinov, V. N.
1986 [1973]   *Marxism and the Philosophy of Language*. Cambridge: Harvard University Press.

Warner, Daniel
1994   Voluntary Repatriation and the Meaning of Return to Home: A Critique of Liberal Mathematics. *Journal of Refugee Studies* 7(2-3):160-74.

Wiley, James
1991   The Relief versus Development Dichotomy: C.I.R.E.F.C.A. and Issues of Refugee Policy in Costa Rica. Thesis (Ph.D.)—State University of New Jersey.
1993   Peace, Reconstruction, and *Repoblaciones* in El Salvador: The case of Comunidad Rutilio Grande. *Conference of Latin Americanist Geographers Yearbook* 19:57-65.
1995   Undocumented Aliens and Recognized Refugees: The Right to Work in Costa Rica. *International Migration Review* 29(2):423-40.

Williams, Raymond
1977   *Marxism and Literature*. Oxford: Oxford University Press.

Williams, Robert G.
1986   *Export Agriculture and the Crisis in Central America*. Chapel Hill: University of North Carolina Press.

Woodward, Ralph Lee
1985   *Central America: A Nation Divided*. New York: Oxford University Press.
1987   La historiografía centroamericana moderna desde 1960. *Anuario de estudios centroamericanos* 13(1):43-65.

Wright, Richard, Adrian J. Bailey, Ines Miyares, and Alison Mountz
   2000   Legal Status, Gender and Employment among Salvadorans in the US. *International Journal of Population Geography*. 6:273–86.
Yundt, Keith W.
   1989   The Organization of American States and Legal Protection to Political Refugees in Central America. *International Migration Review* 23(2):201–18.
Yuval-Davis, Nira
   1997   *Gender and Nation*. Thousand Oaks, Calif.: Sage.
Zúñiga S., María de los Angeles
   1989   *El impacto economico-social del refugiado centroamericano en Costa Rica.* Heredia, Costa Rica: IDESPO.

Index

About the Author

Bridget Hayden holds a Ph.D. in anthropology from the University of Michigan, Ann Arbor. She has taught at Barnard College, in the department of Sociology and Political Science of the Universidad Centroamericana in San Salvador, and at St. Cloud State University. Her research interests focus on the experience and cultural construction of social inequality. This has led her to study how global, regional, and local structures shape social positions in differential ways across time and space, the relationship between these levels of space, and the social construction of space. She is particularly interested in the relationship between political and economic processes, social interaction, and meaning as people draw on available meanings to understand events and create new possibilities.

Her current research interest extends work done for this book. Salvadoran migration, particularly to the United States, is of extraordinary importance to the country economically, politically, and culturally. She is particularly interested in what it means to be Salvadoran when approximately one third of the population lives abroad and those who remain are to a large degree dependent upon that migration. There are two sides to this question: inside and outside the country. What does it mean to be Salvadoran abroad and how does this vary by gender, age, and country of settlement? What does it mean to be Salvadoran inside El Salvador when the country is defined as one of migration and it depends so heavily on the continued participation of Salvadorans abroad? Can El Salvador and Salvadorans develop a sufficiently flexible sense of national identity to include those who left?

DATE DUE